THE HIDDEN PLACES OF

DEVON

By David Gerrard

Regional Hidden Places

Cornwall
Devon
Dorset, Hants & Isle of Wight
East Anglia
Lake District & Cumbria
Lancashire & Cheshire
Northumberland & Durham
Peak District and Derbyshire
Yorkshire

National Hidden Places

England
Ireland
Scotland
Wales

Country Living Rural Guides

East Anglia
Heart of England
Ireland
North East of England
North West of England
Scotland
South
South East
Wales
West Country

Other Guides

Off the Motorway
Garden Centres and Nurseries
of Britain

Published by: Travel Publishing Ltd, Airport Business Centre, 10 Thornbury Road, Estover, Plymouth, Devon PL6 7PP

ISBN13   9781904434863

© Travel Publishing Ltd

First published 1989, second edition 1992, third edition 1996, fourth edition 1998, fifth edition 2000, sixth edition 2003, seventh edition 2005, eighth edition 2007, ninth edition 2009

Printing by: Latimer Trend, Plymouth

Maps by: ©MAPS IN MINUTES/Collins Bartholomew (2009)

Editor: David Gerrard

Cover Design: Lines and Words, Aldermaston

Cover Photograph: Newton Creek, Noss Mayo, Devon
© www.britainonview.com

Text Photographs: © www.britainhistoricsites.co.uk and
© www.picturesofbritain.co.uk

Foreword

This is the 9th edition of *The Hidden Places of Devon* taking you on a relaxed but informative tour of Devon. The guide has been been fully updated and in this respect we would like to thank the Tourist Information Centres in Devon for helping us update the editorial content. The guide is packed with information on the many interesting places to visit throughout the county. In addition, you will find details of places of interest and advertisers of places to stay, eat and drink included under each village, town or city, which are cross referenced to more detailed information contained in a separate, easy-to-use section to the rear of the book. This section is also available as a free supplement from the local Tourist Information Offices.

Devon is a beautiful county dotted with delightful little towns, quaint stone villages and eye-catching landscapes. Its lush green rolling hills are intersected with bright fresh streams and wooded valleys and it is also home to the National Parks of Dartmoor and Exmoor (which it shares with Somerset), two areas of outstanding natural beauty. Both parks have spectacular scenery with bleak uplands and isolated moorland stretching out towards the impressive coastlines of the north and south of the county.

The Hidden Places of Devon contains a wealth of interesting information on the history, the countryside, the towns and villages and the more established places of interest. But it also promotes the more secluded and little known visitor attractions and places to stay, eat and drink many of which are easy to miss unless you know exactly where you are going.

We include hotels, bed & breakfasts, restaurants, pubs, bars, teashops and cafes as well as historic houses, museums, gardens and many other attractions throughout Devon, all of which are comprehensively indexed. Many places are accompanied by an attractive photograph and are easily located by using the map at the beginning of each chapter. We do not award merit marks or rankings but concentrate on describing the more interesting, unusual or unique features of each place with the aim of making the reader's stay in the local area an enjoyable and stimulating experience.

Whether you are travelling around Devon on business or for pleasure we do hope that you enjoy reading and using this book. We are always interested in what readers think of places covered (or not covered) in our guides so please do not hesitate to use the reader reaction form provided to give us your considered comments. We also welcome any general comments which will help us improve the guides themselves. Finally if you are planning to visit any other corner of the British Isles we would like to refer you to the list of other *Hidden Places* titles to be found to the rear of the book and to the Travel Publishing website.

Travel Publishing

Did you know that you can also search our website for details of thousands of places to see, stay, eat or drink throughout Britain and Ireland? Our site has become increasingly popular and now receives over **200,000** visits annually. Try it!

website: **www.findsomewhere.co.uk**

Location Map

Chapter 3

Chapter 4

Chapter 2

Chapter 1

Chapter 5

Chapter 6

Chapter 7

Contents

East Devon and the Jurassic Coast

No less a traveller than Daniel Defoe considered the landscape of East Devon the finest in the world. Acres of rich farmland are watered by the rivers Axe, Otter and Madford, and narrow, winding lanes lead to villages that are as picturesque and interesting as any in England. Steep-sided hills rise towards the coastline where a string of elegant Regency resorts remind the visitor that this part of the coast was one of the earliest to be developed to satisfy the early 19th century craze for sea bathing.

Bounded by the rolling Blackdown Hills to the north, and Lyme Bay to the south, much of the countryside here is designated as of Outstanding Natural Beauty. The best, and for much of the route, the *only* landward way to explore the glorious East Devon coastline is to follow the South West Coast Path, part of the 600-mile South West Peninsula Coast Path which starts at Minehead in Somerset and ends at Shell Bay in Dorset.

East Devon's most famous son is undoubtedly Sir Walter Raleigh who was born at Hayes Barton near Yettington in 1552 and apparently never lost his soft Devon burr – a regional accent regarded then by 16th century London sophisticates as uncouth and much mocked by Sir Walter's enemies at the court of Elizabeth I. The Raleighs' family pew can still be seen in Yettington parish church. The famous picture by Sir John Everett Millais of *The Boyhood of Raleigh* was painted on the beach at Budleigh Salterton with the artist using his two sons and a local ferryman as the models.

Shingle Beach, Beer

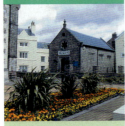

HONITON

Honiton is the "capital" of east Devon, a delightful little town in the valley of the River Otter and the "gateway to the far southwest". It was once a major stopping place on the Fosse Way, the great Roman road that struck diagonally across England from Lincoln to Exeter. Honiton's position on the main traffic artery to Devon and Cornwall brought it considerable prosperity, and its broad, ribbon-like High Street, almost two miles long, testifies to the town's busy past. By the 1960s, this "busyness" had deteriorated into appalling traffic congestion during the holiday season. Fortunately, the construction of a by-pass in the 1970s allowed Honiton to resume its true character as an attractive market town with a street market held on the High Street every Tuesday and Saturday.

Surrounded by sheep pastures, Honiton was the first town in Devon to manufacture serge cloth, but the town became much better known for a more delicate material, Honiton lace. Lace-making was introduced to east Devon by Flemish immigrants who arrived here during the early years of the reign of Elizabeth I. It wasn't long before those who could afford this costly new material were displaying it lavishly as a signal of their wealth and status. By the end of the 17th century, some 5000 people were engaged in the lace-making industry, most of them working from their own homes making fine "bone" lace by hand.

Children as young as five were sent to "lace schools" where they received a rudimentary education in the three Rs of Reading, (W)Riting, and (A)Rithmetic, and a far more intensive instruction in the skills of lace-making. Almost wiped out by the arrival of machine-made lace in the late 1700s, the industry was given a new lease of life when Queen Victoria insisted upon Honiton lace for her wedding dress and created a new fashion for lace that persisted throughout the 19th century. The traditional material is still made on a small scale in the town and can be found on sale in local shops, and on display in **Allhallows Museum.** This part-15th century building served as a school for some 300 years but is now an interesting local museum housing a unique collection of traditional lace and also, during the season, giving daily demonstrations of lace making.

Allhallows Schoolroom was one of the few old buildings to survive a series of devastating fires in the mid-1700s. However, that wholesale destruction had the fortunate result that the new buildings were gracious Georgian residences and Honiton still retains the pleasant, unhurried atmosphere of a prosperous 18th century coaching town.

Another building which escaped the flames unscathed was Marwood House (private) in the High Street. It was built in 1619 by the second son of Thomas Marwood, one of Queen

Elizabeth's many physicians. Thomas achieved great celebrity when he managed to cure the Earl of Essex after all others had failed. (He received his Devonshire estate as a reward). Thomas was equally successful in preserving his own health, living to the extraordinary age of 105.

Honiton boasts the only public art gallery in East Devon. The **Thelma Hulbert Gallery** occupies Elmfield House, an attractive Grade II listed late Georgian/early-Victorian town house which was the home and studio of the artist Thelma Hulbert (1913-1995). Now owned by East Devon District Council, the gallery has strong links with the Hayward Gallery in London which enables it to exhibit works by artists such as David Hockney, Andy Warhol and Roy Lichenstein as well as those of Thelma Hulbert herself.

Some buildings on the outskirts of the town are worth a mention. **St Margaret's Hospital**, to the west, was founded in the middle ages as a refuge for lepers who were denied entry to the town itself. Later, in the 16th century, this attractive thatched building was reconstructed as an almshouse. To the east, an early 19th century toll house known as **Copper Castle** can be seen. The castellated building still retains its original iron toll gates. And just a little further east, on Honiton Hill, stands the massive folly of the Bishop's Tower (private) erected in 1843 and once part of Bishop Edward Copplestone's house. The purpose

Copper Castle, Honiton

of the four-storey stone tower, built in the Italianate style, was apparently to enable the bishop to see his diocese of Llandaff across the Bristol Channel.

On the northern edge of Honiton rises the National Trust-owned **Dumpdon Hill**, an 850feet high steep-sided outcrop which is crowned by a sizeable late-Iron Age fort. Both the walk to the summit and the views over the Otter Valley are breathtaking.

AROUND HONITON

DUNKESWELL

5 miles N of Honiton off the A30

A pleasant country lane leads past **Dunkeswell Abbey**, of which only the 15th century gatehouse survives, the rest of the site now

5

Dunkeswell Abbey

4 THE OLD VICARAGE

Yarcombe

This warm and welcoming B & B is situated in the beautiful surroundings of the Devon countryside.

 see page 141

occupied by a Victorian church of no great charm. A couple of miles further and the road climbs up the hillside to Dunkeswell itself. This little village sits in the heart of the Blackdown Plateau and its main claim to fame is a 900-year-old Norman font in St Nicholas' Church on which is carved a rather crude depiction of an elephant, the earliest known representation of this animal in England. Almost certainly the stonemason had never seen such a beast, but he made almost as good a fist of it as he did with his satirical carvings of a bishop and a doctor. The font was originally located in Dunkeswell Abbey.

To the west of the village, **Dunkeswell Memorial Museum** stands on the site of the only American Navy air base commissioned on British soil during World War II. It is dedicated to the veterans of the US Fleet Air Wing 7 and RAF personnel who served at the base. The museum explores the special role that the servicemen played during the war through a range of exhibits and displays that include artefacts and photographs. There is also a restaurant, a playground for children and a museum shop.

DALWOOD

6 miles E of Honiton off the A35

By some administrative freak, until 1842 the little village of Dalwood, despite being completely surrounded by Devon, was actually part of Dorset. Its other main claim to fame is as the home of the **Loughwood Meeting House**, one of the earliest surviving Baptist chapels in the country. When the chapel was built in the 1650s, the site was hidden by dense woodland, for the Baptists were a persecuted sect who could only congregate in out of the way locations. Under its quaint thatched roof, this charming little building contains a simple whitewashed interior with early 18th century pulpits and pews. The chapel was in use until 1833, then languished for many years until it was acquired by the National Trust in 1969. It is now open all year round with admission by voluntary donation.

About three miles south of Dalwood is another National Trust property, **Shute Barton**, an exceptional example of a medieval manor house which dates from the 1380s. Only two wings of the original building have survived, but they include some remarkably impressive features such as the Great Hall with its massive beamed ceiling, and the ancient kitchen with a huge range capable of roasting an ox whole. Entry is by way of a Tudor gatehouse.

Shute Barton was owned by the Pole family, a local dynasty which is commemorated by some grand monuments in **St Michael's Church.** Amongst them is an overbearing memorial to Sir William Pole which depicts the Master of the Household to Queen Anne standing on a pedestal dressed in full regalia. More appealing is the 19th century sculptured panel, seven feet high and framed in alabaster, which shows Margaret Pole greeting her three little daughters at the gates of heaven.

Close by are **Burrow Farm Gardens,** beautifully landscaped gardens that provide a peaceful place for a relaxing afternoon's outing as well as plenty of interest for keen gardeners. Also on site are a craft shop, tea room and nursery.

Also close to the village is **Lyme Bay Winery** where the traditional craft of making West Country cider is kept very much alive. Using old-fashioned locally farmed cider apples, such as Kingston Black, Dabinett and Yarlington Mill, the winery produces a range of ciders and apple-based drinks that can be purchased at the winery shop.

The Winery includes a range of drinks named after the notorious smuggler Jack

Shute Barton, Shute

Rattenbury (1778-1844), who operated around the Lyme Bay coast between Weymouth and Topsham. Often involved in skirmishes with the Customs and Excise men, Rattenbury, like other smugglers of the time, practised creeping, a local method of hiding contraband from the authorities by sinking barrels on rafts off the coast and then recovering the goods when the excisemen were otherwise occupied.

AXMINSTER

10 miles E of Honiton on the A35/A358

This little town grew up around the junction of two important Roman roads, the Fosse and the Icknield, and was prominent in medieval times because of its Minster beside the River Axe. Its name has entered the language as the synonym for a very superior kind of floor-covering which first appeared in the early 1750s. Wandering around London's Cheapside market, an Axminster weaver named **Thomas Whitty** was astonished to see a

5 BURROW FARM GARDENS

Dalwood

A beautifully landscaped 10-acre garden, the work over the last 40 years of Mary Benger, with a vast array of shrubs and plants.

 see page 142

6 CASTLE INN

Axminster

Situated in the ancient market town of Axminster, the **Castle Inn** is a pleasant town centre pub, offering a warm welcome.

 see page 142

7

7 THE OLD INN

Hawkchurch

Atmospheric old hostelry offering wholesome food, local real ales and 3-star en suite accommodation.

 see page 142

Every June, on the showground just outside Axminster, the Axe Vale Festival of Gardening and Crafts draws visitors from all over the southwest and beyond. This traditional horticultural show also offers a craft marquee, an antiques fair and numerous amusements for children.

huge Turkish carpet, 12 yards long and 8 yards wide. Returning to the sleepy little market town where he was born, Thomas spent months puzzling over the mechanics of producing such a seamless piece of work. By 1755 he had solved the problem, and on midsummer's day that year the first of these luxurious carpets was revealed to the world. The time and labour involved was so prodigious that the completion of each carpet was celebrated by a procession to St Mary's Church and a ringing peal of bells. Ironically, one distinguished purchaser of an Axminster carpet was the Sultan of Turkey who in 1800 paid the colossal sum of £1000 for a particularly fine specimen. But the inordinately high labour costs involved in producing such exquisite hand-tufted carpets crippled Whitty's company. In 1835, their looms were sold to a factory at Wilton. That was the end of Axminster's pre-eminence in the market for top-quality carpets, but echoes of those glorious years still reverberate. **St Mary's Church** must be the only house of worship in Christendom whose floor is covered with a richly-woven carpet.

Opposite the church is the former courthouse which is now home to the **Axminster Museum** where the old police cells can be visited and there are collections of vintage agricultural tools and Axminster carpets.

The town has a market every Thursday and boasts a good range of privately owned shops, amongst them 'River Cottage', a former inn converted by TV presenter Hugh Fearnley-Whittingstall to an organic produce shop and canteen.

COLYTON

7 miles SE of Honiton off the A3052

The tramway that starts at Seaton runs by way of Colyford to this ancient and very appealing small town of narrow winding streets and interesting stone houses. Throughout its long history, Colyton has been an important agricultural and commercial centre with its own corn mill, tannery, sawmill and iron foundry.

Many of the older buildings are grouped around the part-Norman **Church of St Andrew,** a striking building with an unusual 15th century octagonal lantern tower, and a **Saxon Cross** brilliantly reconstructed after its broken fragments were retrieved from the tower where they had been used as

Saxon Cross, Colyton

building material. Nearby is the Vicarage of 1529, and the Old Church House, a part-medieval building enlarged in 1612 and used as a Grammar School until 1928.

Just to the north of Colyton are the exceptional remains of **Colcombe Castle**, which dates from the 16th and 17th centuries, while to the south stands **Great House**, which was built on the road to Colyford by a wealthy Elizabethan merchant. To the west lies **Countryside Park Farway** which offers breathtaking views, woodland nature trails, both traditional and rare breed farm animals and a children's indoor play area. There is also a licensed restaurant.

OTTERY ST MARY

7m SW of Honiton on the B3177

The glory of Ottery St Mary is its magnificent 14th century **Church of St Mary**. From the outside, St Mary's looks part mini-Cathedral, part Oxford college. Both impressions are justified since, when Bishop Grandisson commissioned the building in 1337, he stipulated that it should be modelled on his own cathedral at Exeter. He also wanted it to be "a sanctuary for piety and learning", so accommodation for 40 scholars was provided.

The interior is just as striking. The church's medieval treasures include a brilliantly-coloured altar screen, canopied tombs, and a 14th century astronomical clock showing the moon and the planets which still functions with its original

machinery. The weather vane is a Whistling Cock, with tubes running through the body that make it whistle in the wind. Cromwell's soldiers used the vane as target practice during the Civil War.

Ottery's Vicar during the mid-18th century was the Rev. John Coleridge whose 13th child became the celebrated poet, **Samuel Taylor Coleridge.** The family home near the church has since been demolished but in one of his poems Samuel recalls

> *"my sweet birth-place,*
> *and the old church-tower*
> *Whose bells,*
> *the poor man's only music, rang*
> *From morn to evening,*
> *all the hot Fair-day"*

A bronze plaque in the churchyard wall honours Ottery's most famous son. It shows his profile, menaced by the albatross that features in his best-known poem, *The Ancient Mariner.* Outside the church is a monument erected to commemorate Queen Victoria's Diamond Jubilee; a copy of one of the gateposts at Kensington Palace, it stands on the site originally occupied by the town stocks, which are now to be found in the churchyard.

It's a delight to wander around the narrow, twisting lanes that lead up from the River Otter, admiring the fine Georgian buildings amongst which is an old wool manufactory by the riverside, a dignified example of early industrial architecture. Many visitors walk along the river to see the Tumbling Weir, built in 1790 to supply power

8   VOLUNTEER INN

Ottery St Mary

The **Volunteer Inn** feels genuinely warm and homely and offers comfortable accommodation.

 see page 143

Cadhay Manor, Ottery St Mary

9 RIDGEWAY FARM

Awliscombe, nr Honiton

Set in an area of outstanding natural beauty with stunning views, **Ridgeway Farm** is a traditional 18th century farmhouse with cosy, comfortable accommodation.

 see page 143

10 OLD BRIDWELL HOLIDAY COTTAGES

Uffculme

Idyllic self-catering cottages in the rural countryside hamlet of Old Bridwell.

 see page 144

from the mill stream to the factory.

An especially interesting time to visit Ottery is on the Saturday closest to November 5th. The town's Guy Fawkes celebrations include a time-honoured, if rather alarming, tradition of rolling barrels of flaming tar through the narrow streets.

About a mile northwest of Ottery, **Cadhay** is a beautiful Tudor mansion built around 1550 but incorporating the Great Hall of an earlier mansion built between 1420 and 1470. The house was built for a Lincoln's Inn lawyer, John Haydon, whose great-nephew Robert Haydon later added the exquisite Long Gallery thus forming a unique and attractive courtyard. Opening times are restricted.

Close by is **Escot Fantasy Gardens** & Parkland where visitors can see an arboretum and rose garden along with a collection of wildlife that includes wild boar, pot-bellied pigs, otters and birds of prey. The original gardens in this 1200-acre estate were set out by 'Capability Brown' and have been restored by the land artist and television gardener, Ivan Hicks.

BLACKBOROUGH

10 miles NW of Honiton off the A373

Most of the villages in this corner of East Devon nestle in the valley bottoms, but Blackborough is an exception, standing high on a ridge of the Blackdown Hills. It's a comparatively new settlement which sprang up when whetstone mining flourished here for a period in the early 1800s. RD Blackmore's novel *Perlycross* presents a vivid picture of life in these makeshift mining camps where the amenities of a comfortable life were few and far between.

UFFCULME

13 miles NW of Honiton off the A38

In medieval times, the charming little village of Uffculme, set beside the River Culm, was an important centre for the wool trade. Profits from this booming business helped build the impressive parish church of St Mary around 1450 and to install its splendid rood screen, believed to be the longest in Devon.

Coldharbour Mill, to the west of the village, is one of the few surviving reminders of the county's industrial wool trade. It closed down in 1981 but has since been converted into a Working Wool Museum where visitors can watch the whole process of woollen and worsted manufacture, wander around the carpenters' workshop, a weavers' cottage and the dye room. On most Bank Holidays, the massive 300 horsepower engine in the boiler house is "steamed up"- a spectacular sight. Conducted tours are available and the complex also includes a Mill Shop and a waterside restaurant.

CULMSTOCK

13 miles NW of Honiton on the B3391

Lovers of RD Blackmore's novel *Lorna Doone* will be particularly interested in Culmstock since it was here that the author lived as a boy during the years that his father was the Vicar. One of his playmates in the village was Frederick Temple, another bright boy, and the two friends both went on to Blundell's School at Tiverton where they shared lodgings. Blackmore was to become one of the most successful novelists of his time; Temple entered the church and after several years as Headmaster of Rugby School reached the pinnacle of his profession as Archbishop of Canterbury.

In the centre of the village stands Culmstock's parish church with its famous yew tree growing from the top of the tower. The tree has been growing there for more than 200 years and, despite the fact that its only nourishment is the lime content of the mortar in which it is set, the trunk has now achieved a girth of 18 inches. It's believed that the seed was probably carried up in the mortar used to repair the tower when its spire was demolished in 1776. The church's

more traditional kind of treasures include a magnificently embroidered cope of the late 1400s, now preserved in a glass case; a remarkable 14th century tomb rediscovered during restoration in the 19th century; and a richly-coloured memorial window designed by Burne-Jones.

THE JURASSIC COAST

The coastal stretch to the east of Exmouth has been named the Jurassic Coast because it was formed during the Jurassic period some 185 million years ago. England's first natural World Heritage Site, the 95 miles of coastline from Exmouth to Studland in Dorset are spectacularly beautiful.

Three river valleys, those of the Axe, the Sid and the Otter, cut through the hills of east Devon to meet the sea at Lyme Bay. They provide the only openings in the magnificent 20-mile long stretch of rugged cliffs and rocky beaches. Virtually the only settlements to be found along the seaboard are those which developed around the mouths of those rivers: Seaton, Sidmouth and Budleigh Salterton. The intervening cliffs discouraged human habitation and even today the only way to explore most of this part of the coast is on foot along the magnificent **East Devon Way,** part of the South West Coast Path. Signposted by a foxglove, the footpath travels through the county

About three miles east of Culmstock is Hemyock Castle, built around 1380. Four turrets, a curtain wall, a moat with mallard and moorhen in residence, and a dungeon are all that remains of the Hidon family's sturdy manor house, but it is a peaceful and evocative place. The castle stands behind the church in beautiful grounds and, since it lies close to the head of the lovely Culm valley, is very popular as a picnic spot. Opening times are restricted.

11

11 THE STRAND COFFEE HOUSE

Exmouth

This traditional tearoom serves speciality teas and coffees as well as homemade cakes, scones and soups.

 see page 145

to Lyme Regis just over the county border in Dorset. Four other circular paths link in with the East Devon Way providing other options for walkers to enjoy and explore the quieter and more remote areas away from the coast.

For centuries the little towns along the coast subsisted on fishing and farming until the early 1800s when the Prince Regent's fad for sea bathing brought an influx of comparatively affluent visitors in search of healthy relaxation. Their numbers were augmented by others whose accustomed European travels had been rendered impossible by Napoleon's domination of the Continent. Between them, they transformed these modest little towns into fashionable resorts, imbuing them

with an indefinable "gentility" which still lives on in the elegant villas, peaceful gardens and wide promenades.

EXMOUTH

With its glorious coastal scenery and splendid beach, Exmouth was one of the earliest seaside resorts to be developed in Devon, "the Bath of the West, the resort of the tip-top of the gentry of the Kingdom". Lady Byron and Lady Nelson came to stay and found lodgings in The Beacon, an elegant Georgian terrace overlooking the Madeira Walk and Esplanade. This terrace lay at the heart of life in Regency Exmouth and here can be found the **Assembly Rooms**, where most of the social events were held in the late 18th and early 19th centuries, and also **Nelson House**, the home of Lady Nelson in her later years.

Exmouth's early success suffered a setback when Brunel routed his Great Western line along the other side of the estuary, (incidentally creating one of the most scenic railway journeys still possible in England), and it wasn't until a branch line reached Exmouth in 1861 that business picked up again. The town isn't just a popular resort. Exmouth Docks are still busy with coasters and in summer a passenger ferry crosses the Exe to Starcross. There are also services to Dawlish Warren and from the marina there are cruises along the River Exe to Topsham.

A La Ronde, Exmouth

Exmouth's major all-weather attraction is **The World of Country Life** which offers an Adventure Exhibition Hall, a collection of vintage cars, a Victorian Street, safari train, pirate ship, pets centre and restaurant.

Occupying converted 18th century stables and an adjoining cottage, **Exmouth Museum** provides fascinating insights into the town's rich history and its strong maritime links.

While in Exmouth, you should make a point of visiting what has been described as "the most unusual house in Britain". **A La Ronde** (National Trust) is a fairy-tale thatched house built in 1765 by the sisters Jane and Mary Parminter who modelled it on the church of San Vitale in Ravenna. Despite its name, the house is not circular but has 16 sides with 20 rooms set around a 45 feet high octagon. The sisters lived here in magnificent feminist seclusion, forbidding the presence of any male in their house or its 15 acres of grounds. What, therefore, no gentleman saw during the lifetime of the sisters, was the wonderfully decorated interior that the cousins created. These fabulous rooms, common in Regency times, are rare today. Due to their delicacy, the feather frieze and shell-encrusted gallery can be seen only via closed circuit TV. Throughout the house the vast collection of pieces that the ladies brought back from their extensive travels is on display.

EAST OF EXMOUTH

BUDLEIGH SALTERTON

4 miles E of Exmouth on the B3180

With its trim Victorian villas, broad promenade and a spotlessly clean beach flanked by 500 feet high red sandstone cliffs, Budleigh Salterton retains its 19th century atmosphere of a genteel resort. Victorian tourists "of the better sort" noted with approval that the two-mile long beach was of pink shingle rather than sand. (Sand, apparently, attracted the rowdier kind of holiday-maker). The steeply-shelving beach was another deterrent, and the sea here is still a place for paddling rather than swimming as on some days there is a strong undertow.

One famous Victorian visitor was the celebrated artist Sir John Everett Millais who stayed during the summer of 1870 in the curiously-shaped house called The Octagon (private). It was beside the beach here that he painted his most famous picture *The Boyhood of Raleigh*, using his two sons and a local ferryman as the models. Raleigh's birthplace, Hayes Barton, lies a mile or so inland and remains virtually unchanged. It is not open to the public.

The name Budleigh Salterton derives from the salt pans at the mouth of the River Otter which brought great prosperity to the town during the Middle Ages. The little port was then busy with ships loading salt and wool, but by 1450 the estuary had become blocked by

12 TEA AND TITTLE TATTLE

Budleigh Salterton
Tea and Tittle Tattle, as the name suggests, are rather into their hot beverages and merry conversation.

see page 145

Found on Budleigh Salterton's seafront is Fairlynch Museum, one of very few thatched museums in the country. It houses numerous collections covering all aspects of life through the ages in the lower Otter Valley.

a pebble ridge and the salt pans flooded.

Covering the whole of the river estuary, the **Otter Estuary Nature Reserve** includes areas of salt marsh, tidal mudflats, grazing marsh and redbuds that provide an interesting and varied habitat and an important refuge for over-wintering birds. There are footpaths on both sides of the estuary with viewing platforms (on the western side) and a hide (on the eastern).

To the northeast of the town lies **Bystock Nature Reserve**, a place of heath, grassland, woods and boggy areas that is part of the East Devon Heaths Site of Special Scientific Interest. Despite being occupied by the military during World War II, the reserve is now returning to the heathland that, for centuries, provided rough grazing for cattle. The network of paths crossing the reserve can be quite rough in places and the paths often follow the tops of narrow, raised banks to avoid boggy ground.

EAST BUDLEIGH
6 miles NE of Exmouth off the B3178

Just to the south of the village is Hayes Barton (private), a fine E-shaped Tudor house in which **Sir Walter Raleigh** was born in 1552. The Raleighs' family pew can still be seen in All Saints' Church, dated 1537 and carved with their (now sadly defaced) coat of arms. The church also contains a series of more than fifty 16th century bench-ends which were carved by local artisans into weird and imaginative depictions of their various trades.

A wall memorial in the church commemorates the Revd Ambrose Stapleton who was vicar here for 58 years from 1794 to 1852. He was a popular incumbent, partly it seems because he allowed local smugglers to use the vicarage to hide their brandy barrels.

A mile or so in the other direction is **Bicton Park,** best known for its landscaped gardens which were laid out in the 1730s by Henry Rolle to a plan by André Le Nôtre, the designer of Versailles. There is also a formal Italian garden, a remarkable palm house known as The Dome, a world-renowned collection of pine trees, and a lake complete with an extraordinary summer house, The Hermitage. Its outside walls are covered with thousands of tiny wooden shingles, each one individually pinned on so they look like the scales of an enormous fish.

Bicton Park Gardens, East Budleigh

Inside, the floors are made from deer's knucklebones. The Hermitage was built by Lady Louise Rolle in 1839 as an exotic summer-house; any occupation during the winter would have been highly inadvisable since the chimney was made of oak.

OTTERTON

7 miles NE of Exmouth off the B3178

This delightful village has a charming mix of traditional cob and thatch cottages, along with other buildings constructed in the distinctive local red sandstone, amongst them the tower of St Michael's parish church. Nearby stands a manor house which was built in the 11th century as a small priory belonging to Mont St Michel in Normandy. It is now divided into private apartments.

An interesting feature of this village of white-painted and thatched cottages is the little stream that runs down Fore Street. At the bottom of the hill, this beck joins the River Otter, which at this point has only a couple of miles to go before it enters the sea near Budleigh Salterton. There's a lovely riverside walk in that direction, and if you go northwards the path stretches even further, to Ottery St Mary some nine or ten miles distant.

HARPFORD

11 miles NE of Exmouth off the A3052

In an attractive setting on the east bank of the River Otter with wooded hills behind, Harpford has a 13th century church with an

Dartford Warbler

impressive tower and, in its churchyard, a memorial cross to the **Revd Augustus Toplady** who was vicar of Harpford for a couple of years in the mid-1700s. In 1775 Augustus wrote the hymn *Rock of Ages, cleft for me*, which has proved to be one of the most durable contributions to English hymnody.

If you cross the footbridge over the river here and follow the path for about a couple of miles you will come to **Aylesbeare Common**, an RSPB sanctuary which is also one of the best stretches of heathland in the area. Bird watchers may be lucky enough to spot a Dartford warbler, stonechats, or tree pipits, and even hear the strange song of the nightjar.

SIDMOUTH

Sidmouth's success, like that of many other English resorts, had much to do with Napoleon Bonaparte. Barred from the Continent and their favoured resorts by the Emperor's conquest of Europe, the leisured classes were forced to find diversion and

The Domesday Book recorded a mill on the River Otter at Otterton, almost certainly on the site of the present Otterton Mill. This handsome, part-medieval building was restored to working order in the 1970s by Desna Greenhow, a teacher of Medieval Archaeology. Visitors can now buy packs of flour ground by the same methods that were in use long before the compilers of the Domesday Book passed through the village. The site also includes a craft centre, shop and restaurant.

14 SOUTHERN CROSS GUEST HOUSE & TEA ROOMS

Newton Poppleford

The **Southern Cross Guest House** offers award winning B&B accommodation and is also home to the celebrated **Southern Cross Tea Rooms**

see page 146

15 THE LONGHOUSE BED & BREAKFAST

Sidmouth

Surrounded by woodland, the Longhouse sits just below the top of Salcombe hill, at six hundred feet above sea level, with views across Sid Bay and Sidmouth town.

 see page 147

*One of the Sidmouth's early visitors was Jane Austen, who came here on holiday in 1801 and, according to Austen family tradition, fell in love with a clergyman whom she would have married if he had not mysteriously died or disappeared. Later, in the 1830s, William Makepeace Thackeray visited and the town featured as Baymouth in his semi-autobiographical work **Pendennis** (published in 1848). During the Edwardian age, Beatrix Potter was a visitor on several occasions.*

entertainment within their own island fortress. At the same time, sea bathing had suddenly become fashionable so these years were a boom time for the south coast, even as far west as Sidmouth which until then had been a poverty-stricken village dependent on fishing.

Sidmouth's spectacular position at the mouth of the River Sid, flanked by dramatic red cliffs soaring to over 500 feet and with a broad pebbly beach, assured the village's popularity with the newcomers. A grand Esplanade was constructed, lined with handsome Georgian houses, and between 1800 and 1820 Sidmouth's population doubled as the aristocratic and well-to-do built substantial "cottages" in and around the town. Many of these have since been converted into impressive hotels such as the Beach House, painted strawberry pink and white, and the Royal Glen which in the early 19th century was the residence of the royal **Duke of Kent.** The duke came here in 1819 in an attempt to escape his numerous creditors, and it was here that his infant daughter, Princess Victoria, later Queen Victoria, saw the sea for the first time.

Trying to evade his many creditors, the duke had his mail directed to Salisbury. Each week he would ride there to collect his letters but in Sidmouth itself he couldn't conceal his delight in his young daughter. He would push Victoria in a little carriage along the mile-long Regency Esplanade,

stopping passers-by to tell them to look carefully at the little girl – "for one day she would be their Queen". Half a century later, his daughter presented a stained-glass window to Sidmouth parish church in dutiful memory of her father.

A stroll around the town reveals a wealth of attractive Georgian and early-Victorian buildings. Amazingly for such a small town, Sidmouth boasts nearly 500 listed buildings. Curiously, it was the Victorians who let the town down. Despite being the wealthiest nation in the world at that time, with vast resources at its command, its architects seemed incapable of creating architecturally interesting churches and the two 19th century Houses of the Lord they built in Sidmouth display a lamentable lack of inspiration. So ignore them, but it's worth seeking out the curious structure known as the **Old Chancel,** a glorious hotch-potch of styles using bits and pieces salvaged from the old parish church and from just about anywhere else, amongst them a priceless window of medieval stained glass.

Also well worth a visit is **Sidmouth Museum**, near the seafront, which provides a vivid presentation of the Victorian resort, along with such curiosities as an albatross's swollen foot once used as a tobacco pouch. There's also an interesting collection of local prints, a costume gallery and a display of fine lace. One of the most striking exhibits in the museum is the "Long Picture" by

Hubert Cornish which is some 8 feet (2.4 metres) long and depicts the whole of Sidmouth seafront as it was around 1814.

Close to the seafront is the **Sid Vale Heritage Centre** which portrays the varied history of this elegant resort through old photographs, costumes, Victoriana and artefacts that once belonged to famous residents. The geology and archaeology of the area are also explored. On certain days guided tours of the town leave from here led by the museum staff.

Set atop cliffs overlooking Lyme Bay, **Connaught Gardens** are named after Queen Victoria's third son, the Duke of Connaught, who formally opened them in 1934. Most weeks throughout the summer at least one band is playing here and there are occasional outdoor theatre performances.

Sidmouth boasts one of the few public access observatories in Britain: the **Norman Lockyer Observatory**. It has a planetarium and large telescopes, and a radio station commemorating the contribution of Sir Ambrose Fleming, a local hero, to the invention of the radio valve.

AROUND SIDMOUTH

SIDFORD

2 miles N of Sidmouth on the A375

As its name suggests, Sidford stands beside a narrow stretch of the River Sid – one of the shortest rivers in England – that rises from spring-fed waters to the east of Ottery St Mary and tumbles and twists down a narrow valley for just four miles before entering Lyme Bay at Sidmouth. The village is famous for its Norman **Packhorse Bridge**, dating from the 12th century, which has played an important part in local history over the centuries, not least during the Civil War when there was a skirmish here in 1644.

SIDBURY

3 miles N of Sidmouth on the A375

St Peter & St Giles' Church at Sidbury boasts the unique amenity of a Powder Room. In fact, the room over the porch contained not cosmetics, but gunpowder which was stored there by the military during the fearful days when Napoleon was expected to land in England at any moment. The church is also notable for its Saxon crypt, rediscovered during restoration in 1898. It's a rough-walled room just nine feet by 10 located under the chancel floor. Other treasures include a remarkable 500-year-old font with a square iron lock intended to protect the holy water in the basin from witches, and a number of curious carvings on the Norman tower.

Sidbury is also home to the last working watermill on the River Sid and, now carefully restored, it is open to the public as **Sidbury Mill and Art Gallery**. Although it is nearly 100 years since the mill's massive waterwheel turned, it remains a feature of the village; the gallery displays arts and crafts by local artists.

16 NORMAN LOCKYER OBSERVATORY

Sidmouth

Public access observatory commemorating Norman Lockyers lifetime achievements

 see page 148

Demure though it remains, Sidmouth undergoes a transformation in the first week of August each year when it plays host to the Sidmouth Folk Week, a cosmopolitan event which attracts a remarkable variety of morris dancers, folk singers and even clog dancers from around the world.

17 ROSE COTTAGE

Sidbury

Delightful 17th century former estate house office offering 4-star quality en suite B&B accommodation.

 see page 149

18 THE HARBOUR INN

Axmouth

Traditional 12th century old English pub, with cosy bars, dining rooms and oak beams.

 see page 150

To the northeast of Sidbury is one of east Devon's hidden gems – **Sand House and Gardens**. Situated in a quiet valley, this historic house dates principally from the Elizabethan era and has been in the unbroken ownership of the same family since 1561. Members of the family lead guided tours of the house, where a wealth of period interior features can be seen; the gardens, which extend for six acres, incorporate a sunny terrace, shady woodland, manicured lawns and colourful borders.

Above the village to the southwest stands **Sidbury Castle**, not a castle at all but the site of a hilltop Iron Age fort from which there are some spellbinding views of the coastline extending from Portland Bill to Berry Head.

BRANSCOMBE

5 miles E of Sidmouth off the A3052

The coastal scenery near Branscombe is some of the finest in the south west with great towers of chalk rising from overgrown landslips. The village itself is a picturesque scattering of farmhouses and thatched cottages with an interesting National Trust property within its boundaries – **Branscombe Manor Mill, Old Bakery and Forge**. Regular demonstrations are held at the Manor Mill which is still in working order. The water-powered mill provided flour for the adjacent bakery which, until 1987, was the last traditional bakery operating in Devon. Its vintage baking

equipment has been preserved and the rest of the building is now a tearoom. The Forge is still working and the blacksmith's ironwork is on sale to visitors.

The land around Branscombe's beach with its long expanse of pebbles and painted coastal huts, is also owned by the National Trust. The beach entered the national consciousness in January 2007 when a container ship, the *MSC Napoli* got into difficulties during a gale and was grounded about 100 yards from the beach. Some of the ship's containers broke open and their contents were washed on to the beach. The flotsam included barrels of wine, shoes, hair care products, beauty cream, steering wheels, exhaust pipes, gearboxes, nappies, foreign language bibles and even BMW motorbikes. As the word spread, the beach was invaded by scavengers, many of whom made away with rich pickings until the police closed the beach 24 hours after the *Napoli* had grounded. It was not until 7 months later that the stricken ship was taken by tug to a dry dock at the Harland and Wolff shipyard in Belfast.

BEER

7 miles E of Sidmouth on the B3174

Set between the high white chalk cliffs of Beer Head and Seaton Hole, this picturesque fishing village is best known for the superb white freestone which has been quarried here since Roman times. Much prized for carving, the results can be seen in countless Devon churches, and most notably in the cathedrals at Exeter, Winchester, and St Paul's, as well as at the Tower of London and in Westminster Abbey. Conducted tours around the vast, man-made complex of the **Beer Quarry Caves** leave visitors astonished at the sheer grandeur of the lofty halls, vaulted roofs and massive supporting pillars of natural stone. Not surprisingly, this complex underground network recommended itself to smugglers, amongst them the notorious Jack Rattenbury who was a native of Beer and published his *Memoirs of a Smuggler* in 1837.

A family attraction here is **Pecorama** which sits on the cliff top high above the village and has an award-winning miniature railway, spectacular Millennium Gardens, the Peco Model Railway Exhibition, play areas and superb sea views.

SEATON

8 miles E of Sidmouth on the B3172

Set around the mouth of the River Axe, with red cliffs on one side and white cliffs on the other, Seaton was once a quite significant port. By the 16th century, however, the estuary had filled up with stones and pebbles, and it wasn't until moneyed Victorians came and built their villas (and one of the first concrete bridges in the world, in 1877) that Seaton was accorded a new lease of life. The self-confident architecture of those times gives the little town an

attractive appearance which is enhanced by its pedestrianised town centre, well-maintained public parks and gardens, manicured bowling greens, extensive walled promenade, pretty harbour and vast pebbled beach.

From Seaton, an appealing way of travelling along the Axe Valley is on the **Seaton Tramway** whose colourful open-topped tramcars trundle along a three-mile route following the course of the River Axe to the villages of Colyford and Colyton. The area is noted for its abundant wild bird life. Really dedicated tram fans, after a short lesson, are even permitted to take over the driver's seat.

From Seaton, eastwards, the **South West Coast Path** follows the coastline uninterruptedly all the way to Lyme Regis in Dorset. Considered by naturalists as the last and largest wilderness on the southern coast of England, this area of unstable cliffs, wood and scrub is also a haven for wildlife.

19 BEAUMONT

Seaton

Enjoying an unrivalled location in the seaside town of Seaton, Beaumont provides the ideal getaway for those wanting to enjoy the delights the area has to offer.

 see page 151

Seaton Promenade

Exeter and the Exe Valley

The valley of the River Exe is dominated by the city of Exeter and the city in turn is dominated by its superb cathedral, one of the finest examples of the Decorated style of architecture in the country. The city was once an important port but today the area around the harbour where the old warehouses and port buildings are situated has been given a new lease of life with speciality shops, cafés, restaurants and visitor attractions.

The Exe estuary stretches for six miles from Exeter to the sea and is a place of international importance that supports an amazing diversity of bird life. A journey upstream through the Exe Valley from Exeter reveals quaint scattered villages set amidst glorious countryside. This area is known as "Red Devon" because the soil here has a distinctive colour derived from the red Permian rocks that underlie it. Unlike most land in Devon, this is prime agricultural land, fertile, easily worked and, for some reason, particularly favourable for growing swedes to which it imparts a much sought after flavour. Man-made additions to the pastoral landscape include Iron Age forts at Cadbury and

Woodbury, and some splendid stately homes at Knighthayes Court, Powderham Castle and Killerton House.

The only town of any size in the valley is Tiverton which developed around its medieval castle and later enjoyed great prosperity through the wool trade.

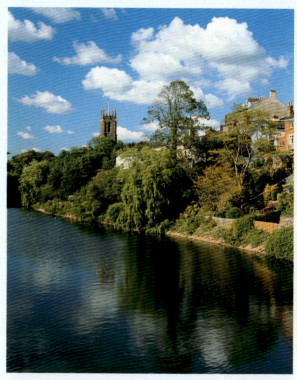

St Peters Church, Tiverton

21

Exeter

Popular city centre café offering extensive menu based on fresh, locally-sourced ingredients.

see page 152

EXETER

A lively and thriving city with a majestic Norman cathedral, many fine old buildings, and a wealth of excellent museums, Exeter's history stretches back for more than two millennia. Its present High Street was already in place some 200 years or more before the Romans arrived, part of an ancient ridgeway striking across the West Country. The inhabitants then were the Celtish tribe of the Dumnonii and it was they who named the river Eisca, "a river abounding in fish".

The Romans made Isca their south-western stronghold, surrounding it with a massive defensive wall. Most of that has disappeared, but a spectacular *caldarium,* or **Roman Bath House** was uncovered in the Cathedral Close in 1971.

In the Dark Ages following the Roman withdrawal, the city was a major ecclesiastical centre and in AD670 King Cenwealh founded an abbey on the site of the present cathedral. That, along with the rest of Exeter, was ransacked by the Vikings in the 9th century. They occupied the city twice before King Alfred finally saw them off.

The Normans were next on the scene, although it wasn't until 20 years after the Battle of Hastings that William the Conqueror finally took possession of the city after a siege that lasted 18 days. He ordered the construction of **Rougemont Castle,** the gatehouse and tower of which still stand at the top of Castle Street. Here, planted in and around the original moat of the castle, and with a section of the Roman walls as a backdrop, are **Rougemont Gardens** – a tranquil haven in the heart of this bustling city.

During the following century, the Normans began building **St Peter's Cathedral,** a work not completed until 1206. Half a century later, however, everything except the two sturdy towers was demolished and the present cathedral took shape. These years saw the development of the Decorated style, and Exeter is a sublime example of this appealing form of church architecture. In the

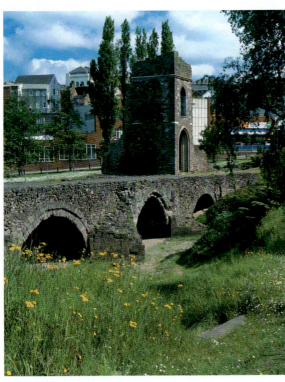

Medieval Exe Bridge, Exeter

300 feet long nave, stone piers rise 60 feet and then fan out into sweeping arches. Equally impressive is the west front, a staggering display of more than 60 sculptures, carved between 1327 and 1369. They depict a curious mix of Biblical characters, soldiers, priests and a royal flush of Saxon and Norman kings.

Other treasures include an intricately-carved choir screen from about 1320, an astronomical clock built in 1376 which is one of the oldest timepieces in the world and reputed to be the inspiration for the children's nursery rhyme *Hickory, Dickory Dock*, a monumental organ , a minstrels' gallery with a wonderful band of heavenly musicians, a monumental organ, and a colossal throne with a canopy 59 feet high, carved in wood for Bishop Stapledon in 1316.

Another remarkable carving can be found beneath the misericord seats in the choir stalls where, amongst other carvings, there is one of an elephant. However, as the carver had no model to work from he has given the animal tusks that look like clubs and rather eccentric feet. It has been suggested that the carving was based on the first elephant to come to Britain as a gift to Henry III in 1253. The carver had probably heard stories of the creature and made up the rest.

In 1941 much of the old part of the city was destroyed by a German air raid and, although the cathedral survived, it was badly damaged. When restoration work

Exeter Quayside

began in 1943, a collection of wax models was discovered hidden in a cavity. Including representations of human and animal limbs, the complete figure of a woman and a horse's head, they are thought to have been brought here by pilgrims who would place their wax models on the tomb of Bishop Edmund Lacy. By placing a model of an injured or withered limb on the tomb the pilgrims believed that they would be cured of their affliction.

Such is the grandeur of the cathedral that other ecclesiastical buildings in Exeter tend to get overlooked. But it's well worth seeking out **St Nicholas' Priory**, an exceptional example of a small Norman priory. The Priory re-opened to the public in April 2008 after a two-year programme of conservation work. Adorned with quality replica furniture and painted in the bright colours of the period, the Priory is now presented as the 1602 home of the wealthy Hurst family. Visitors can experience

•

An interesting medieval building in Exeter is The Tucker's Hall in Fore Street, built in 1471 for the Company of Weavers, Fullers (Tuckers) and Shearmen. Inside there is some exceptional carved panelling, a collection of rare silver, and a huge pair of fulling shears weighing over 25 pounds and almost 4 feet long. Nearby Parliament Street claims to be the world's narrowest street - just 45 inches at its widest and less than 25 inches at its narrowest.

•

Customs House, Exeter

Exeter

Dating from 14th century, the medieval passages under Exeter High Street are a unique ancient monument.

 see page 152

Tudor life including Elizabethan music, costume, food, games and stories. They can also view the original Priory cellar with its chunky Norman pillars, the 15th century kitchens, and the parlour with its original Tudor plaster ceiling. The church of **St Mary Steps** also repays a visit just to see its beautifully-preserved Norman font, and its ancient "Matthew the Miller" tower clock, named after a medieval miller noted for his undeviating punctuality. The church stands in Stepcote Hill, a narrow cobbled and stepped thoroughfare which until as late as 1778 was the main road into Exeter from the west.

The remarkable **Guildhall** in the High Street has been in use as a Town Hall ever since it was built in 1330, making it one of the oldest municipal buildings in the country. Its great hall was remodelled around 1450, and the Elizabethans added a striking, if rather fussy,

portico but the interior is still redolent of the Middle Ages.

Exeter's one-time importance as a port is reflected in the dignified **Custom House**, built in 1681, and now the centrepiece of **Exeter Historic Quayside**, a fascinating complex of old warehouses, craft shops, cafés, and the **Seahorse Nature Aquarium** which is specially dedicated to these beautiful and enigmatic creatures. There are riverside walks, river trips, Canadian canoes and cycles for hire, and a passenger ferry across the river to the **Piazza Terracina** which explores five centuries of Exeter's trading connections around the world. The museum contains an extraordinary collection of boats, amongst them an Arab dhow, a reed boat from Lake Titicaca in South America, and a vintage steam launch. A special attraction of the museum is that visitors are positively encouraged to step aboard and explore in detail the many craft on show.

Other excellent museums in the city include the **Devonshire Regiment Museum** (regimental history); the **Rougemont House Museum** near the castle which has a copious collection of costumes and lace; and the Bill Douglas Centre for the History of Cinema and Popular Culture. The **Bill Douglas Centre** concentrates very much on optical entertainments and, in particular, films. While the stars of over a century of movies are well represented, along with the history of the cinema, the centre also looks at other forms of visual entertainment from prehistoric shadow plays, through 18th century peep shows to Victorian optical toys and magic lanterns. The hundreds of items on display were collected by the film-maker Bill Douglas and his friend Peter Jewell and, after Bill's death in 1991, the collection was donated to the University of Exeter. The centre is located on the University's main campus.

One of the city's most unusual attractions lies beneath its streets: the maze of **Underground Passages** constructed in the 14th and 15th centuries to bring water from springs beyond the city walls. A guided tour of the stone-vaulted caverns is an experience to remember.

Although Exeter is linked to the sea by the River Exe, the 13th century Countess of Devon, with a grudge against the city, built a weir across the river so that boats could sail no further upstream than Topsham. Some 300 years passed before action was taken by the city and the world's first ship canal was constructed to bypass the weir. Originally only three feet deep, this was changed to 14 feet over the years and the **Exeter Ship Canal** continued to be used until the 1970s. However, the M5 motorway, which crosses the canal on a fixed height bridge too low to allow big ships to pass, finally achieved what the Countess of Devon began so many centuries ago.

Exeter University campus is set on a hill overlooking the city, and

the grounds, laid out by Robert Veitch in the 1860s, offer superb views of the tors of Dartmoor. The landscape boasts many rare trees and shrubs, and the University has followed Veitch's example by creating many new plantings, including areas devoted entirely to Australasian plants. **Exeter University Sculpture Walk** comprises more than 20 sculptures, including works by Barbara Hepworth and Henry Moore, set out both in the splendid grounds and within the university buildings.

To the southwest of the city lies the **Devon and Exeter Racecourse**, one of the most scenic in the country and one that is considered to be Britain's favourite holiday course.

AROUND EXETER

CADBURY

10 miles N of Exeter off the A3072

To the north of this delightful hamlet is **Cadbury Castle**, actually an Iron Age fort. It was built high on the hilltop, about 700 feet above sea level, and it's claimed that the views here are the most extensive in Devon. On a good day Dartmoor and Exmoor are in full view, and the Quantocks and Bodmin Moor can also be seen.

A little more than a mile away stands **Fursdon House** which has been lived in by the Fursdon family since around 1260. The varied architecture reflects the many additions made over the centuries. Some fascinating family memorabilia, including old

22 POACHERS INN

Ide

This inn provides wonderful food, great ales and a comfortable nights sleep, what else is needed?

 see page 153

23 THE THREE TUNS

Silverton

Delightful thatched inn in attractive village, offering excellent home-cooked food and en suite accommodation.

 see page 154

scrapbooks, are on display; there's an excellent collection of 18th century costumes and textiles, and amongst the family treasures is a letter from Charles I written during the Civil War. Opening times are restricted.

BICKLEIGH

12 miles N of Exeter on the A396

Running due north from Exeter, the Exe Valley passes through the heart of what is known as "Red Devon". The soil here has a distinctive colour derived from the red Permian rocks that underlie it. Unlike most land in Devon, this is prime agricultural land, fertile, easily-worked and, for some reason, particularly favourable to growing swedes to which it gives a much sought-after flavour.

One of the most charming villages in the Exe Valley is Bickleigh. With its riverside setting and picturesque thatched cottages with lovingly-tended gardens, Bickleigh is one of Devon's most photographed villages. It also boasts two of the area's most popular attractions. **Bickleigh Mill** has been developed as a craft centre and farm stocked with rare breeds, while across the river is **Bickleigh Castle,** actually a moated and fortified manor house with an impressive gatehouse dating back to the late 1300s. Even older is the detached chapel which was built in the 11th century. The castle is no longer open on a regular basis but you can hold your wedding reception there and stay in one of the 15 bedrooms in the thatched courtyard cottages.

Bickleigh's unique 5-arched bridge has spanned the River Exe since 1630 and is reputed to have been the inspiration for the famous Simon and Garfunkel song *Bridge Over Troubled Water.*

Railway buffs will enjoy the **Devon Railway Centre & Model World** housed in the Victorian station buildings. It has 15 different working model railway layouts and various museum collections, and provides unlimited train rides on two railways - one narrow gauge, the other miniature. There's also a riverside picnic area, crazy golf and refreshments.

A popular attraction at Bickleigh is the **Maize Maze,** created from a field of maize beside the River Exe. The theme of the 10-acre maze changes each year

Bickleigh Village

- in 2008 it commemorated the centenary year of the author Ian Fleming with a design depicting Sean Connery as James Bond together with an Aston Martin DB5.

TIVERTON

16 miles N of Exeter on the A396

The only town of any size in the Exe valley is Tiverton, originally Twyfyrde, or two fords, for here the Exe is joined by the River Lowman. The town developed around what is now its oldest building, **Tiverton Castle**, built at the command of Henry I in 1106.

Grand Western Canal, nr Tiverton

Unfortunately, the castle found itself on the wrong side during the Civil War. General Fairfax himself was in charge of the successful onslaught in 1645. A few years later Parliament decreed that the castle should be "slighted" - destroyed beyond any use as a fortification. Cromwell's troops observed the letter of their instructions, sparing those parts of the castle which had no military significance, and leaving behind them a mutilated, but still substantial, structure which is still lived in.

During the Middle Ages, the citizens of Tiverton seem to have had a very highly-developed sense of civic and social responsibility. Throughout the town's golden age as a wool town, from the late 1400s until it reached its zenith in the 18th century, prosperous wool merchants put their wealth to good use. Around 1613, George Slee built himself a superb Jacobean mansion in St Peter Street, the

Great House, and in his will bequeathed the huge sum of £500 to establish the **Slee Almshouses** which were duly built right next door. Later almshouses, founded by John Waldron (in Welbrook Street), and John Greenway (in Gold Street) are still in use. As well as funding the almshouse, John Greenway also devoted another sizeable portion of his fortune to the restoration of **St Peter's Church** in 1517. He added a sumptuous porch and chapel, their outside walls richly decorated with carvings depicting sailing ships of the time.

The wool magnate Peter Blundell chose a different method of demonstrating his beneficence by endowing Tiverton with a school. It was in the **Old Blundell's School** building of 1604, by the Lowman Bridge, that the author RD Blackmore received his education. He later used the school as a setting for the first chapter of his novel, *Lorna Doone*. Now a highly-regarded public

•

A quay on the south-eastern edge of Tiverton marks the western end of the Grand Western Canal which was built in the early 19th century with the idea of linking the River Exe to Bridgewater and the Bristol Channel. It was never fully completed and finally closed in 1920. In recent years, an attractive stretch from Tiverton quay to the Somerset border has been restored and provides a pleasant easy walk. Horse-drawn barge trips along the canal are also available.

•

school, "Blundell's" moved to its present location on the edge of town in 1880.

The **Tiverton Museum of Mid Devon Life** is one of the largest social history museums in the southwest, containing some 15 galleries in all. It's particularly strong on the Great Western Railway, and agriculture – it has a nationally important collection of farm wagons. One entire gallery is devoted to John Heathcoat who developed his original lace-making machine at a Tiverton mill in the early 1800s.

The more one reads of Devon in the early to mid-18th century, the more one becomes convinced that there must have been a serial arsonist abroad. So many Devonshire towns during this period suffered devastating fires. Tiverton's conflagration occurred in 1731, but one happy outcome of the disaster was the building of **St George's Church,** by common consent the finest Georgian church in the county, furnished with elegant period ceilings and galleries.

A few miles north of Tiverton, up the Exe Valley, is **Knightshayes Court** a striking Victorian Gothic house designed by William Burges in 1869. It remains a rare survivor of his work. The grand and opulent interiors, blending medieval romanticism with lavish Victorian decoration, became too much for the owner, Sir John Heathcoat-Amory, the lace manufacturer. So he sacked Burges and employed the less imaginative but competent John Diblee Crace. Covered over during the time of the backlash against the High Victorian style, the rooms have been returned to their original grandeur by the National Trust who were given the building by the builder's son in 1973. The house is surrounded by extensive grounds that include a water-lily pond, topiary and some rare shrubs.

BAMPTON

21 miles N of Exeter on the B3190/B3227

In medieval times Bampton was quite an important centre of the wool trade but it's now best known for its annual **Exmoor Pony Sale**, held in late October. Throughout the rest of the year, though, it's a wonderfully peaceful place with some handsome Georgian cottages and houses, set beside the River Batherm, a tributary of the Exe. To the north of the village, a tree-crowned motte marks the site of Bampton Castle. Bampton's parish church

Knightshayes Court, Tiverton

of St Michael and All Angels is popular with collectors of unusual memorials. A stone on the west side of the tower replicates a memorial of 1776 which records the strange death of the parish clerk's son who was apparently killed by a falling icicle. The inscription is remarkably insensitive and reads:

Bless my I I I I I (eyes),
Here he lies,
In a sad pickle,
Killed by an icicle.

BROADCLYST

5½ miles NE of Exeter on the B3181

Just to the north of the village and set within the fertile lands between the Rivers Clyst and Culm, lies the large estate of **Killerton House & Garden**, centred around the grand 18th century mansion house that was the home of the Acland family. Furnished as a comfortable family home, the house contains a renowned costume collection and a Victorian laundry. While the house provides some interest it is the marvellous grounds laid out by John Veitch in the 1770s that make a visit here special. Veitch introduced many rare trees to the arboretum along with rhododendrons, magnolias and herbaceous borders. In the parkland are several interesting structures including a 19th century chapel and the Dolbury Iron Age hill fort. Here, too, can be found **Marker's Cottage** dating from the 15th century and containing 16th century paintings, and **Forest**

Cottage, originally a gamekeeper's cottage. Circular walks around the grounds and estate provide ample opportunity to discover the wealth of plant, animal and birdlife that thrives in this large estate.

Also part of the Killerton Estate is **Newhall Equestrian**, a working thoroughbred stud breeding National Hunt horses that provides visitors with a unique opportunity to look behind the scenes at the work involved in producing horses ready for the races. The centre is housed in restored listed buildings and includes a coach house with Royal horse-drawn vehicles, an equestrian art gallery, saddlers, children's pets corner and a tearoom.

BRADNINCH

9 miles NE of Exeter off the B3181

This pleasant little village stands on what used to be the main Exeter to Taunton road but it is now, thankfully, bypassed. Of particular note here is the striking parish church, with its crenellated tower spouting gargoyles; inside, there is a magnificent 16th century rood screen beautifully coloured in gleaming red, blue and gold.

CLYST ST MARY

4 miles E of Exeter on the A376/A3052

A couple of miles east of Clyst St Mary is **Crealy Park**, a large all-weather entertainment centre offering a wide range of attractions for children, including the largest indoor PlayZone in the country, bumper boats and go-karts, a farm nursery and pony rides.

Just to the northeast of Bradninch is Diggerland, an exciting adventure park set in glorious Devon countryside. Visitors have the opportunity of driving real JCBs, mini-tractors, quad bikes and dumpers, as well as numerous other rides and activities for the whole family.

29

A mile or so to the east of Woodbury is the famous Woodbury Common viewpoint. More than 560 feet high, it provides spectacular vistas across the Exe estuary to Dartmoor, and along the south Devon coast. It's easy to understand why an Iron Age tribe chose this spot to build their massive fort whose huge ramparts lie close to the viewpoint.

TOPSHAM
3 miles SE of Exeter off the A376

It's not surprising to find that the whole of the charming old town of Topsham has been declared a conservation area. Its narrow streets are lined with fine examples of 17th and 18th century merchants' houses, many built in the Dutch style with curved gable ends. There's a wealth of specialist and antique shops, and some stunning views over the Exe estuary with its extensive reed beds, salt marshes and mud banks. These provide an important winter feeding ground and summer breeding area for birds from all over the world. The estuary is also home to the largest winter flocks of avocets in the county. There are walks along the banks of the estuary that lead right from Exeter to the coast at Exmouth.

Housed in one of the town's finest late 17th century buildings, is **Topsham Museum** which also has a courtyard and estuary garden with fine views out over the River Exe. Along with the furnished period rooms, the museum holds an excellent local history collection that portrays Topsham's maritime, commercial and shipbuilding past. The museum also has a café serving home-made teas in its riverside gardens.

WOODBURY
7 miles SE of Exeter on the B3179

St Swithin's Church at Woodbury has achieved a rather sad kind of fame because of the Revd. J.

Loveband Fulford who in 1846 cut great chunks out of its medieval rood screen so that his parishioners could see him more clearly. Fortunately he left untouched the fine 15th century font made from Beer stone, the Jacobean pulpit, and the interesting memorials.

Just outside the town is the **Nigel Mansell World Of Racing** attraction which displays Formula 1 cars, and has a trophy room and specially designed cinema celebrating Nigel Mansell's remarkable career.

LYMPSTONE
8 miles SE of Exeter off the A376

It's a delight to wander around the old part of Lympstone with its narrow streets, small courts and ancient cottages. Set beside the estuary of the River Exe, Lympstone looks across the water to the impressive outline of Powderham Castle. There's a tiny harbour with a slipway and, on the beach, an Italianate clock tower erected in 1885 by a Mr W. H. Peters in commemoration of his wife, Mary Jane, who was noted for her good works amongst the poor of the village. The tower is now owned by the Landmark Trust and can be rented.

POWDERHAM
7 miles S of Exeter off the A379

Set in a deer park beside the River Exe, **Powderham Castle** has been the home of the Courtenay family, Earls of Devon since 1390. The castle stands in a beautiful setting in an ancient deer park alongside

Powderham Castle

the River Exe and is at the centre of a large traditional estate of about 4000 acres. The present building is mostly 18th century and contains some fine interiors, a breathtaking Grand Staircase, and historic family portraits – some of them by Sir Joshua Reynolds, a Devon man himself.

Outside there are the extensive grounds to explore that include the beautiful 18th century woodland walk, the tranquil Rose Garden and the Secret Garden, where children can pat and chat to a variety of pet animals. A tractor and trailer ride takes visitors around the grounds and to see the working blacksmith and wheelwright. There's also a restaurant and tearooms here along with a Country Store selling all manner of locally produced goods and foods.

KENTON

7 miles S of Exeter on the A379

Founded in Saxon times, this picturesque village is famed for its glorious 14th century **All Saints Church**. The tower stands over 100 feet high and is decorated with a wonderful assortment of ornate carvings. Inside, there is more rich carving in the south porch and in the Beer stone arcades of the nave.

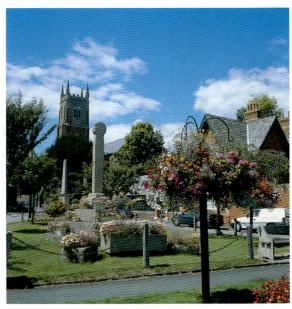

Kenton Village

31

25 HALDON BELVEDERE

Higher Ashton

This stunning apartment is set in Lawrence Castle, built in 1788 and offers magnificent views over Exeter and the surrounding Devon countryside.

   see page 156

26 THE VANILLA POD AT THE CRIDFORD INN

Teign Valley

Fine dining and wines at the à la carte restaurant in this beautiful 14th century Inn in the Teign Valley.

  see page 157

The pulpit is a 15th century original which was rescued and restored after it was found in pieces in 1866, and the massive rood screen, one of the finest in Devon, is a magnificent testimony to the 15th century woodcarver's art.

DUNCHIDEOCK

7 miles SW of Exeter off the A30

A beautifully located village, Dunchideock hugs the sides of a deeply-sloping combe. At the northern end, the modest red sandstone church of St Michael has an unusual number of noteworthy internal features. There's a medieval font, a set of carved pew ends and a richly-carved rood screen which at one point makes a surprising diversion around three sides of an octagonal roof column. Amongst the monuments is one to Major-General Stringer Lawrence, the "Father of the Indian Army", who in 1775 left a legacy of £50,000 to his lifelong friend, Sir Robert Palk. Palk proceeded to build himself a mansion, Haldon House, half a mile to the south, along with a folly in memory of his benefactor. Known locally as Haldon Belvedere, or Lawrence Castle, this tall triangular

structure stands on the summit of Haldon Ridge and can be seen for miles around.

CREDITON

8 miles NW of Exeter on the A377

Very few Britons have managed to become fully-fledged Saints, so Crediton is rather proud that one of this small and distinguished group, **St Boniface**, was born here in AD680. The infant was baptised with the name Wynfrith but on becoming a monk he adopted the name Boniface. He rose swiftly through the ranks of the Benedictine Order and in AD731 was sent by the Pope to evangelise the Germans. Boniface was remarkably successful, establishing

Church of the Holy Cross, Crediton

Christianity in several German states. At the age of 71, he was created Archbishop of Mainz but three years later, he and 53 members of his retinue were ambushed and murdered. They were on their way to the great monastery at Fulda in Hesse which Boniface had founded and where he was now laid to rest.

Boniface was greatly revered throughout Germany and a few years later the Pope formally pronounced his sanctification, but it was to be almost 1200 years before the town of his birth accorded him any recognition. Finally, in 1897, the people of Crediton installed an east window in the town's grand, cathedral-like **Church of the Holy Cross** depicting events from his life. A few years later, a statue of the saint was erected in the gardens to the west of the church.

The interior of the early 15th century church is especially notable for its monuments which include one to Sir John Sully who fought alongside the Black Prince and lived to the age of 105, and another to Sir William Peryam, a commissioner at the trial of Mary, Queen of Scots. Most impressive of all, though, is the richly ornamented arch in memory of Sir Henry Redvers Buller, commander-in-chief during the Boer War and the hero of the Relief of Ladysmith. Also of interest is the Lady Chapel of 1300 which housed Crediton's famous grammar school from the time of Edward VI until 1859 when it moved to its present site in the High Street.

27 THE LAMB INN

Sandford

This 16th century coaching house hosts spectacular bedrooms, great food and a wonderful atmosphere.

 see page 158

28 THE CROWN & SCEPTRE

Newton St Cyres

Traditional country pub, serving great food and drink, perfect for all the family, with riverside beer garden.

see page 159

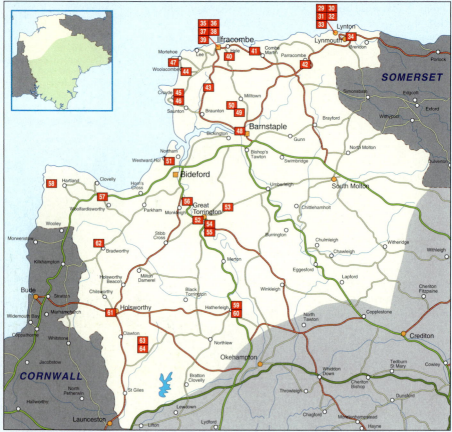

North Devon

The most striking feature of North Devon is the magnificent stretch of coastline that extends from Hartland Point to the Somerset border. It presents not only spectacular scenery but also some fine sandy beaches. Several of the popular holiday resorts along the coast were developed during the late 1700s and early 1800s during the craze for sea bathing initiated by George III and his son, the Prince Regent. Another popular resort, however, was developed following the success of Charles Kingsley's *Westward Ho!* and took the name of the famous novel.

North Devon has another major literary connection - with Henry Williamson whose *Tarka the Otter* is set in the area between the rivers Torridge and Taw. The Tarka Trail links many of the towns and villages that feature in the book.

To the east of Ilfracombe are the twin villages of Lynton and Lynmouth, linked by a unique water-powered cliff railway. Their particularly romantic setting led

Victorians to describe this area as the "English Switzerland". And no visit to this part of the county should miss out the village of Clovelly, the unbelievably quaint community that tumbles down a steep hillside to the sea.

The only towns of any size - Ilfracombe, Barnstaple and Bideford, are all either on, or close to the coast while, inland, small unspoilt villages of thatched and whitewashed cottages range from the pleasant to the astoundingly picturesque.

Devon Coast Path, nr Lynton

LYNTON

Lynton and Lynmouth, though often mentioned in the same breath, are very different in character. Lynton is the younger of the two settlements and sits atop a great cliff 600 feet high; Lynmouth, far below, clusters around the junction of the East and West Lyn rivers just before they reach the sea.

Lynton is a bright and breezy village, its houses and terraces mostly Victorian. The **Exmoor Museum**, housed in a restored 16th century house, has an interesting collection of the tools and products of bygone local craftsmen and other exhibits relating to the area.

If you are visiting Lynton in August, you won't be able to avoid the odd characters standing in gardens and doorways, sitting on roofs or shinning up drainpipes. Don't worry – they are just participating in the **Lynton & Lynmouth Scarecrow Festival,** a popular event that has become the largest and longest running such festival in the West Country.

Lynton has its own cinema, next to the impressive Town Hall, that shows all the latest releases while the old Methodist Chapel is home to the work of **Lyn Valley Art and Craft Centre** which showcases Exmoor textiles, pottery, glass, ceramics, woodwork, jewellery, sculptures, textiles, pictures, paintings, and much more

Castle Rock, Valley of the Rocks

all under one roof.

A recent addition to the attractions here is the re-opening of part of the **Lynton and Barnstaple Railway**, a narrow gauge railway which was closed in 1935. A group of volunteers have restored Woody Bay Station on the main A39 road, together with a 1-mile stretch of track, a restoration programme which will long continue. Passengers can travel by both steam and diesel along the track.

To the west of Lynton, about a mile or so along a minor road, is one of the most remarkable natural features in Devon, the **Valley of the Rocks.** When the poet Robert Southey visited the area in 1800, he was most impressed by this natural gorge *"covered with huge stones...the very bones and skeletons of the earth; rock reeling upon rock, stone piled upon stone, a huge terrific mass".* In *Lorna Doone*, the author RD Blackmore transforms the site into the "Devil's Cheesering" where Jan Ridd visits Mother Meldrun who is sheltering under "eaves of lichened rock". And it was after walking along the clifftop path, more than 1300 feet above the sea, in company with William Wordsworth and his sister Dorothy, that Samuel Taylor Coleridge was inspired to write his immortal *Rime of the Ancient Mariner.*

An unusual attraction in the valley is its herd of feral goats, introduced here in the 1970s. A good time to see them is in January when the nannies give birth to their kids.

AROUND LYNTON

LYNMOUTH

1 mile E of Lynton on the A39

Lynton is connected to its sister village Lynmouth by an ingenious cliff railway which, when it opened on Easter Monday 1890, was the first of its kind in Britain. A gift from Sir George Newnes, the publisher and newspaper tycoon, the railway is powered by water, or rather by two 700-gallon water tanks, one at each end of the 450 feet track. When the tank at the top is filled, and the one at the bottom emptied, the brakes are released and the two passenger carriages change place.

One of the most picturesque villages in Devon, Lynmouth also has a tiny harbour surrounded by lofty wooded hills. From the Quay trips around the bay to the lighthouse and smugglers caves are available. The curious Rhenish Tower at the end of the Quay was built in the late 1850s by a General Rawdon to store salt water to supply his house with sea baths. And do seek out Mars Hill, an eye-ravishing row of thatched cottages.

Understandably, this lovely setting acts as a magnet for artists and craftspeople. People like Peter Allen, for example, whose **Lynmouth Pottery** is very much a pottery with a difference. For one thing, it's a working pottery and one of the few places where you can try out your own skills at the potter's wheel. (Children too are encouraged to have a go). If you're not totally ashamed of the result,

32 SEAWOOD HOTEL

Lynton

Guests can expect first class service at this stunning hotel which enjoys fabulous views of the bay at Lynmouth.

 see page 163

33 SINAI HOUSE

Lynway

Quality en suite B&B accommodation in former vicarage set on steep hillside above Lynton.

 see page 162

HIDDEN PLACES OF DEVON

34 RIVER LYN VIEW

Lynmouth

River Lyn View is beautifully
situated just a stroll away
from the picturesque
Lynmouth harbour.

 see page 164

*For centuries, the people
of Lynmouth subsisted on
agriculture and fishing,
especially herring fishing
and curing. By good
fortune, just as the
herring shoals were
moving away to new
waters, the North Devon
coast benefited from the
two new enthusiasms for
"romantic" scenery and
sea bathing. Coleridge
and Wordsworth arrived
here on a walking tour in
the 1790s, Shelley wrote
fondly of his visit in
1812, and it was Robert
Southey, later Poet
Laureate, who first used
the designation "the
English Switzerland" to
describe the dramatic
scenery of the area. The
painter Gainsborough
had already described it
as "the most delightful
place for a landscape
painter this country can
boast".*

Peter Allen will then fire the
finished item and post it on to you.
Many a visitor to Lynmouth
Pottery has discovered an
unsuspected talent for turning
slippery clay into a quite
presentable decorative piece.

More hands-on experience is
offered at the **Exmoor Brass
Rubbing and Hobby Craft
Centre** on Watersmeet Road. The
first collection of brass rubbings
was made by a man named Craven
Ord between 1790 and 1830. His
collection is now housed in the
British Museum but because of his
method – pouring printer's ink into
the engraved lines and then
pressing a sheet of damp tissue
paper on the brass – the results are
often very poor. It was the
Victorians who developed a process
using heelball (shoemaker's black
wax) and white paper that is still in
use today. The Centre provides all
the necessary materials and friendly
instruction.

Adjacent to the Parish Church
is the **Lyn Model Railway**, a
superb L.N.E.R. layout covering the
period from 1929 to 1939 - a real
delight for children and adults alike.
At the crossroads you will find the
Glen Lyn Gorge, a visitor
attraction designed to allow an
insight into the benefits of working
with nature. Part of the river flow
here is used to provide the hydro-
electric needs of the village and
visitors can see how it all works,
with the opportunity to work the
waterwheels and fire water
cannons. Lovely woodland walks
take you into the gorge, passing the

turbines and water-operated
machines, and by the waterfalls
leading to an impressive ravine.

If you continue along
Watersmeet Road you will come to
the popular beauty spot of
Watersmeet, where the East Lyn
river and Hoar Oak Water come
together. An 1832 fishing lodge,
Watersmeet House, stands close by.
A National Trust property, it is
open during the season as a café,
shop and information centre where
you can pick up leaflets detailing
some beautiful circular walks,
starting here, along the East Lyn
valley and to Hoar Oak Water.

Lynmouth's setting beside its
twin rivers is undeniably beautiful,
but it has also proved to be
tragically vulnerable. On the night
of August 16th, 1952, a cloudburst
over Exmoor deposited nine inches
of rain onto an already saturated
moor. In the darkness, the normally
placid East and West Lyn rivers
became raging cataracts and burst
their banks. Sweeping tree trunks
and boulders along with it, the
torrent smashed its way through
the village, destroying dozens of
houses and leaving 34 people dead.
That night saw many freak storms
across southern England, but none
matched the ferocity of the deluge
that engulfed this pretty little
village. The Flood Memorial Hall
has an exhibition that details the
events of that terrible night.

An earlier exceptional storm, in
1899, involved the Lynmouth
lifeboat in a tale of epic endurance.
A full-rigged ship, the *Forest Hall,*
was in difficulties off Porlock, but

38

the storm was so violent it was impossible to launch the lifeboat at Lynmouth. Instead, the crewmen dragged their three-and-a-half ton boat, the *Louisa,* the 13 miles across the moor. Along the way they had to negotiate Countisbury Hill, with a gradient of 1000 feet over two miles, before dropping down to Porlock Weir where the *Louisa* was successfully launched and every crew member of the stricken ship was saved.

MARTINHOE

4 miles W of Lynton on minor road off the A39

Set amidst rolling fields above spectacular cliffs some 700 feet high, the small village of Martinhoe was occupied in Roman times as a signal station keeping an eye out for any aggressive activity by the Silurian tribes of Wales on the other shore of the Bristol Channel.

Martinhoe boasts what some argue is the highest waterfall in the West Country - it all depends on how you define a waterfall. **Hollow Brook Falls** descend 600 feet to the sea in a series of cascades, including two drops of 150 feet each. Coastal waterfalls are quite common on the North Devon and Exmoor coast but unusual elsewhere in Europe apart from the Norwegian fjords.

ILFRACOMBE

Ilfracombe takes its floral decorations very seriously – during the 1990s the town was a consistent winner of the Britain in Bloom Competition. Between June and October the town goes "blooming mad" with streets, parks and hotels awash with flowers. Ilfracombe also promotes itself as a "Festival Town" offering a wide variety of events. They include a Victorian Celebration in mid-June when local people don period costumes. A grand costume ball and a fireworks display all add to the fun. There's the National Youth

35 THE STEAK HOUSE

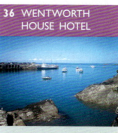

Ilfracombe

This family run restaurant provides very high quality meat in a comfortable and spacious setting.

 see page 165

36 WENTWORTH HOUSE HOTEL

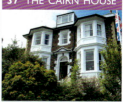

Ilfracombe

An elegant Victorian B&B, whose attentive hosts offer comfortable accommodation alongside good old fashioned hospitality and cuisine.

 see page 166

37 THE CAIRN HOUSE

Ilfracombe Harbour

Ilfracombe

A friendly, family run bed and breakfast hotel with its own licensed bar, beautiful gardens and coastal bedroom views.

 see page 167

38 SHERBORNE LODGE

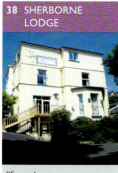

Ilfracombe

Graham and Alison provide comfortable accommodation in warm and welcoming surroundings.

 see page 168

39 THE ILFRACOMBE CARLTON HOTEL

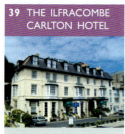

Ilfracombe

Attractive 2 star hotel in the heart of the exciting holiday resort town of Ilfracombe.

 see page 169

Arts Festival in July, a Fishing Festival in early August, a Carnival Procession later that month, and many more.

A fairly recent addition to the town's amenities is **The Landmark Theatre**, a striking building with what looks like two gleaming white truncated cooling towers as its main feature. This multi-purpose arts centre has a 480-seat theatre, cinema screening facilities, a spacious display area and a café-bar with a sunny, sea facing terrace. Next door to the Landmark Theatre, in Runnnymede Gardens, is the **Ilfracombe Museum** which opened in 1932 and has a variety of displays ranging from Bats to Buddhas.

With a population of around 11,000, Ilfracombe is the largest seaside resort on the North Devon coast. Up until 1800, however, it was just a small fishing and market town relying entirely on the sea both for its living and as its principal means of communication. The boundaries of the old town are marked by a sheltered natural harbour to the north, and, half-a-mile away to the south, a part-Norman parish church boasting one of the finest medieval waggon roofs in the West Country.

The entrance to Ilfracombe harbour is guarded by Lantern Hill, a steep-sided conical rock which is crowned by the restored medieval **Chapel of St Nicholas**. For centuries, this highly conspicuous former fishermen's chapel has doubled as a lighthouse, the light being placed in a lantern at the western end of the building. St Nicholas must surely be the only ecclesiastical building in the country to be managed by the local Rotary Club – it was they who raised the funds for its restoration. From the chapel's hilltop setting there are superb views of Ilfracombe, its busy harbour and the craggy North Devon coastline.

Like so many west country resorts, Ilfracombe developed in response to the early-19th century craze for sea bathing and sea water therapies. The **Tunnel Baths,** with their extravagant Doric façade, were opened in Bath Place in 1836, by which time a number of elegant residential terraces had been built on the hillside to the south of the old town.

The arrival of a branch railway line from Barnstaple in 1874 brought an even larger influx of visitors to Ilfracombe. Much of the town's architecture, which could best be described as "decorated Victorian vernacular", dates from this period, the new streets spreading inland in steeply undulating rows. Around the same time the harbour was enlarged to cope with the paddle steamers bringing in tourists from Bristol and South Wales. Today, visitors can take advantage of regular sailings from that harbour to Lundy Island, as well as cruises along the spectacular Exmoor coast.

Standing beside the harbour is the **Ilfracombe Aquarium,** housed in the former lifeboat house. It contains an impressive collection of both freshwater and marine species in carefully re-created natural habitats. Worth a visit is the

Hele Corn Mill and Pottery

fun fish retail area here.

For walkers, the **South West Coast Path** from Ilfracombe provides some spectacular scenery, whether going west to Capstone Point, or east to Hillsborough Hill.

Just to the east of Ilfracombe, at Hele Bay, **Hele Corn Mill & Pottery** is unique in North Devon. Dating back to the 16th century, the mill has been lovingly restored from near dereliction and is now producing 100% wholemeal stone-ground flour for sale. In Robin Gray's pottery, you can watch him in action at the potter's wheel and try your own skill in fashioning slippery clay into a more-or-less recognisable object. If you really want to keep the result, the pottery will fire and glaze it, and post it on to you.

Half a mile or so south of the mill, set in a secluded valley, **Chambercombe Manor** is an 11th century mansion which was first recorded in the *Domesday Book*. It still retains much of its original architecture and is in a wonderful state of preservation. The manor stands in 16 acres of woodland and landscaped gardens and is well known for its paranormal phenomena - it has been researched on many occasions and in 2006 was the focus of Living TV's *Most Haunted* series. Visitors have access to eight rooms displaying period furniture from Elizabethan to Victorian times, can peek into the claustrophobic Priest's Hole, and test their sensitivity to the spectral presences reputed to inhabit the Haunted Room. The Coat of Arms bedroom was once occupied by Lady Jane Grey and it is her family's arms that are displayed above the fireplace. Outside, the beautiful grounds contain wildfowl ponds, a bird sanctuary and an arboretum.

AROUND ILFRACOMBE

BERRYNARBOR

3 miles E of Ilfracombe off the A399

Nestling in a steep-sided combe, Berrynarbor is a wonderfully unspoilt village of quaint cottages and narrow streets set around **St Peter's Church** which, with its 96 feet high tower, is one of the grandest churches in North Devon. Inside, there's an interesting

40 CHAMBERCOMBE MANOR

Ilfracombe

Displaying period furniture from Elizabethan times up to the Victorian era, this is a delightful house that allows visitors to soak up the atmosphere of what was also a family home.

 see page 168

41

41 THE ROYAL MARINE

Combe Martin

Delightful seaside hotel, with impressive restaurant and views of the beach and Hangman cliffs.

see page 170

A remarkable architectural curiosity in Combe Martin is The Pack o' Cards Inn, built by Squire George Ley in the early 18th century with the proceeds of a highly successful evening at the card table. This Grade II listed building represents a pack of cards with four decks, or floors, 13 rooms, and a total of 52 windows. Inside there are many features representing the cards in each suit.

Watermouth Cove, Berrynarbor

collection of monuments, many of them memorials of the Berry family, once the owners of the nearby 15th century manor house which later became the village school.

On the coast to the northeast of Berrynarbor is the pretty cove of Watermouth and the Victorian folly, **Watermouth Castle,** which has been transformed into a family theme park. In the castle's great hall, there's a collection of suits of armour and visitors can enjoy mechanical music demonstrations. Elsewhere, there are displays on Victorian life, antique pier machines, a room devoted to model railways and, down in the depths of the dungeon labyrinths, fairy tales come to life.

COMBE MARTIN

4 miles E of Ilfracombe on the A399

Just a short distance from Berrynarbor, on the other side of the River Umber, is another popular resort, Combe Martin. There's a good sandy beach here and a short walk will take you to one of the secluded bays. An added attraction, especially for children, is the large number of rock pools amongst the bays. In the village itself, the main street is more than two miles long, reputed to be the longest in the country and featuring a wide selection of inns, cafés and shops. As well as the **Combe Martin Museum**, there is also the **Wildlife and Dinosaur Park** where life-sized animated dinosaurs lurk in the woods. The 25-acre site also shelters 250 species of real animals, including a large and lively collection of apes and monkeys. Within the park are animal handling areas, an "Earthquake Ride", a dinosaur museum and oriental gardens. There's an otter pool and daily sea lion shows and falconry displays, and if you book ahead you can experience the unique thrill of swimming with the sea lions.

STOWFORD

12 miles SE of Ilfracombe off the A399

Exmoor Zoological Park is home to more than 170 species of unusual and exotic animals and birds. The residents of the 12 acres of gardens here range from pygmy marmosets to tarantulas, from penguins to catybara. Children can enjoy close encounters with many of the more cuddly animals, there are informative talks by the keepers but, as at any zoo, the most magnetic visitor attraction is the feeding time for the various animals.

To the north of the Park lies **Wistlandpound Reservoir** around part of which a Nature Reserve has been established. A tranquil place that is home to a variety of wildlife, it has a waymarked path around the lake where fly fishing for rainbow trout is available with a permit.

PARRACOMBE

13 miles SE of Ilfracombe off the A39

The redundant **Church of St Petroc** is notable for its marvellously unspoilt interior, complete with 15th century benches, 17th century box pews, a Georgian pulpit and a perfectly preserved musician's gallery. Perhaps most striking of all is the unique gated screen between the chancel and the nave which bears a huge tympanum painted with the royal arms, the Lord's Prayer, the Creed and the Ten Commandments. We owe the

church's survival to John Ruskin who led the protests against its intended demolition in 1879 after another church was built lower down the hill.

WEST DOWN

3 miles S of Ilfracombe off the A361

This village of whitewashed houses beside the River Caen is noted for its tiny church whose nave is barely 15 feet wide. Mostly rebuilt in the 17th and 18th centuries, the church has, nevertheless, retained a fine oak roof that dates from the 14th century, a Norman font that was discovered beneath the floor, and a rare wooden figure of Sir John Stowforth, Justice of the Common Pleas in the 1300s. Here, he is shown wearing the still colourful robes of a Serjeant-at-Law.

WOOLACOMBE

7 miles SW of Ilfracombe on the B3343

The wonderful 3-mile-long stretch of golden sands at Woolacombe is justifiably regarded as the finest beach in North Devon. This favoured resort lies between two dramatic headlands, both of which are now in the care of the National Trust. The sands and rock pools lying between these two outcrops are a delight for children, (along with the swing boats and donkey rides), and surfers revel in the monster waves rolling in from the Atlantic.

Back in the early 1800s, Woolacombe was little more than a hamlet whose few residents sustained a precarious livelihood by fishing. Then, suddenly, the leisured

42 THE FOX & GOOSE

Parracombe
Riverside village pub with delightful traditional interior and serving outstanding cuisine.

 see page 171

43 THE FOXHUNTERS INN

West Down
300 year old family friendly hostelry of exceptional charm and character, varied menu and en suite rooms.

 see page 172

44 THE ROCKS HOTEL

Woolacombe
Recently modernised and refurbished, and offering quality B&B accommodation just 300 yards from the beach

see page 173

To the south of Woolacombe rises Potters Hill, a conical hill that was given to the National Trust in 1935. The path cut up the hill to the summit, from where there are glorious views, was constructed to celebrate King George V's Silver Jubilee while the cairn on the hilltop was a Millennium project. To the southeast lies the higher and wider hill of Woolacombe Down, a former sea-cliff that now supports a wealth of wildlife including some rare species of beetles and moths.

45 MOORSANDS

Croyde Bay

This friendly B & B is a warm and welcoming place to stay all year round.

see page 173

classes were seized by the craze for sea bathing initiated by George III at Weymouth and enthusiastically endorsed by his successor George IV at Brighton. Inspired by the economic success of those south coast towns, the two families who owned most of the land around Woolacombe, the Fortescues and the Chichesters, began constructing villas and hotels in the Regency style, elegant buildings which still endow the town with a very special charm and character. Many friends of the Fortescue and Chichester families regarded their initiative as a suicidally rash enterprise. Woolacombe was so remote and the roads of North Devon at that time still so primitive, little more than cart tracks. "Who," they asked, "would undertake such an arduous journey?" During the first few years only a trickle of well-to-do visitors in search of a novel (and comparatively inexpensive resort) found their way to Woolacombe. But their word of mouth recommendations soon ensured a steady flow of tourists, a flow which has swelled to a flood over subsequent years. The town recently won the England for Excellence Gold Award for best family resort, and was dubbed Best British Beach by the *Mail on Sunday*.

Just outside the town, **Once Upon a Time** provides a huge variety of entertainment for younger children, - indoor and outdoor play areas, crazy golf, a young scientist's room, children's driving school, train rides, animated fairy tales, an ocean of plastic balls to play through in the Wild Boar Adventure Trail, and much more.

GEORGEHAM

6 miles SW of Ilfracombe off the B3231

It was in Georgeham that **Henry Williamson** settled in 1921 and where he wrote his most famous novel, *Tarka the Otter,* which was published in 1927. 'Tarka' lived in the land between the Taw and Torridge rivers and many of the small villages and settlements feature in the story. The writer lived a very simple life in a wooden hut that he built himself. After World War II, he farmed for a while in Norfolk but returned to Georgeham where he died in 1947. He is buried in the graveyard of St George's Church.

CROYDE

7 miles SW of Ilfracombe on the B3231

One of the prettiest villages in Devon, Croyde is renowned for its excellent beach with, just around the headland, another three-mile stretch of sands at Saunton Sands, one of the most glorious, family-friendly sandy beaches in the West Country. The sands are backed by 1000 acres of dunes known as **Braunton Burrows.** The southern part of this wide expanse is a designated nature reserve noted for its fluctuating population of migrant birds as well as rare flowers and insects.

Also noted for its abundant wildlife is **Baggy Point,** just northwest of Croyde. This headland of Devonian rock (so named because the rock was first

Croyde Village

46 CROYDE HOLIDAY BUNGALOWS

Croyde

The two bungalows Gilonica and Seashells offer peaceful and a relaxing solution to the beach holiday genre.

 see page 174

47 LUNDY HOUSE HOTEL

Mortehoe

This spectacular hotel has excellent facilities and offers stunning views towards Lundy Island while offering all guests a friendly, personal service.

 see page 174

identified in this county) is a popular nesting place for seabirds, including herring gull, fulmar, shag and cormorant. Grey seals can often be seen from here.

Running northwestwards from the cliffs is a shoal known as Baggy Leap. In 1799, *HMS Weazle* was driven onto the shoal during a gale and all 106 souls on board perished.

LEE

2 miles W of Ilfracombe off the A361

This pleasing small village with a population of some 250 souls boasts several attractive buildings. These include the centuries-old Grampus Inn, the Old Mill of 1560, the Old Post Office of 1706 and the thatched Old Maids Cottage (private).

To the west of the village is Lee Abbey, now home to a Christian community offering retreats, conference facilities and a holiday centre.

MORTEHOE

4 miles W of Ilfracombe off the B3343

Mortehoe is the most north-westerly village in Devon and its name, meaning "raggy stump", reflects the rugged character of the Morte Peninsula. In this pretty stone-built village set on the cliff-top, Mortehoe's part-Norman **St Mary's Church** is certainly worth a visit. It's a small cruciform building with a 15th-century open-timbered wagon roof, an interesting early 14th century table tomb, a bell in the tower which may be the oldest

45

48 MARSHALS

Barnstaple

Popular town centre pub noted for its real ales, good home-made food and regular live music sessions.

 see page 175

in Devon, and a wonderful series of grotesquely carved Tudor bench ends. The church is also notable for the large mosaic of 1905 which fills the chancel arch. Designed by Selwyn Image, the Slade Professor of Art at Oxford, the mosaic was created by the same craftsmen who did the mosaics in St Paul's Cathedral.

In the village centre, the **Mortehoe Heritage Centre** occupies the Cart Linhay building and also serves as a local Tourist Information Centre. It contains a museum which has sections dealing with the local farming communities, the railway and the history of ship wrecks in the area.

A short walk from Mortehoe village leads you to the dramatic coastline, mortally dangerous to ships, but with exhilarating views across to Lundy Island. Much of this clifftop area is in the guardianship of the National Trust which also protects nearby **Barricane Beach** (remarkable for being formed almost entirely of sea shells washed here from the

Caribbean), and the three-mile stretch of Woolacombe Sands.

To the north of Mortehoe is **Bull Point Lighthouse**, another popular destination for walkers, while, to the south, there is another footpath that takes in the splendid natural viewpoint of Morte Hill.

BARNSTAPLE

Barnstaple enjoys a superb location at the head of the Taw estuary, at the furthest point downstream where it was possible to ford the river. The first bridge across the Taw was built in the late 1200s, but the present impressive structure, 700 feet long with 16 arches and known locally as the Long Bridge, dates from about 1450 although it has been altered and widened many times.

Visitors will immediately realise that Barnstaple takes its floral decorations very seriously. The town began its association with the Britain in Bloom movement in 1991 and just five years later crowned its efforts by winning the Gold award for the "Prettiest Floral Town in Europe" in the Entente Florale Competition. Wherever you turn you may well find a magnificent display, - a hay cart full of flowers outside the police station and civic centre, for example, a giant postage stamp modelled in blossoming plants outside the Post Office, or a stunning model of a train (again, all created in flowers) at the entrance to the railway station.

The town's love of floral

River Taw, Barnstaple

exuberance may be one of its most endearing features but Barnstaple is also the administrative and commercial capital of the region, a pre-eminence it already enjoyed when the *Domesday Book* recorded the town as one of only four boroughs in the county. Back then, in 1086, Barnstaple had its own mint and, already, a regular market. More than nine centuries later, the town still hosts produce markets every Tuesday and Friday, but the **Pannier Market** is open every weekday. This huge, glass-roofed building covering some 45,000 square feet was built in 1855 and its grandiose architecture resembles that of a major Victorian railway station, (London's St Pancras springs to mind). The Market takes it name from the pannier baskets, (two wicker baskets connected by a leather strap draped across the back of a donkey, pony or horse), in which country people in those days would carry their fruit and vegetables to town.

Just across the road from the Pannier Market is **Butchers Row,** a quaint line of booth-like Victorian shops built mostly of wood and with brightly painted wooden canopies. When they were built, back in 1855, they were occupied exclusively by butchers, but now you'll find a much wider variety of goods on sale – seaweed amongst them. Every week during the summer season at least 300 pounds of this succulent algae are sold, most of it ending up as a breakfast dish, served with bacon and an egg on top.

St Anne's Chapel, Barnstaple

In Barnstaple's High Street stands the rather austere **Guildhall,** built in the Grecian style in 1826 and now housing some interesting civic memorabilia – portraits, municipal regalia and silverware – which are occasionally on display. Nearby, the **Church of St Peter and St Paul** dates back to the early 1300s. After having its spire twisted by a lightning strike in 1810, it suffered even more badly later that century under the heavy hand of the Victorian restorer, Sir Gilbert Scott. Much more appealing are the charming 17th century **Horwood's Almshouses** nearby, and the 15th century **St Anne's Chapel** which served for many years as the town's Grammar School. During the late 17th century John Gay, author of *The Beggar's Opera,* was numbered amongst its pupils. The town has other literary associations. William Shakespeare visited in 1605 and it was the sight of its narrow streets

Barnstaple has two railway stations but only one is still functioning. This is the northern terminus of the Tarka Line, a lovely 39-mile route that follows the gentle river valleys of the Yeo and the Taw where Tarka the Otter had his home. The railway is actually the main line route to Exeter but has been renamed in honour of one of the area's major visitor attractions. Walkers along the Tarka Trail will know Barnstaple well as the crossover point in this figure-of-eight long-distance footpath. Inspired by Henry Williamson's celebrated story of **Tarka the Otter,** the 180-mile trail wanders through a delightful variety of Devon scenery – tranquil countryside, wooded river valleys, rugged moorland, and a stretch of the North Devon coast, with part of the route taking in the Tarka Line railway in order to get the best views of the locations described in the novel.

Housed in a grand Victorian residence at the end of the Long Bridge in Barnstaple is the Museum of Barnstaple and North Devon where visitors can see displays on the geology, natural history and archaeology of north Devon. Detailed displays include Roman finds, North Devon pottery and the Royal Devon Yeomanry.

bustling with traders that inspired him to write *The Merchant of Venice*. The diarist Samuel Pepys married a 15-year-old Barnstaple girl in 1655.

As at Tiverton, the 17th century well-to-do residents of Barnstaple were given to charitable endowments. As well as Thomas Horwood's almshouses, Messrs. Paige and Penrose both bequeathed substantial funds for almshouses, and in 1659 Thomas' wife, Alice, paid for the building in Church Lane of a school for "20 poor maids". It is now a coffee house.

A slightly later building of distinction is **Queen Anne's Walk**, a colonnaded arcade with some lavish ornamentation and surmounted by a large statue of the Queen herself. Opened in 1708, it was used by the Barnstaple wool

merchants who accepted that any verbal bargain they agreed over the Tome Stone was legally binding. The building stands on the old town quay from which, in 1588, five ships set sail to join Drake's fleet against the Armada. The building is now home to the **Barnstaple Heritage Centre** where more can be found out about this ancient town and one of its most enduring industries, pottery, which has been made here continuously since the 13th century. One of the country's most traditional terracotta potteries is **Brannam's**, which was established in 1879. It is famous for its range of kitchenware that has been successfully combining style, quality and functionality for many years. Local Fremington red clay is used and visitors can try their hand at creating their own pot . There's also a museum, shop and restaurant on site.

AROUND BARNSTAPLE

BRAUNTON

6 miles NW of Barnstaple on the A361

Braunton claims the rather odd distinction of being the largest village in Devon. It is certainly a sizeable community, spreading along both sides of the River Caen, with some handsome Georgian houses and a substantial church reflecting Braunton's relative importance in medieval times. The church is dedicated to St Brannoc, a Celtic saint who arrived here

Marwood Hill Gardens, nr Barnstaple

from Wales in the 6th century. It's said that his bones lie beneath the altar of the present 13th century church, a story which may well be true since the building stands on the site of a Saxon predecessor. What is certainly true is that the church contains some of the finest 16th century carved pews to be found anywhere in England. Many of the carvings depict pigs, a clear allusion to the ancient tradition that St Brannoc was instructed in a dream to build a church where he came across a sow and her litter of seven pigs. Arriving in North Devon the saint happily discovered this very scene at the spot where Braunton's church now stands.

There is further evidence of Saxon occupation of this area to be found in **Braunton Great Field**, just to the southwest of the village. This is one of very few remaining examples of the Saxon open-field strip system still being actively farmed in Britain. Around 350 acres in total, the field was originally divided into some 700 half-acre strips, each of them a furlong (220 yards) long, and 11 yards wide. Each strip was separated by an unploughed "landshare" about one foot wide. Throughout the centuries, many of the strips have changed hands and been combined, so that now only about 200 individual ones remain.

MARWOOD

3 miles N of Barnstaple off the B3230

This ancient village is home to **Marwood Hill Gardens** which offers visitors some 18 acres of

trees and shrubs, many of them rare and unusual. The collection was started more than half a century ago and now includes an enormous number and variety of plants. The gardens are home to the national collections of astilbe, iris and tulbaghia where 18 acres of pastureland have been transformed into a spectacular water garden with three lakes that are surrounded by herbaceous plants, trees and shrubs. Home to the National Collections of Astilbe, Iris and Tulbaghia, the gardens also feature the Folly and the Scented Arbour as well as the largest Bog Garden in the West Country that links the lakes. Throughout the year there is plenty of interest – from the spring magnolias to the brilliant autumnal colours. The gardens are open daily from dawn to dusk and there are plants for sale, including rare and unusual species.

MUDDIFORD

4 miles N of Barnstaple on the B3230

From Barnstaple to Ilfracombe, the B3230 winds through a pretty valley, passing along the way through attractive small villages. Despite the rather unappealing name, Muddiford is one of them. The village really did get its name from the "muddy ford" by which medieval travellers used to cross the river here.

ARLINGTON

7 miles NE of Barnstaple on the A39

Arlington Court is an imposing National Trust property which was

49 RING O' BELLS

Prixford, nr Barnstaple

Local produce is at the heart of the menu, which offers mouth-watering dishes and an array of wines, spirits, beers and ales to choose from.

 see page 175

50 MARWOOD HILL GARDENS

Marwood, nr Barnstaple

A stunning labour of love; 20 acres of glorious gardens, lakes and tea room serving home cooked treats.

 see page 176

Surrounded by hundreds of acres of wooded grounds, Broomhill Sculpture Gardens near Muddiford provides a showcase for more than 300 examples of contemporary sculptures created by over 60 international artists. They are displayed in the 10-acre grounds of a small late-Victorian hotel which also has an art gallery.

home to the Chichester family from 1534 until the last owner, Rosalie Chichester, died childless in 1949. (Sir Francis Chichester, famous as an aviation pioneer and as the first solo round-the-world sailor, was born two miles away at Shirwell). The present house was built in 1822 to an unambitious design by the Barnstaple architect, Thomas Lee, and extended some 40 years later by Sir Bruce Chichester who also added the handsome stable block. When he died in 1881, he left the house and its 2,775-acre park to his daughter Rosalie, along with a staggering mountain of debts. Only 15 years old when she inherited the estate, Rosalie managed to keep it intact and stayed on at Arlington Court until her death at the age of 83.

The interior today is really a museum reflecting Rosalie's varied interests. There are displays of her collections of porcelain, pewter, shells, snuff boxes, and more than a hundred model ships, some made by French soldiers captured during the Napoleonic wars.

Intriguingly, Rosalie never saw the most valuable work of art amongst her possessions. After her death, a watercolour by William Blake was discovered on top of a wardrobe where it had lain forgotten for over 100 years. It is now on display in the white drawing room.

During her lifetime, Rosalie Chichester transformed the grounds of Arlington Court into something of a nature reserve. She ordered the building of an eight-mile long perimeter fence to protect the native wildfowl and heron populations. The Shetland ponies and Jacob sheep grazing the fields today are descendants of those introduced by Rosalie. Another of her eclectic interests is evident in the 18th century stable block which houses a unique collection of horse-drawn carriages she saved from destruction.

LANDKEY
2 miles SE of Barnstaple off the A361

Landkey boasts a fine church with some impressive memorials (well worth visiting) and also the distinction of being the only village bearing this name in Britain. Historians believe that it is derived from *Lan*, the Celtic word for a church, and the saint to which it was

Arlington Court

dedicated, Kea. An enduring legend claims that St Kea rowed over from Wales with his personal cow on board determined to convert the pagans of north Devon to Christianity. Sadly, these benighted people were not persuaded by his eloquence, so they chopped off his head. Not many public speakers could cope with that kind of negative response, but St Kea calmly retrieved his severed head and continued, head in hand, to preach the Gospel for many years.

Just outside the village, **Miss Piggyland, Rabbit World and Indoor Jungle World** has been trading as a farm park and rare breed centre since 1992 with the aim of providing an educational glimpse into times and lifestyles past. It is set in beautiful, unspoilt North Devon countryside, and centres around a Grade II listed, 15th century Devon farm house. There are more than 50 acres of lovely countryside and nature walks to explore, including lime kilns, badger sets, rivers and lakes. There are many animals to see and feed as well as activities for the young ones, whatever the weather.

SWIMBRIDGE

5 miles SE of Barnstaple on the A361

For almost half a century from 1833 this attractive village was the home of the **Rev. John "Jack" Russell**, the celebrated hunting parson and breeder of the first Jack Russell terriers. A larger than life character, he was an enthusiastic master of foxhounds and when his Bishop censured him

for pursuing such an unseemly sport for a man of the cloth, he transferred the pack into his wife's name and continued his frequent sorties. He was still riding to hounds in his late 70s and when he died in 1880 at the age of 87, hundreds of people attended his funeral. Russell was buried in the churchyard of St James', the church where he had been a diligent pastor. He was gratefully remembered for his brief sermons, delivered as his groom waited by the porch with his horse saddled and ready.

Mostly 15th century, the **Church of St James** is one of Devon's outstanding churches, distinctive from outside because of its unusual lead-covered spire. Inside, there is a wealth of ecclesiastical treasures: a richly carved rood screen spanning both the nave and the aisles, an extraordinary 18th century font cover in the shape of an elongated octagonal "cupboard", a fine 15th century stone pulpit supported by a tall pedestal and carved with the figures of saints and angels, and a wonderful nave roof with protective angels gazing down. Collectors of unusual epitaphs will savour the punning lines inscribed on a monument here to John Rosier, a lawyer who died in 1658:

*Lo, with a Warrant
sealed by God's decree
Death his grim Seargant
hath arrested me
No bayle was to be given,
no law could save
My body from the prison of the grave.*

Just outside Swimbridge, in beautiful unspoilt countryside, lies North Devon Farm Park. Centred around a traditional 15th century Devonshire farmhouse, the park aims to offer a glimpse into the lifestyles of those living on the land in the past while also providing numerous activities for everyone that include an all-weather indoor play area, an outdoor assault course, tractor rides, dog handling and ferret racing. Two of its most popular attractions are the shire horses Jack and Derby.

The village itself has some elegant Georgian houses and a pub which in 1962 was renamed after Swimbridge's most famous resident. Jack Russell societies from around the world frequently hold their meetings here.

COBBATON

6 miles SE of Barnstaple off the A377

The hamlet of Cobbaton is home to the largest private collection of military vehicles and wartime memorabilia in the southwest. Owner Preston Isaac started the **Cobbaton Combat Collection** as a hobby but admits that "it got out of hand!" His schoolboy's box of treasures has grown to comprise more than 60 World War II military vehicles, including tanks and artillery, along with weapons and equipment from all over the world as well as thousands of smaller items. For visitors' convenience, a NAAFI truck is on duty to provide snacks and drinks and the Quartermaster's Stores offers a

Cobbaton Combat Collection

range of surplus uniforms, de-activated guns, militaria, books and souvenirs.

BISHOPS TAWTON

2 miles S of Barnstaple on the A377

Bishop's Tawton takes its name from the River Taw and the medieval Bishop's Palace that stood here until the reign of Henry VIII and of which a few fragments still stand. The village today is not over-endowed with listed buildings but it can boast a very unusual one, a sociable three-seater outside lavatory which has been accorded Grade II Listed status. This amenity has not been used for 40 years or more (and the brambles which have invaded it would make it rather uncomfortable to do so) but it still looks perfectly serviceable.

ATHERINGTON

7 miles S of Barnstaple on the B3217

A landmark for miles around, **St Mary's Church** stands in the picturesque square of this hilltop village and is notable for a feature which is unique in Devon – a lavishly carved and alarmingly top-heavy rood loft. Created by two carvers from Chittlehampton in the 1530s, it is an exceptionally fine example of their craft. The church also contains striking effigies of Sir John Wilmington, who died in 1349, and his wife; a window of medieval glass; and well-preserved brasses of Sir John Basset, (died 1529), his two wives and 12 children.

HIGH BICKINGTON

8 miles S of Barnstaple on the B3217

Two miles south of Atherington is another hilltop village. Standing at almost 600 feet above sea level, the village commands excellent views in all directions. It boasts a fine 16th century inn, The George, which is set amongst a delightful group of thatched cottages, and a parish church dating back to the 1100s which is renowned for its exceptional collection of carved bench and pew ends. There are around 70 of them in all: some are Gothic (characterised by fine tracery); others are Renaissance (characterised by rounded figures). More recent carving on the choir stalls depicts an appealing collection of animals and birds.

BIDEFORD

Dubbed the "Little White Town" by Charles Kingsley, this attractive town set beside the River Torridge was once the third busiest port in Britain. The first bridge across the shallow neck of the Torridge estuary was built around 1300 to link Bideford with its aptly-named satellite village, East-the-Water. That bridge must have been very impressive for its time. It was 670 feet long, and built of massive oak lintels of varying length which created a series of irregular arches between 12 and 25 feet apart. Legend has it that the reason for the varying arch sizes is because the local parishes contributed to the

Bideford

funding of the bridge in varying amounts and the size of the arches reflects their contributions. These erratic dimensions were preserved when the bridge was rebuilt in stone around 1460, (the old bridge was used as scaffolding), and despite widening during the 1920s they persist to this day. Unusually, Bideford Bridge is managed by an ancient corporation of trustees, known as *feoffees,* whose income, derived from property in the town, not only pays for the upkeep of the bridge but also supports local charities and good causes. A high-level bridge a mile or so downstream, opened in 1987, has relieved some of the traffic congestion and also provides panoramic views of the town and the Torridge estuary.

Bideford received its Market Charter from Henry III in 1272, (on May 25th to be precise) and markets still take place every

Tuesday and Saturday. Since 1883 they have been held in the splendid **Pannier Market** building, reckoned to be one of the best surviving examples of a Victorian covered market. Along with local produce, there's a huge selection of gifts, crafts, and handmade goods on offer: "Everything from Antiques to Aromatherapy!"

Devon ports seemed to specialise in particular commodities. At Bideford it was tobacco from the North American colonies which brought almost two centuries of prosperity until the American War of Independence shut off supplies. Evidence of this golden age can still be seen in the opulent merchants' residences in Bridgeland Street, and most strikingly in the **Royal Hotel** in East-the-Water, a former merchant's house of 1688 with a pair of little-seen plasterwork ceilings which are perhaps the finest and most extravagant examples of their kind in Devon.

Devil's Kitchen, Lundy Island

It was while he was staying at the Royal Hotel that Charles Kingsley penned most of *Westward Ho!* A quarter of a million words long, the novel was completed in just seven months. There's a statue of Kingsley, looking suitably literary, on Bideford Quay. Broad and tree-lined, the Quay stands at the foot of the narrow maze of lanes which formed the old seaport.

Just round the corner from the Quay, on the edge of Victoria Park, is the **Burton Museum & Art Gallery**, opened in 1994. The museum contains some interesting curios such as Bideford harvest jugs of the late 1700s, and model ships in carved bone made by French prisoners during the Napoleonic wars. The gallery has frequently changing exhibitions with subjects ranging from automata to kites, quilts to dinosaurs, as well as paintings by well-known North Devon artists. The museum also has a craft gallery, shop, workshop, lecture area and coffee shop. Starting at the Burton Gallery, guided walks around the town are available.

The town's strong maritime connection is represented by the *Kathleen & May*, which is moored on the River Torridge next to the old bridge. This historic three-masted schooner has been restored and the guided tours of the ship take in the cosy captain's cabin, the cramped crew's quarters and the vast hold that carried coal, bricks, slate and even gunpowder. There is also an information centre, with

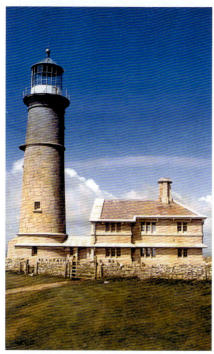

Old Lighthouse, Lundy Island

derives from the Norse *lunde ey*, meaning puffin island, and these attractive birds with their multi-coloured beaks are still in residence, along with many other species. More than 400 different species of birds have been spotted on Lundy, and you might also see one of the indigenous black rats which have survived only at this isolated location. The island has a 13th century castle and a lighthouse, both offering accommodation, a church, a pub and a shop selling souvenirs and the famous stamps.

AROUND BIDEFORD

WESTWARD HO!

2 miles NW of Bideford on the B3236

Is there any other place in the world that has been named after a popular novel? Following the huge success in 1855 of Charles Kingsley's tale of Elizabethan derring-do, a company was formed to develop this spectacular site with its rocky cliffs and two miles of sandy beach. The early years were troubled. A powerful storm washed away the newly-built pier and most of the houses. When Rudyard Kipling came here in 1874 as a pupil at the United Services College he described the place as "twelve

51 THE VILLAGE INN

Westward Ho!

Mid-18th century former farmhouse offering outstanding food and beautifully appointed rooms..

 see page 177

early prints and documents along with a collection of interesting artefacts, and a gift shop selling souvenirs.

Another form of transport is explored at the former **Bideford Railway Station**, now a museum, which displays many fascinating objects of local railway interest. Outside, several railway vehicles are parked on a length of re-laid track.

One excursion from Bideford that should not be missed is the day trip to **Lundy Island** on the supply boat, the *MS Oldenburg*. Lundy is a huge lump of granite rock, three miles long and half a mile wide, with sheer cliffs rising 500 feet above the shore. Its name

Just a couple of miles southwest of Westward Ho! is The Big Sheep, which has been described as "a working farm turned wacky tourist attraction." Along with 'one dog and his ducks', sheep racing and the horse whisperers, there is a huge indoor adventure play area for children and, more conventionally, cheese making, sheep shearing and sheepdog trialling demonstrations. The Big Sheep, which has its own brewery, is open daily from April to the end of October.

bleak houses by the shore". Today Westward Ho! is a busy holiday resort well worth visiting for its two miles of golden sands, recently awarded a Blue Flag, and the nearby **Northam Burrows Country Park**, almost 1000 acres of grazed burrows rich in flora, fauna and migratory birds, and offering tremendous views across Bideford Bay.

The Park is also home to the oldest 18-hole links golf course in England. The **Royal North Devon Golf Course** was laid out in 1864 by 'Old Tom Morris' and it is considered to represent a true test of the game.

An unusual event at Westward Ho! is the **Pot Walloping Festival** which takes place in late spring. Local people and visitors join together to throw pebbles which have been dislodged by winter storms back onto the famous ridge, after which pots of a different kind also get a walloping.

NORTHAM

2 miles N of Bideford on the A386

Northam is said to have been where Hubba the Dane attacked

Devon and was repelled by either Alfred the Great or the Earl of Devon. Another tale recounts that in AD1069, three years after King Harold had been slain at the Battle of Hastings, his three sons landed at Northam in an attempt to regain their father's throne. They came from Ireland with an invasion force of more than 60 ships but their rebellion was mercilessly suppressed at a site just to the south of the town. To this day, it is known as **Bloody Corner**.

APPLEDORE

3 miles N of Bideford on the A386

Overlooking the Taw-Torridge estuary, Appledore is a delightful old-world fishing village of narrow winding lanes and sturdy fishermens' cottages from the 18th and 19th centuries. All types of fishing can be arranged here and you can even go crabbing from the quayside. The streets of the old quarter are too narrow for cars although not, it seems, for the occasional small fishing boat which is pulled up from the harbour and parked between the buildings.

A hundred years ago,

River Torridge, Appledore

Appledore had several boat and ship repair yards building and maintaining wooden schooners, ketches and barques. Nowadays, the Covered Shipyard, the largest in Europe at its time of construction, builds large ocean going steel hulled vessels.

It seems appropriate that the **North Devon Maritime Museum** should be located in this truly nautical setting. Housed in a former ship-owner's residence, the museum contains a wealth of seafaring memorabilia, a photographic exhibit detailing the military exercises around the estuary in preparation for the D-Day landings during World War II, a reconstructed Victorian kitchen, and much more.

A stroll along Bude Street is recommended. Art and craft galleries have gathered here amongst the Georgian style "Captains" houses, and it's particularly colourful during the **Appledore Visual Arts Festival** in late May-early June when one of the many events is a door decorating competition.

Signal Box, Instow

INSTOW

3 miles N of Bideford on the B3233

The older part of this delightful village lies inland from the Torridge estuary while, looking out over the magnificent beach, there are some early 19th century villas. Here, too, is the **Instow Signal Box** that was built in 1873 to control the crossing gates and the passing loop at Instow Station. It has been restored and is now the first Grade II listed signal box in the country. Visitors can see its machinery, gate wheel and instruments as well as 'pull off' a re-instated signal.

Just south of the village are **Tapeley Park Gardens,** some 35 acres of grounds on the eastern bank of the River Torridge. From here there are excellent views across the estuary and over to Lundy Island. Along with the lake reached by a woodland walk, there are masses of hydrangeas, rhododendrons and camellias. As well as the renovated Italian terraces and the restored walled kitchen garden, Tapeley has an organic permaculture garden where fruit, vegetables, nuts and herbs are mixed together using companion planting. There is also a children's play area and a variety of animals and pets to entertain the youngsters.

GREAT TORRINGTON

7 miles SE of Bideford on the A386

A good place to start exploring Great Torrington is at **Castle Hill**

52 THE GLOBE HOTEL

Torrington

Beautifully refurbished rooms and an amazing *à la carte* menu, make this hotel in the picturesque town of Torrington a popular spot with holiday-makers and locals alike.

  see page 178

53 THE CORNER HOUSE

High Bullen

A charming place to stay, offering first class hospitality as soon as guests arrive until the time they depart.

 see page 179

which commands grand views along the valley of the River Torridge. (There's no view of the castle: that was demolished as long ago as 1228: its site is now a bowling green). On the opposite bank of the river is the hamlet of Taddiport where the tiny 14th century church by the bridge was originally the chapel of a leper hospital: its inmates were not permitted to cross over into Torrington itself.

Not many churches in England have been blown up by gunpowder. That was the fate however of the original **Church of St Michael and All Angels.** It happened during the Civil War when General Fairfax captured the town on February 16th, 1645. His Royalist prisoners were bundled into the church which they had been using as an arsenal. In the darkness, the 80 barrels of gunpowder stored there were somehow set alight and in the huge explosion that followed the church was demolished, 200 men lost their lives, and Fairfax himself narrowly escaped death. The present spacious church was built five years later, one of very few in the country erected during the Commonwealth years. At the **Torrington 1646** attraction at Castle Hill, you can learn about the Battle of Torrington, the Civil War and what it would have been like to be a Roundhead or Cavalier in the 17th century.

The **Torrington Museum** is an ideal place to discover the history of this small Devon town through the centuries. The

collections here cover agriculture, transport, domestic life and local industries. The museum also has a collection of artefacts on the life and work of William Keble-Martin, the author of the *Definitive Book on Wild Flowers* and a vicar in the town for nine years.

In Fore Street, is the Plough Arts Centre, a theatre, cinema and art gallery sharing the one building which was formerly the Plough Inn.

Today, the town's leading tourist attraction is **Dartington Crystal** where visitors can see skilled craftsmen blowing and shaping the crystal, follow the history of glass-making from the Egyptians to the present day, watch a video presentation, and browse amongst some 10,000 square feet of displays. The enterprise was set up in the 1960s by the Dartington Hall Trust to provide employment in an area of rural depopulation: today, the beautifully designed handmade crystal is exported to more than 50 countries around the world.

Torrington's **May Fair** is still an important event in the local calendar, and has been since 1554. On the first Thursday in May, a Queen is crowned, there is maypole dancing in the High Street, and a banner proclaims the greeting *"Us be plazed to zee 'ee".*

About a mile south of Great Torrington on the A3124, the Royal Horticultural Society's **Rosemoor Garden** occupies a breathtaking setting in the Torridge Valley. The 40-acre site includes mature planting in Lady Anne Palmer's

Rosemoor Garden, nr Great Torrington

54 RHS GARDEN ROSEMOOR

Great Torrington

The Royal Horticultural Society Garden **Rosemoor** is acclaimed by gardeners throughout the world.

 see page 180

55 APARTMENTS AT ROSEMOOR

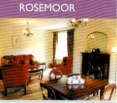

Great Torrington

Apartments at Rosemoor offer quality self-catering accommodation in a delightful setting.

 see page 180

magnificent garden and arboretum; a winding rocky gorge with bamboos and ferns beside the stream, and a more formal area which contains one of the longest herbaceous borders in the country. There are trails for children, a picnic area and an award-winning Visitor Centre with a licensed restaurant, plant centre and shop.

MERTON

10 miles SE of Bideford on the A386

This village is home to **Barometer World and Museum**, a remarkable collection that was begun by Edwin Banfield, a retired bank manager in the early 1970s. Along with housing the largest collection of English barometers on public display in the world, the museum is home to an exhibition that charts the development of domestic barometers from the 1680s to the present day as well as other unusual items that have been used, over the years, to predict the weather. Perhaps most extraordinary of all these bizarre devices is the Tempest Prognosticator that was designed by Dr George Merryweather and exhibited by him at the Great Exhibition of 1851. Styled on an Indian temple, the 'machine' uses live leeches to determine whether a storm is on its way!

DOLTON

11½ miles SE of Bideford on the B3217

Situated above the wooded Torridge Valley, this village clusters around its parish Church of St Edmund's that boasts a true treasure – a font that dates back more than 1,000 years. Made from two pieces of a Saxon cross, the intricate carvings on the font depict a fantastic menagerie of winged

56 THE CYDER PRESSE

Weare Gifford

Late 18th century former farmhouse noted for excellent food, well-kept real ales and comfortable B&B rooms.

  see page 181

dragons and writhing serpents with yet more dragons emerging from the upturned head of a man. Their relevance to the Christian message may be a little obscure but there is no denying their powerful impact.

MONKLEIGH

5 miles S of Bideford on the A388

Monkleigh parish church contains a striking monument, an ornate canopied tomb containing the remains of **Sir William Hankford** who was Lord Chief Justice of England in the early 1400s. He lived at nearby Annery Park and the story goes that having been troubled by poachers Sir William instructed his gamekeeper to shoot anyone he found in the park at night. The gamekeeper did indeed see a figure passing through the park, fired and discovered to his horror that he had killed his master.

Found in the outbuildings of a small holding near the village is **Monkleigh Pottery**, where Richard Champion, a traditional craft potter who specialises in hand thrown stoneware pottery works. Visitors are welcome to come to see the pots being made, which include dinner services, vases and planters. There is also a picnic and children's play area.

WEARE GIFFARD

5 miles S of Bideford off the A386

This appealing village claims to be the longest riverside village in England, straggling for almost two miles along the banks of the Torridge. Weare Giffard

(pronounced *Jiffard*) has a charm all its own, suspended in time it seems to belong to the more peaceful days of half a century ago. The villagers have even refused to have full street lighting installed, so avoiding the "street furniture" that blemishes so many attractive places.

Another attraction in the village is a fine old 15th century manor house, **Weare Giffard Hall**. Although its outer walls were partially demolished during the Civil War, the splendid gatehouse with its mighty doors and guardian lions has survived. Inside, the main hall has a magnificent hammer-beam roof, and several of the other rooms are lined with Tudor and Jacobean oak panelling. For centuries, the house was the home of the Fortescue family and in the nearby church there is an interesting "family tree" with portraits of past Fortescues carved in stone.

WOOLFARDISWORTHY

11 miles SW of Bideford off the A39

Naturally, you don't pronounce Woolfardisworthy the way it looks. The correct pronunciation is *Woolsery*. The extraordinary name goes back to Saxon times when the land was owned by Wulfheard who established a *worthig*, or homestead, here.

A mile or so north of the village, alongside the A39, is another family entertainment complex, the **Milky Way Adventure Park**. The park includes a huge indoor play area (for both children and adults) where you can test your archery and laser target shooting skills, a Pets Corner where children are encouraged to cuddle the animals, a Bird of Prey Centre, a Sheep Dog Training and Breeding Centre, "Toddler Town" - a safe play area for very young children, a Sports Hall, a miniature railway, and a "Time Warp Adventure Zone".

CLOVELLY

12 miles SW of Bideford off the A39

Even if you've never been to Devon, you must have heard of this unbelievably quaint and picturesque village that tumbles down a steep hillside in terraced levels. Almost every whitewashed and flower-strewn cottage is worthy of its own picture postcard and from the sheltered little harbour there is an enchanting view of this unique place. One reason Clovelly is so unspoilt is that the village has belonged to the Rous family since 1738 and they have ensured that it has been spared such modern defacements as telegraph poles and "street furniture".

The only access to the beach and the beautifully restored 14th century quay is on foot or by donkey, although there is a Land Rover service from the Red Lion Hotel for those who can't face the climb back up the hill. The only other forms of transport are the sledges which are used to deliver weekly supplies. During the summer months there are regular boat trips around the bay, and the *Jessica Hettie* travels daily to Lundy Island with timings that allow

passengers to spend some six hours there, watching the seals and abundant wildlife.

The skipper of the *Jessica Hettie,* Clive Pearson, is also a potter. In 1992 he opened **The Clovelly Pottery** which displays an extensive range of items made by Cornish and Devon potters. In the nearby workshop, for a small fee, you can try your own hand at throwing a pot.

This captivating village has some strong literary connections. It features as "Steepway" in the story *A Message from the Sea* by Dickens

57 THE MILKY WAY ADVENTURE PARK

Woolfardisworthy, nr Bideford

Set in magnificent grounds and bursting with rollercoasters, rides and live shows, families will have trouble deciding what to do next at this fun-filled adventure park.

 see page 182

Clovelly Cobbled Street

The oldest cottage in Clovelly is Crazy Kate's Cottage (private) which overlooks the harbour and is named after a fisherman's widow who died in 1736. Kate Lyall used to watch her husband from the upper window as he fished in the bay. One day, a squall blew up just outside the harbour and Kate watched in horror as her husband drowned. From that time on, she became demented. One day, she put on her wedding dress and walked into the sea to join her husband in his watery grave.

58 THE CHURCH OF ST NECTAN

Hartland

The Parish Church of St Nectan has many interesting features and is well worth a visit.

 see page 183

and Wilkie Collins. Charles Kingsley (*The Water Babies; Westward Ho!*) was at school here in the 1820s and the **Kingsley Museum** explores his links with the village. Next door, the **Fisherman's Cottage** provides an insight into what life was like here about 80 years ago. And the award-winning Visitor Centre, modelled on a traditional Devon long barn, has an audio-visual show narrating the development of Clovelly from around 2000BC to the present day.

Clovelly Court Gardens are a perfect example of a Victorian walled kitchen garden with some impressive glasshouses sheltering peaches, apricots, melons and grapes. The unique maritime micro-climate also allows the growth of tender and exotic plants.

The parking fee charged at Clovelly also covers admission to Fisherman's Cottage and the Kingsley Museum.

HARTLAND

15 miles SW of Bideford on the B3248

This pleasant village with its narrow streets and small square was once larger and more important than Bideford. Hartland was a royal possession from the time of King Alfred until William the Conqueror and continued to be a busy centre right up to the 19th century. It was at its most prosperous in the 1700s and some fine Georgian buildings survive from that period. But the most striking building is the parish **Church of St Nectan** which stands about 1.5 miles west of the

village. This is another of Devon's "must-see" churches. The exterior is impressive enough with its 128 feet high tower, but it is the glorious 15th century screen inside which makes this church one of the most visited in the county. A masterpiece of the medieval woodcarvers' art, its elegant arches are topped by four exquisitely fretted bands of intricate designs. The arches are delicately painted, reminding one yet again how colourful English churches used to be before the vandalism of the Puritan years.

In the churchyard is the grave of Allen Lane who, in 1935, revolutionised publishing by his introduction of Penguin Books, paperback books which were sold at sixpence (2.5p) each.

From the village, follow the signs to **Hartland Abbey.** Founded in 1157, the abbey was closed down in 1539 by Henry VIII who gave the building and its wide estates to William Abbott, Sergeant of the Royal wine cellars. His descendants still live here. The house was partly rebuilt in the mid-18th century in the style known as Strawberry Hill Gothic, and in the 1850s the architect George Gilbert Scott added a front hall and entrance. The abbey's owner, Sir George Stucley, had recently visited the Alhambra Palace in Spain which he much admired. He asked Scott to design something in that style and the result is the elegant Alhambra Corridor with a blue vaulted ceiling with white stencilled patterns. The abbey has a choice collection of pictures, porcelain and furniture acquired over many generations and, in the former Servants' Hall, a unique exhibition of documents dating from 1160. There's also a fascinating Victorian and Edwardian photographic exhibition which includes many early photographs. Outside, the extensive grounds include woodland gardens of camellias and rhododendrons, a bog garden, 18th century walled gardens and a recently restored gazebo overlooking the sea. In 2005, the Abbey provided a striking location for the film *Shell Seekers*.

Hartland Point

A mile further west is **Hartland Quay**. Exposed to all the wrath of Atlantic storms, it seems an inhospitable place for ships, but it was a busy landing-place from its building in 1566 until the sea finally overwhelmed it in 1893. Several of the old buildings have been converted into a comfortable hotel; another is now a museum recording the many wrecks that have littered this jagged coastline.

About three miles to the north of the Quay, reached by winding country lanes, is **Hartland Point.** On Ptolemy's map of Britain in Roman times, he names it the "Promontory of Hercules", a fitting name for this fearsome stretch of upended rocks rising at right angles to the sea. There are breathtaking sea and coast views and a lighthouse built in 1874.

MILFORD

16 miles SW of Bideford off the A39

In Speke valley, just north of the village, and only a short walk from the famous **Spekes Mill Mouth Coastal Waterfall**, are **Docton Mill and Gardens**. The mill dates back to Saxon times and only ceased working in 1910; the superb gardens were created in 1980 around the existing river, leats and ponds.

SOUTH MOLTON

This pleasant old market town, thankfully now bypassed by the A361 North Devon link road, has been a focus of the local agriculture-based economy since Saxon times. In common with many such towns throughout Devon, it was a centre of the wool trade in the late Middle Ages. The town still flourishes as a market town with a main market day on Thursday and an extra pannier market on Saturday.

Unusually, the town has two Royal Charters, one from Elizabeth I in 1590 and another from Charles II in 1684. They are commemorated

63

Just to the north of South Molton is Quince Honey Farm where the mysterious process of honey-making is explained in a series of displays and demonstrations. This is the world's largest exhibition of living honey bees, their hives all safely behind glass. A viewing gallery gives an overhead view of the process of honey-making and the shop offers a full range of honey and honey products, including delicious Devonshire honey ice cream.

each year with an Old English Fayre held in June. The original charters can both be seen in the **Town Museum** along with one of the oldest fire engines in the country. It was bought by the town in 1746 for £46.

In the heart of the old town lies Broad Street, so broad as to be almost a square, and distinguished by some handsome Georgian and Victorian civic architecture. Among the noteworthy buildings to be found here are the **Market Hall and Assembly Rooms,** the eccentric **Medical Hall** with its iron balcony and four Ionic columns, and the Palladian-style **Guildhall** of 1743 which overhangs the pavement in a series of arches. A useful Heritage Trail Guide, obtainable from the Tourist Information Centre, provides an excellent introduction to these notable buildings.

AROUND SOUTH MOLTON

NORTH MOLTON

3 miles NE of South Molton off the A399 or A361

Tucked away in the foothills of Exmoor, North Molton was once a busy wool and mining town. At intervals from Elizabethan times until the late 1800s, copper and iron were extracted from the hills above the town and transported down the valley of the River Mole and on to the sea at Barnstaple. Evidence of abandoned mine workings are still visible around the town as well as remains of the old

Mole Valley tramway.

North Molton's 15th century parish **Church of All Saints** reflects the small town's former industrial importance. It's a striking building with a high clerestory and a 100 feet pinnacled tower which seems rather grand for this rather remote community. Several notable features have survived. There's a part-medieval "wine-glass" pulpit complete with sounding board and trumpeting angel, a rood screen, some fine Jacobean panelling, and an extraordinary 17th century alabaster monument to Sir Amyas Bampfylde depicting the reclining knight with his wife Elizabeth reading a book and their 12 sons and five daughters kneeling nearby. The figures are delightfully executed, especially the small girl with plump cheeks holding an apple and gazing wide-eyed at her eldest sister.

Also interesting is the church clock which was purchased in 1564 for the then exorbitant price of £16.14s 4d. However, it proved to be a sound investment since it remained in working order for 370 years before its bells chimed for the last time in 1934.

Just to the west of the church is a fine 16th century house, Court Barton (private). The iconoclastic biographer and critic Lytton Strachey (1880-1932) stayed here with a reading party in 1908. It seems that the eminent writer greatly enjoyed his stay, reporting enthusiastically on the area's *"mild tranquillities"*, and a way of life which encompassed *"a surplusage of beef and Devonshire cream,.....a village shop with bulls'-eyes,.....more cream and then more beef and then somnolence".*

MOLLAND

6 miles E of South Molton off the A361

Hidden away in a maze of lanes skittering across the foothills of Exmoor, Molland is one of Devon's "must-visit" villages for anyone interested in wonderfully unspoilt churches. Following the sale of the village in the early 1600s, **St Mary's Church** stood within the estates of the Courtenay family. During and following the Commonwealth years, the Courtenays remained staunch Catholics and showed no interest in restoring or modernising the Protestant parish church. So today you will still find a Georgian screen and tiers of box-pews, whitewashed walls, an elaborate three-decker pulpit crowned by a trumpeting angel and a colourful Royal Arms blazoned with the name of its painter, Rowlands. Despite their Catholic principles, three late-17th and early-18th century members of the Courtenay family are commemorated by some typically flamboyant monuments of the time. Also within Molland parish lies Great Champson, the farm where in the 18th century the Quartly family introduced and developed their celebrated breed of red North Devon cattle.

WEST ANSTEY

9 miles E of South Molton off the B3227

The tiny hamlet of West Anstey lies just a mile or so from the Somerset border. **The Two Moors Way** passes by just a little to the east and the slopes on which the hamlet stands continue to rise up to the wilds of Exmoor. Despite being so small, West Anstey nevertheless has its own church, which boasts a fine Norman font and an arcade from the 1200s but is mostly 14th century. The area around West Anstey is one of the emptiest parts of Devon – grand open country dotted with just the occasional farm or a tiny cluster of cottages.

BISHOP'S NYMPTON

3 miles SE of South Molton off the A361

Bishop's Nympton, King's Nympton, George Nympton, as well as several Nymets, all take the Nympton or Nymet element of their names from the River Yeo which in Saxon and earlier times was known as the Nymet, meaning "river at a holy place". Bishop's Nympton has a long sloping main street, lined with thatched cottages, and a 15th century church whose lofty, well-proportioned tower is considered one of the most beautiful in Devon. For many years the church had a stained glass window erected in Tudor times at the expense of Lady Pollard, wife of Sir Lewis, an eminent judge and leading resident of the village. Sir Lewis told the author of *The Worthies of Devon*, John Prince, that he was away on business in London at the time and the details of the window's design were entrusted to his wife. At the time Sir Lewis left for town, he and his wife already had 21 children - 11 sons and 10 daughters. "But his lady caused one more child than she then had to be set there: presuming that, usually conceiving at her husband's coming home, she should have another. Which, inserted in expectation, came to pass in reality". The oddest thing about the story is that Lady Pollard not only correctly predicted the forthcoming child, but also its sex.

CHULMLEIGH

8 miles S of South Molton off the A377

With its narrow cobbled lanes, courtyards and quiet squares, Chulmleigh is a delight to explore. Sprawled across the hills above the leafy valley of the Little Dart river, it is one of several attractive small towns in mid-Devon which

Chulmleigh Church

prospered from the wool trade in the Middle Ages and then declined into sleepy, unspoilt communities. Chulmleigh's prosperity lasted longer than most since it was on the old wagon route to Barnstaple but in 1830 one of the newfangled turnpike roads was constructed along the Taw valley, siphoning off most of its trade. A quarter of a century later the Exeter to Barnstaple railway was built along the same route, the final straw for Chulmleigh as a trade centre. But this charming small town has been left with many original thatched cob cottages which cluster around a fine 15th century church noted for its lofty pinnacled tower and, inside, a wondrously carved rood screen that extends 50 feet across the nave and aisles.

To the south of Chulmleigh is **Eggesford Forest** where, in 1919, the newly-formed Forestry Commission planted its first tree. This event is commemorated by a stone unveiled by the Queen in 1956. The stone also marks the planting of more than one million acres of trees by the Commission. There are two walks through the forest, each about one mile long, which provide visitors with the opportunity of seeing the red deer that live here.

LAPFORD

12 miles S of South Molton on the A377

Remarkably, this small community still has its own railway station. Passenger numbers have been much augmented since British Rail's rather prosaic "Exeter to Barnstaple route" was re-christened as the **"Tarka Line"**. The original name may have been lacklustre but the 39-mile journey itself has always been delightful as it winds slowly along the gentle river valleys of the Yeo and the Taw.

Lapford stands high above the River Yeo, its hilltop church a famous local landmark for generations: *"when yew sees Lapford church yew knows where yew'm be"*. It's well worth a visit since the 15th century rood screen inside is regarded as one of the most exquisitely fashioned in the country. There are five bands of the most delicate carving at the top and above them rise modern figures of the Holy Family, (Jesus, Mary and John), surmounted by the original ornamental ceiling with its carved angels gazing down from the nave roof.

WINKLEIGH

8 miles N of Okehampton on the A3124

This attractive village with its open views across to Dartmoor is believed to have been a beacon station in prehistoric times. When the Normans arrived they built two small castles, one at each end of the village. They were probably intended as bases for hunting in the nearby park – the only Devon park to be mentioned in the *Domesday Book*. For centuries Winkleigh was an important local trading centre with its own market, fair and borough court. Today, it's a peaceful little place with thatched cottages nestling up to the mainly 15th century church which has a richly carved and painted wagon roof where 70 golden-winged angels stand guard over the nave.

DOLTON

12 miles SW of South Molton on the B3217

Dolton clusters around its parish church of St Edmund's which boasts a real treasure, a Saxon font more than 1000 years old. Its

intricate carvings depict a fantastic menagerie of winged dragons and writhing serpents, with yet more dragons emerging from the upturned face of a man. Their relevance to the Christian message may be a little obscure but there's no denying their powerful impact.

Just to the northwest lies the **Halsdon Nature Reserve** that encompasses an extremely pretty valley of deciduous trees and pasture along with a mile and a half stretch of the River Torridge. This river is particularly important for its otter population and these creatures can be found in the reserve along with a wide variety of birds.

MEETH

14 miles SW of South Molton on the A386

A mile or so north of Hatherleigh, the A386 crosses the River Torridge and a couple of miles further is the pleasant little village of Meeth whose Old English name means "the meeting of the streams". Indeed, a small brook runs down the hillside into the Torridge. From the early 1700s, Meeth and the surrounding area was noted for its "pipe" and "ball clay" products, generically known as pottery clay. There are still extensive clay works to the northwest of the village.

But for cyclists and walkers Meeth is much better known as the southern terminus of the **Tarka Trail Cycle / Walkway** which runs northwards through Bideford and Barnstaple.

One traditional rural industry does thrive in Winkleigh - the Winkleigh Cider Company has been producing the West Country's favourite tipple at Western Barn since 1916. The company uses only locally grown apples which are pressed from October to early December. Visitors at this time can watch the operation, before the cider is fermented in the 100-year-old vats. The premises are open from Monday to Saturday throughout the year and there's a site shop selling local crafts and personal gifts along with the company's own products.

59 THE BRIDGE INN

Hatherleigh

This newly refurbed pub is a great place to stay and explore Devon from.

 see page 183

60 THOMAS ROBERTS HOUSE

Hatherleigh

Thomas Roberts House is an elegant and comfortable Georgian House offering B&B and with a sense of history.

 see page 184

HATHERLEIGH

17 miles SW of South Molton on the A386

This medieval market town, which has held a market every Tuesday since 1693, has been popular for many years as a holiday base for fishermen trying their luck on the nearby River Torridge and its tributary which runs alongside the small town.

A good starting point for an exploration of this attractive town with its cob and thatch cottages is the Tarka Country Information Point at **Hatherleigh Pottery** where there are exhibits detailing the life and countryside in and around this 1000-year-old town. You can also pick up leaflets to guide you around Hatherleigh's narrow streets. The Pottery itself has showrooms displaying colourful hand-thrown ceramics, textile items, original prints and greetings cards.

Hatherleigh was owned by Tavistock Abbey from the late 900s until the Dissolution of the Monasteries in the 1540s and the picturesquely thatched George Hotel is believed to have been built around 1450 as the abbot's court house. The London Inn also dates from around that time and the Old Church House is thought to be even older.

The town would have possessed an even finer stock of early buildings were it not for a devastating fire in 1840 which destroyed much of the old centre. Fortunately, the 15th century **Church of St John the Baptist** escaped the flames. Set high above the Lew valley, the church's red sandstone walls and sturdy tower still provide a striking focus for this pleasant rural community. Although the church survived the great fire of 1840, a century-and-a-half later hurricane force winds, generated during the storms of January 1990, swashed against its spindly tower and tossed it through the roof of the nave. Thankfully, nobody was in the church at the time.

In mid-July, the **Hatherleigh Arts Festival** takes place, 4 days of contemporary arts, including theatre, concerts, art exhibitions, street theatre and workshops. All year round art is visible in the various sculptures scattered around the town, notably the larger than life "Sheep" sculpture in the town's car park.

For a superb view of the surrounding countryside, make your way to the Monument erected in memory of Colonel William Morris, a hero of the Charge of the Light Brigade.

Until 1966, the Okehampton to Bude railway ran through Hatherleigh. In that year it was closed as part of the notorious "Beeching Cuts". The last train on the Hatherleigh to Bude line, a prized local amenity, steamed its way into Cornwall on May 16th, 1966, then to a siding, and then to rust. Long stretches of the old track bed of the railway now provide some attractive walking.

There's more good walking at **Abbeyford Woods,** about a mile to the east of the village, with a particularly lovely stretch running alongside the River Okement.

Barbara Pearson Sculpture Shelter, Holsworthy

HOLSWORTHY

Wednesday is a good day to visit Holsworthy. That's when this little town, just four miles from the Cornish border, holds its weekly market. This is very much the traditional kind of street market, serving a large area of the surrounding countryside and with locally-produced fresh cream, butter, cheese, and vegetables all on sale. The town gets even livelier in early July when it gives itself over to the amusements of the three-day-long **St Peter's Fair**. The Fair opens with the curious old custom of the Pretty Maid Ceremony. Back in 1841, a Holsworthy merchant bequeathed a legacy to provide a small payment each year to a local spinster, under the age of 30 and noted for her good looks, demure manner and regular attendance at church. Rather surprisingly, in view of the last two requirements, the bequest still finds a suitable recipient each year.

Holsworthy's most striking architectural features are the two Victorian viaducts that once carried the railway line to Bude. The viaducts stride high above the southern edge of the town and, since they now form part of a footpath along the old track, it's possible to walk across them for some stunning views of the area.

An interesting feature in the parish church is an organ built in 1668 by Renatus Hunt for All Saints Church, Chelsea. In 1723, it was declared worn out but was nevertheless purchased by a Bideford church. There it gave good service for some 140 years before it was written off once again. Removed to Holsworthy, it has been here ever since.

Just off the Market Square, **Holsworthy Museum** features displays about an era of bygone rural life and is run with enthusiasm by a band of dedicated volunteers.

The area around Holsworthy is particularly popular with cyclists. There are three clearly-designated routes starting and finishing in the town, and it also lies on the **West Country Way**, a 250-mile cycle route from Padstow to Bristol and Bath which opened in the spring of 1997.

AROUND HOLSWORTHY

SHEBBEAR

7 miles NE of Holsworthy off the A388

This attractive village is set around a spacious square laid out in the Saxon manner with a church at one end and a hostelry at the other. Lying in a hollow just outside St Michael's churchyard is a huge lump of rock, weighing about a ton, which is known as the **Devil's Stone**. According to local legend, the boulder was placed here by Old Nick who challenged the villagers to move it, threatening that disaster would strike if they could not. Every year since then, on November 5th (a date established long before the Gunpowder Plot of 1605), a curious ceremony has taken place. After sounding a peal of bells, the bell ringers come out of the church and set about the stone with sticks and crowbars. Once they have successfully turned the stone over, they return in triumph to the bell tower to sound a second peal. The story is recounted in greater detail in the village hostelry, The Devils Stone Inn.

SHEEPWASH

9 miles E of Holsworthy off the A3072 or A386

Sheepwash is yet another Devon community to have been devastated by fire. The conflagration here occurred in 1742 and the destruction was so great that for more than 10 years the village was completely deserted. Slowly, the villagers returned, built new houses in stone, and today if you want the essence of Devon distilled into one location, then the village square at Sheepwash is just about perfect. Along one side stands the famous Half Moon Inn, renowned amongst fishermen; on another, the old church tower rises above pink-washed thatched cottages, while in the centre, cherry trees shelter the ancient village pump.

Just south of the village, a minor road crosses the River Torridge and there's a rather heartening story about the bridge here, **Sheepwash Bridge.** Until well into the 1600s, the only way of crossing the river was by means of stepping stones. One day, when the river was in full spate, a young man attempting to return to the village was swept away and drowned. His father, John Tusbury, was grief-stricken but responded to the tragedy by providing money to build a bridge. He also donated sufficient funds for it to be maintained by establishing the Bridgeland Trust and stipulating that any surplus income should be used to help in the upkeep of the church and chapel. The Trust is still in operation and nowadays also funds outings for village children and pensioners.

NORTHLEW

10 miles SE of Holsworthy off the A3072 or A3079

As at Sheepwash, the thatched cottages and houses stand around a large central square which is dominated by a charming 15th century church standing on the hilltop above the River Lew. The church is noted for its Norman remains and the exceptional (mainly Tudor) woodwork in the roof, bench ends and screen. Also of interest is one of the stained glass windows which features four saints. St Thomas, to whom the church is dedicated, is shown holding a model of the church; St Augustine, the first Archbishop of Canterbury, holds the priory gateway, while St Joseph carries the Holy Grail and the staff which grew into the

famous Glastonbury thorn tree. The fourth figure is simply clad in a brown habit and carries a bishop's crozier and a spade. This is St Brannock who is credited with being the first man to cultivate the wild lands of this area by clearing woodland and ploughing and could therefore be regarded as the patron saint of farmers.

CLAWTON

3 miles S of Holsworthy, on the A388

A good indication of the mildness of the Devon climate is the number of vineyards which have been established over the last 30 years or so. **Clawford Vineyard** in the valley of the River Claw is a good example. Set in more than 78 acres of vines and orchards, the vineyard's owners welcome visitors to sample their home-grown wines and ciders, and in the autumn to watch that year's vintage being produced.

63 BRADDON COTTAGES & FOREST

Ashwater

This unique low carbon holiday opportunity is a must for the environmentally conscious holidaymakers.

 see page 187

64 EAST LAKE FARM

East Chilla

This 150 acre working farm is a great base from which to explore the surrounding Devon and Cornwall countryside.

 see page 188

North Dartmoor

High, wild and bleak, Dartmoor is the south of England's only true wilderness and it is easy for walkers to lose their way in the rolling granite uplands, particularly when the mists descend unexpectedly and with great speed. Roughly 30 miles long and 22 miles wide, the Dartmoor National Park covers an area of some 365 square miles and it rises to a height of more than 2000 feet. The highest and most dramatic area of the moor lies to the northwest, on Okehampton Common, where High Willhays and Yes Tor rise to a height of 2038 feet and 2029 feet respectively. Although not so high, Brent Tor is one of the moorland's most striking features since crowning its 1000-feet summit is a 12th century church. From here, on a clear day there are superb views across Dartmoor, westwards to Bodmin Moor and southwards to the sea at Plymouth Sound.

Several of Devon's rivers have their source on the moorland and some have given rise to another feature of the moorland – waterfalls. In particular there is Lydford Gorge where the suddenly narrowing valley of the River Lyd creates the impressive 100 feet White Lady Waterfall and a series of whirlpools. On the eastern edge of the National Park and in the valley of the River Bovey is the Becky Falls Woodland Park while, close by, in the valley of the River Teign, there is England's highest waterfall, Canonteign Falls.

White Lady Waterfall, Lydford

Dartmoor is perhaps most closely associated with Sir Arthur Conan Doyle who, in his spine-chilling novel *The Hound of the Baskervilles*, made the moorland bleaker and more sinister than it is in reality. This most famous of all the Sherlock Holmes tales was inspired by stories told to Conan Doyle by his Dartmoor guide, Harry Baskerville. Although he took the liberty of changing some of the geography of the moorland, the novel has brought many visitors to Dartmoor since it was first published.

Within this area of North Dartmoor there is only one town of any size, Okehampton, and it is there we begin our tour of the region.

OKEHAMPTON

The old travel-writer's cliché of a "county of contrasts" can't be avoided when describing the landscape around Okehampton. To the north and west, the puckered green hills of North Devon roll away to the coast; to the south, lie the wildest stretches of Dartmoor with the great peaks of **High Willhays** and **Yes Tor** rising to more than 2000 feet. At this height they are, officially, mountains but quite puny compared with their original altitude: geologists believe that at one time the surface of Dartmoor stood at 15,000 feet above sea level. Countless centuries of erosion have reduced it to a

plateau of whale-backed granite ridges with an average height of around 1200 feet. After so many millions of years of erosion, the moor has become strewn with fragments of surface granite, or moorstone. It was because of this ready-to-use stone that Dartmoor became one of the most populous areas of early Britain, its inhabitants using the easily quarried granite to create their stone rows, circles, and burial chambers. Stone was also used to build their distinctive hut-circles of which there are more than 1500 scattered across the moor.

From Celtic times Okehampton has occupied an important position on the main route to Cornwall. Romantically sited atop a wooded hill and dominating the surrounding valley of the River Okement are the remains of **Okehampton Castle** (EH). This is the largest medieval castle in Devon and the ruins are still mightily impressive even though the castle was dismantled on the orders of Henry VIII after its owner, the Earl of Devon, was convicted of treason.

A good place to start a tour of the town is the **Museum of Dartmoor Life,** housed in a former mill with a restored water wheel outside. Here, in the three galleries, the story of life on Dartmoor, down the ages, is told and, in particular, the museum displays illustrate how the moorland has shaped the lives of its inhabitants and vice versa. In the surrounding courtyard, you will also find a gift shop and a tea-room. Amongst the town's many interesting buildings are the 15th

Meldon Reservoir, nr Okehampton

century **Chapel of Ease,** and the **Town Hall**, a striking three-storey building erected in 1685 as a private house and converted to its current use in the 1820s. And don't miss the wonderful Victorian arcade within the shopping centre which is reminiscent of London's Burlington Arcade.

Okehampton is also the hub of the **Dartmoor Railway,** part of the former Southern Railway main line from London to Plymouth and Cornwall. This was once the route of the famous Atlantic Coast Express and the Devon Belle Pullman. Today, the company runs trains from Crediton and climbs into the National Park, terminating at Meldon Viaduct. Okehampton Station has been restored to its 1950s appearance, complete with buffet and licensed bar. Sampford Courtenay Station, 3.5 miles to the east was re-opened in 2004 and provides access to pleasant walking routes, including the Devon Heartlands Way footpath. To the west, Meldon Quarry Station is the highest station in southern England. It has two visitor centres, a buffet with licensed bar, a picnic area and a spectacular verandah giving wonderful views of Dartmoor's highest tors and the Meldon Reservoir dam.

AROUND OKEHAMPTON

SAMPFORD COURTENAY

5 miles NE of Okehampton

A charming and unspoilt village with a fine medieval church,

Sampford Courtenay is notable for its picturesque assortment of cottages, many of them thatched and built of cob. This local building material is created by mixing well-sieved mud with straw. This is then built up in sections. It was the local tradition to limewash the outside of the cottages at Whitsuntide, a process that helps to preserve the cob. This simple material is surprisingly durable and will last indefinitely provided it has a "good hat", that is, if the thatched roof is well looked after. Another unusual feature of the village is that every road out of it is marked by a medieval stone cross.

NORTH TAWTON

7 miles NE of Okehampton off the A3072 or A3124

Well-known nowadays to travellers along the Tarka Trail, the small market town of North Tawton was once an important borough governed by a portreeve, an official who was elected each year until the end of the 19th century. This scattered rural community prospered in medieval times but the decline of the local textile industry in the late 1700s dealt a blow from which it never really recovered, - the population today is still less than it was in 1750. The little town also suffered badly from the ravages of a series of fires which destroyed most of the older and more interesting buildings. However, a few survivors can still be found, most notably Broad Hall (private) which dates back to the 15th century.

65 PREWLEY MOOR ARMS

Sourton Down

This is a lovely public house ideally situated on the edge of Dartmoor.

 see page 189

Samford Courtney was the unlikely setting for the start of the Prayer Book Revolt of 1549. It was originally initiated as a protest against Edward VI's introduction of an English prayer book, but when the undisciplined countrymen marched on Exeter, it degenerated into a frenzy of looting and violence. Confronted by an army led by Lord Russell, the rioters were soon overwhelmed and several unfortunate ringleaders executed.

66 COPPER KEY INN

North Tawton

This traditional 16th century inn has everything; good food, great service and a warm and welcoming atmosphere.

 see page 189

67 THE SEVEN STARS

South Tawton

The Seven Stars offers a beautiful location, great locally sourced food and friendly staff.

 see page 190

In a field close to the town is **Bathe Pool,** a grassy hollow that is said to fill with water at times of national crises or when a prominent person is about to die. The pool reportedly filled at the time of the death of Nelson, the Duke of Wellington and Edward VII, and also just before the outbreak of World War I.

STICKLEPATH

2 miles E of Okehampton off the A30

Set beside the River Taw, the little village of Sticklepath boasts one of the most interesting exhibits of industrial archaeology in Devon. From 1814 to 1960, **Finch Foundry** (National Trust) was renowned for producing the finest sharp-edged tools in the West Country. The three massive waterwheels are now working again, driving the ancient machinery, and pounding rhythms of the steam hammer and rushing water vividly evoke that age of noisy toil.

SOUTH ZEAL

4 miles E of Okehampton off the A30

South Zeal is yet another of the many Devon villages which have good reason to be grateful for the major road-building undertakings of the 1970s. The village sits astride what used to be the main road from Exeter to Launceston and the Cornwall coast, a road which as late as 1975 was still laughably designated on maps of the time as a "Trunk (major) Road". The "Trunk Road" was actually little more than a country lane but it was also the only route

available for many thousands of holiday-makers making their way to the Cornish resorts. Today, the village is bypassed by the A30 dual carriageway.

Isolated in the middle of the broad main street stand a simple medieval market cross and St Mary's Chapel, rebuilt in 1713. Nearby is the Oxenham Arms, an ancient hostelry believed to have been established in the 12th century. Charles Dickens stayed here in the 1840s. He was snowed in but put the time to good use by writing part of *The Pickwick Papers*.

To the south of the village rises the great granite hump of Dartmoor. On its flanks, for the few years between 1901-9, the villagers of South Zeal found sorely needed employment in a short-lived copper mine.

WHIDDON DOWN

7 miles E of Okehampton off the A30

About a mile south of the village stands the **Spinsters' Rock**, the best surviving chambered tomb in the whole of Devon. According to legend, three spinsters erected the dolmen one morning before breakfast, an impressive feat since the capstone, supported by just three uprights seven feet high, weighs 16 tons.

BELSTONE

2 miles SE of Okehampton off the A30

Surrounded by the magnificent scenery of the Dartmoor National Park, Belstone is a picturesque village with a triangular village green, complete with stocks and a stone commemorating the coronation of George V, and a church dating back to the 13th century.

A path from Belstone village leads up to the ancient standing stone circle known as the **Nine Stones,** although there are actually well over a dozen of them. Local folklore asserts that these stones under Belstone Tor were formed when a group of maidens was discovered dancing on the Sabbath and turned to stone. The problem with this story is that the stone circle was in place long before the arrival of Christianity in England. It is also claimed that the mysterious stones change position when the clock strikes noon. What is certain is that the view across mid-Devon from this site is quite breathtaking.

Another path from Belstone leads south to a spot on the northern edge of Dartmoor where the ashes of the Poet Laureate, Ted Hughes, were scattered and where a granite stone was placed to his memory.

For lovers of solitude, this is memorable country, unforgettably evoked by Sir Arthur Conan Doyle in *The Hound of the Baskervilles.* Recalling the villain's fate in that book, walkers should beware of the notorious "feather beds" – deep bogs signalled by a quaking cover of brilliant green moss.

DREWSTEIGNTON

10 miles SE of Okehampton off the A30

This appealing village stands on a ridge overlooking the valley of the

River Teign and the celebrated beauty spot near the 400-year-old **Fingle Bridge**. Thatched cottages and a medieval church stand grouped around a square, very picturesque and much photographed.

To the south of the village, Prestonbury Castle and Cranbrook Castle are not castles at all but Iron Age hilltop fortresses. **Castle Drogo** (National Trust) on the other hand, looks every inch the medieval castle but in fact was constructed between 1911 and 1930 – the last castle to be built in England. Occupying a spectacular site on a rocky outcrop 900 feet above sea level, with commanding views over Dartmoor, it was built to a design by Lutyens for the self-made millionaire Sir Julius Drewe on land once owned by his Norman ancestor, Drogo de Teigne. Lutyens' preliminary sketches envisaged a house of heroic size, but practicalities and the intervention of World War I caused the dimensions to be reduced by about two-thirds. Nevertheless, the granite and oak castle, finally completed in 1930, is one of Lutyens' most remarkable works. It combines the grandeur of a medieval castle with the comforts

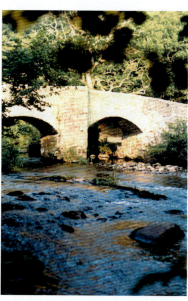

Fingle Bridge, Drewsteignton

68 CASTLE DROGO

Drewsteignton

The last castle to be built in England, this remarkable work by Sir Edwin Lutyens occupies a spectacular position above the Teign gorge.

 see page 190

47 CYPRIAN'S COT

Chagford

An early 16th century grade II listed building of great charm and character offering quality en suite B & B accommodation.

 see page 191

of the 20th century. Surrounding Sir Julius's dream home is an impressive garden which displays colour and interest all year round.

CHAGFORD

10 miles SE of Okehampton off the A382

An ancient settlement and one of the original four Stannary Towns, chartered in 1305, where tinners brought their metal for assay and stamping. Chagford occupies a beautiful setting between the pleasant wooded valley of the

North Teign river and the stark grandeur of the high moor. In the centre of the town stands the former **Market House**, a charming octagonal building erected in 1862. Around the square are some old style family shops providing interesting shopping and scattered around the town are distinctive old thatched granite buildings, many dating from the 1500s.One of these is **Endecott House** (private) which is named after one of the Pilgrim Fathers who became the governor of Massachusetts.

St Michael's Church, mostly 15th century, has an elaborate monument to Sir John Wyddon who died in 1575. But the church is better known because of the tragic death of one of his descendants here in October 1641. **Mary Whiddon** was shot at the altar by a jilted lover as she was being married, an incident that is said to have inspired RD Blackmore's *Lorna Doone*. Mary's tombstone bears the inscription "Behold a Matron yet a Maid". Her ghost is thought to haunt Whiddon Park Guest House - a young woman dressed in black appeared there on the morning of a wedding reception due to take place later that day.

The famous Dartmoor guide, James Perrot, lived in Chagford between 1854 and 1895, and is buried in St Michael's churchyard. It was he who noted that some of the farms around Chagford had no wheeled vehicles as late as 1830. On the other hand, Perrot lived to see the town install electric street

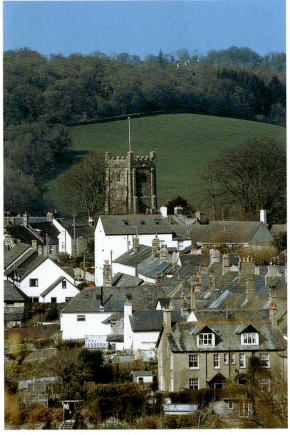

Chagford Village

lighting in 1891 making Chagford one of the first communities west of London to possess this amenity.

It was Perrot also who began the curious practice of letterbox stamp collecting. He installed the first letterbox at Carnmere Pool near the heart of the moor so his Victorian clients could send postcards home, stamped to prove they had been there. Today, there are hundreds of such letterboxes scattered all over Dartmoor.

To the west of Chagford, an exceptionally pleasant lane leads upstream from Chagford Bridge through the wooded valley of the North Teign river. (For 1.5 miles of its length, this lane is joined by the Two Moors Way, the long-distance footpath which runs all the way from Ivybridge on the southern edge of Dartmoor to the Bristol Channel coast.) A rock beside the river known as the **Holed Stone** has a large round cavity. If you climb through this, local people assure you, a host of afflictions from rheumatism to infertility will be cured.

The land to the south of Chagford rises abruptly towards Kestor Rock and Shovel Down, the sites of impressive Bronze Age settlements and, a little further on, the imposing Long Stone stands at the point where the parishes of Gidleigh and Chagford end and Duchy of Cornwall land begins.

LYDFORD

In Saxon times, there were just four royal boroughs in Devon: Exeter,

Fernworthy Stone Circle, nr Chagford

Barnstaple, Totnes and, astonishingly, Lydford which is now a pleasant small town still occupying the same strategic position on the River Lyd which made it so important in those days. In the 11th century, the Normans built a fortification here which was superseded 100 years later by the present **Lydford Castle**, an austere stone fortress which for generations served the independent tin miners of Dartmoor as both a court and a prison. The justice meted out here was notoriously arbitrary. William Browne of Tavistock (1590-1643) observed:

I oft have heard of Lydford law,
How in the morn they hang and draw
And sit in judgement after.

Lydford parish is the largest in England, encompassing the whole of the Forest of Dartmoor. For many centuries the dead were brought down from the moor along the ancient Lych Way for burial in St Petroc's churchyard. A tombstone near the porch bears a lengthy and laboriously humorous

Lydford Gorge, nr Tavistock

narrow 100 feet high waterfall. Back in the 17th century, the then remote Lydford Gorge provided a secure refuge for a band of brigands who called themselves the Gubbinses. Their leader was a certain Roger Rowle, (dubbed the "Robin Hood of the West"), whose exploits are recounted in Charles Kingsley's novel *Westward Ho!*

AROUND LYDFORD

STOWFORD

5 miles NW of Lydford off the A30

An unusual feature in the churchyard of St John's Church is a stone by the gate that is carved in the Ogham script with the word 'Gunglei' and this is believed to be the name of a Roman soldier who was buried here some 1600 years ago. Inside the church are two monuments to the Harris family: John who died in 1767 and Christopher who departed this life in 1718. The latter is curious not only for showing Christopher in the costume of a Roman centurion but also because "the figures are life-size down to the waist and then stunted as if the sculptor had grown weary of them."

BROADWOODWIDGER

7 miles NW of Lydford off the A30

Just to the northeast of this village lies **Roadford Lake**, a reservoir that was completed in 1990 and that has, among its many visitor

epitaph to the local watchmaker, George Routleigh, who died in 1802. The inscription includes the statement that George's life had been:

> *Wound up in hope of being taken in and by his Maker and of being thoroughly cleansed and repaired and set going in the world to come.*

To the southwest of the village, the valley of the River Lyd suddenly narrows to form the 1.5 mile long **Lydford Gorge** (NT), one of Devon's most spectacular natural features. Visitors can follow the riverside path to the Devil's Cauldron, or wander along the two-mile walk to the White Lady, a attractions, a Victorian steam launch, the *SL Elegance*, which takes passengers on a trip around the lake between April and October. There is a network of footpaths around most of the lake, although the northern area has been designated a Special Protection Zone to allow wildlife a safe haven.

Formerly known as Dingles Steam Village, this attraction now operates as **Dingles Fairground Heritage Centre**. A facility unique in the UK, the centre is home to the National Fairground Collection and features some superb displays of fairground art, vintage rides, stalls, shows and memorabilia.

LIFTON

8 miles NW of Lydford off the A30

Standing on the banks of the River Lyd, Lifton was an important centre of the wool trade in medieval times, like so many other Devon towns and villages, but the Dartmoor sheep tended to have rather coarse fleeces due to the cold pastureland on which they lived. So the good weavers of Lifton petitioned Henry VII "by reason of the grossness and stubbornness of their district" to allow them to mix as much lambs' wool and flock with their wool "as may be required to work it."

South Dartmoor

Despite its bleak and wild landscape Dartmoor has been inhabited for centuries: the moorland was dotted with settlements and there is a wealth of Neolithic tombs and Bronze Age remains. In particular, at Merrivale, there is a series of remains, including stone circles, burial chambers, standing stones and a group of stone huts which are some of the largest and most interesting Bronze Age remains on Dartmoor. The row of 150 stones on Stall Moor, near Cornwood, is believed to be the longest prehistoric stone row in the world.

Along with prehistoric remains, the moorland is littered with the remains of commercial activity as tin has been mined here since at least the 12th century. This activity has left the moor pitted with the scars of disused mine working, ruined pump and smelting houses, although most of them are now softened by a cloak of bracken and heather. Tin and, later copper, lead, iron and even arsenic mining, brought wealth to the area and Devon had four Stannary towns –Tavistock, Chagford, Ashburton and Plympton – which were the only places licensed to weigh and stamp the metal. It was near the centre of the moor, at Crockern Tor, between 1474 and 1703 that the Stannary Court, the administrative body of the Dartmoor miners, met. Of the industrial remains to be seen in Dartmoor one of the most impressive is

Wheal Betsy, a restored pumping station dating from the 18th century. On the outskirts of Dartmoor, on the border with Cornwall, is Morwellham Quay. A historic village, copper mine and port, this is now an open-air museum that brings vividly to life a busy 19th century community.

Another imposing man-made structure is the dreaded Dartmoor Prison at Princetown. It was originally built in the early 1800s to house prisoners-of-war from the Napoleonic Wars. Visitors will easily understand why it was built here since it lies at the centre of an inhospitable tract of stony moorland.

By contrast, Widecombe in the Moor, the village made famous by Uncle Tom Cobleigh and all, is an altogether more inviting place. The September Fair that Uncle Tom and his friends were making their way towards is still held each year but this attractive and picturesque village is worth a visit at any time of year.

Dartmoor Stream, nr Tavistock

TAVISTOCK

This handsome old town is one of Devon's four stannary towns, so named from the Latin word for tin – *stannum*. These towns – the others are Ashburton, Chagford and Plympton – were the only places licensed to weigh and stamp the metal extracted from the moor.

For most of its recorded history, Tavistock has had only two owners: Tavistock Abbey and the Russell family. The Benedictine abbey was founded here, beside the River Tavy, in around AD974, close to a Saxon stockade or *stoc*, now incorporated into the town's name. The town grew up around the abbey and, following the discovery of tin on the nearby moors in the 12th century, both flourished.

Then, in 1539, Henry VIII closed the abbey and gave the building, along with its vast estates to John Russell whose family, as Earls and Dukes of Bedford, owned most of the town until 1911. The present town centre is essentially the creation of the Russell family. After virtually obliterating the once-glorious abbey, they created a completely new town plan. Later, in the 1840s, Francis the 7th Duke diverted some of the profits from his copper mines to build the imposing **Guildhall** and several other civic buildings. He also rebuilt the Bedford Hotel, and constructed a model estate of artisans' cottages on the western side of the town. A statue of the duke stands in Bedford Square while, at the western entrance to the town, there is a statue of Sir Francis Drake who is believed to have been born at nearby Crowndale. The statue may look familiar as it is identical to the one standing on Plymouth Hoe – Tavistock's is the original while the one in Plymouth is a copy.

Beside Drake's statue is the **Fitzford Gate**, the original gatehouse of a private residence that no longer exists. This squat, castellated building has a lurid tale attached to it. According to local

Fitzford Gate, Tavistock

stories, several times a year the ghost of Lady Howard rides through the gates in a coach made of bones, drawn by headless horses and preceded by a fierce hound with glowing red eyes. This gruesome procession travels to Okehampton church where Lady Howard gets down from the coach, picks a blade of grass from the churchyard and, clutching it to her chest, returns to Fitzford Gate. She endures this spectral event, it is said because she had murdered all her four husbands – despite her fourth husband, in fact, outliving her.

One of the legacies of the abbey is the annual three-day fair, granted in 1105, which has now evolved into **Goose Fair**, a wonderful traditional street fair held on the second Wednesday in October. Tavistock was also permitted to hold a weekly market which, more than 900 years later, still takes place every Friday in the Pannier Market, a building that was another gift to the town from the 7th duke. There's also an antiques and crafts market on Tuesdays, and a Victorian market on Wednesdays when many of the stallholders appear in period costume.

Also on the western side of Tavistock can be found the beginning of the **Tavistock-Morwellham Canal**, which was built in the early 19th century at a time when the town and surrounding area was experiencing a copper boom. The force behind the construction of the canal, which began in 1803, was John Taylor, a young engineer and the manager of

The Meadows, Tavistock

the Wheal Friendship mine. It was designed to follow the countryside's contours as far as Morwell Down, through which a tunnel a third of a mile long carried the 4½-mile canal on to Morwellham on the Cornish border. The tunnel took more than 13 years to complete, long after the rest of the canal, but by 1872 this waterway had closed as it could no longer compete with the railway that arrived in Tavistock in the late 1850s.

AROUND TAVISTOCK

MILTON ABBOT

6 miles NW of Tavistock on the B3362

Situated high above the Tamar Valley, Milton Abbot is distinguished by the Regency

85

70 EDGECUMBE ARMS

Milton Abbot

Brilliant hosts have bought this property back to life and it is now buzzing once again.

 see page 191

masterpiece, **Endsleigh House**, that was designed for the Duke and Duchess of Bedford by the architect Sir Jeffry Wyattville. Built in the *cottage ornè* style in about 1810, the house comprises the main building and a children's wing that are linked by a curved terrace. Georgina, the Duchess of Bedford, was an ardent gardener and she commissioned the famous landscape designer Humphry Repton to create the arboretum that rises behind the house and contains more than 1000 specimen trees. Repton also laid out the broad terraces that step down to the River Tamar. Today this Grade I listed house is run as a designer hotel by Olga Polizzi. She has restored the gardens in their original style and these are open to the public.

BRENT TOR

4½ miles N of Tavistock off the A386

Brent Tor, an 1100 feet-high volcanic plug that rears up from

the surrounding countryside is one of the most striking sights in the whole of Dartmoor. Perched on its summit is the **Church of St Michael of the Rocks**, the fourth smallest complete church in England. St Michael's is only 15 feet wide and 37 feet long and has walls just 10 feet high but three feet thick. Constructed of stone that was quarried from the rock beneath, the church is surrounded by a steep churchyard that contains a surprising number of graves considering its precarious and seemingly soil-less position. Sometimes lost in cloud, the scramble to the summit of Brent Tor is rewarded on a clear day with magnificent views of Dartmoor, Bodmin Moor and the sea at Plymouth Sound.

LEWTRENCHARD

8 miles N of Tavistock off the A30

A pleasant village situated in a wooded valley, where between 1881 and 1924, the Rev Sabine Baring-Gould was squire then rector. Best known as the composer of the hymn, *Onward, Christian Soldiers,* Baring-Gould was also a prolific prose writer. He regularly produced two or three books a year – novels, historical works such as *Curious Myths of the Middle Ages,* and books on Devon legends and folklore. Baring-Gould nevertheless found time to restore St Peter's Church. His most remarkable success was the creation of a

Church of St Michael, Brent Tor

replica of a medieval screen that his grandfather, also a rector here, had destroyed. The grandson found enough pieces remaining for the replica to be made. It is very impressive with an elaborate canopied loft decorated with paintings of 23 saints.

The Revd. Sabine scandalised Victorian society by marrying a Lancashire mill girl but the union proved to be a happy one and they had a huge family. One local story tells how, one day, emerging from his study, the rector saw a little girl coming down the stairs. "You look nice, my dear, in your pretty frock," he said, vaguely remembering that a children's party was under way. "Whose little girl are you?" "Yours, papa," she answered and burst into tears.

Wheal Betsy, nr Mary Tavy

MARY TAVY

3 miles NE of Tavistock on the A386

The twin villages of Mary Tavy and Peter Tavy stand on opposite banks of the River Tavy and each takes its name from the saint of its parish church. Roughly twice the size of its east bank twin, Mary Tavy lies in the heart of Dartmoor's former mining area. Just to the north of the village stands a survivor from those days. **Wheal Betsy** (National Trust), a restored pumping engine house, was once part of the Prince Arthur Consols mine that produced lead, silver and zinc.

In the village churchyard is the grave of William Crossing, the historian of the moor whose magisterial guide, first published in the early 1900s, is still in print.

PETER TAVY

3 miles NE of Tavistock off the A386

The twin village of Mary Tavy, Peter Tavy stands on the opposite bank of the River Tavy and is linked to its twin by a bridle path. The smaller of the two, Peter Tavy has changed little since William Crossing, the historian of Dartmoor, came here in 1909 and described "a quiet little place, with a church embosomed in trees, a chapel, a school and a small inn." Inside the impressive medieval church, with its octagonal tower and four pinnacles, is a poignant memorial to the five daughters of a 17th century rector. The oldest of them was less than a year old when she died:

> They breathed awhile and looked
> the world about
> And, like newly-lighted candles,
> soon went out.

MERRIVALE

4½ miles E of Tavistock on the B3357

An excellent starting point for exploring the southwest section of

71 THE PETER TAVY INN

Peter Tavy

15th century free house offering a delicious and eye-catching menu, a winner with all the family.

 see page 192

87

To the east of Merrivale can be found the Merrivale Antiquities, a series of Bronze Age remains that are some of the largest and most interesting on Dartmoor. Sometimes hard to distinguish from the natural rocks that litter the landscape, here can also be found stone circles, burial chambers, standing stones and groups of circular huts.

Dartmoor, Merrivale is home to the last of the area's granite quarries that closed in 1997. The quarry once produced a record 1500 tons of stone in a single firing.

POSTBRIDGE

14 miles E of Tavistock on the B3212

In prehistoric times, the area around Postbridge was the "metropolis" of Dartmoor as the wealth of Bronze Age remains bears witness. Today, the village is best known for its **Clapper Bridge** which probably dates back to the 13th century and is the best preserved of all the Devon clapper bridges. Spanning the East Dart River, the bridge is a model of medieval minimalist construction with just three huge slabs of granite laid across solid stone piers. Not wide enough for wheeled traffic, the bridge would originally have been used by pack horses following the post road from Exeter into Cornwall.

Clapper Bridge, Postbridge

Two miles along the road to Moretonhampstead, **Warren House Inn** claims to be the third highest tavern in England. It used to stand on the other side of the road but in 1845 a fire destroyed that building. According to tradition, when the present inn was built its landlord carried some still-smouldering turves across the road to the hearth of his new hostelry and that fire has been burning ever since. It's a pleasant enough sight in summer and must have been even more welcome in the winter of 1963. In that year, the Warren House Inn was cut off by heavy snow drifts some 20 feet deep for almost three months and supplies had to be flown in by helicopter. Such a remote inn naturally generates some good tales. Like the one about the traveller who stayed here one winter's night and opening by chance a large chest in his room discovered the body of a dead man. "Why!", said the landlord when confronted with the deceased, "tis only feyther! 'Twas too cold to take 'un to the buryin', so mother salted 'un down!"

PRINCETOWN

9 miles E of Tavistock on the B3212

Princetown, best known for its forbidding prison, stands 1400 feet above sea level in an area of the moor which is notorious for its atrocious climate. It gets doused with 80 to 100 inches of rain a year, more than three times the average for Exeter which is less than 20 miles away.

That a settlement should be

located here at all was the brainchild of one man, Sir Thomas Tyrwhitt, the owner of a local granite quarry. He proposed that a special prison should be built here to house the thousands of troops captured during the Napoleonic wars. They were becoming too numerous and unruly for the prison ships moored in Plymouth Sound. The work was completed in 1809 by the prisoners themselves using granite from Sir Thomas' quarry. Paid at the rate of sixpence (2.5p) a day, they also built the main east-west road across the moor which is now the B3212. Yet another of their constructions was the nearby Church of St Mary, a charmless building in whose churchyard stands a tall granite cross in memory of all those prisoners whose bodies lie in unmarked graves. (The mortality rate of the inmates in the early 1800s was 50%). Since around 1900, prisoners' graves have been marked just with their initials and date of death. The lines of small stones are a gloomy sight.

At one time the prison held as many as 9000 French and, later, American inmates but by 1816, with the cessation of hostilities, the prison became redundant and was closed. Princetown virtually collapsed as a result and it wasn't until 1823 that its granite quarries were given a new lease of life with the building of the horse-drawn Dartmoor Railway, another of Sir Thomas Tyrwhitt's initiatives. The prison was eventually re-opened for long-serving convicts in 1850 and

Dartmoor Prison, Princetown

since then it has been considerably enlarged and upgraded. It is currently in use as a medium security prison with around 640 inmates. The **Dartmoor Prison Heritage Centre** has exhibits detailing the history of the institution.

Also in the town is the National Park's **Moorland Visitors' Centre** which contains some excellent and informative displays about the moor, and also stocks a wide range of books, maps and leaflets. The centre is housed in the former Duchy Hotel where Sir Arthur Conan Doyle stayed while writing some chapters of *The Hound of the Baskervilles,* much of which is set in Dartmoor. Having 'killed off' his pipe-smoking detective in his previous novel, Sir Arthur was touring the county when he stumbled on local stories of a spectral hound that haunted the moorland. These local tales were based on Squire Cabell of Brook, near Buckfastleigh, a man so evil that, when he died in 1677, a

72 SAMPFORD MANOR

Sampford Spiney

Idyllic granite Manor farm house seeped in history, on the edges of the wilds of Dartmoor.

 see page 193

73 THE ROYAL OAK INN

Meavy

This real old-fashioned village inn oozes class and history- perfect for families.

 see page 194

pack of fire-breathing hounds were said to have emerged from the moor to carry his soul to Hell.

There are many walks into the moorland from Princetown including the **Tyrwhitt Trails**, named after the town's founder, and also the **Princetown Railway Path**, which follows the disused railway to King's Tor.

DARTMEET

13 miles E of Tavistock off the B3357

Dartmeet is a picturesque spot where the boulder-strewn East and West Dart rivers join together. At their junction, a single-span packhorse bridge was built in the 1400s; its remains can still be seen just upstream from the more modern road bridge.

Rising in the boggy plateau of north Dartmoor, the Dart and its tributaries drain a huge area of the moor. The river then flows for 46 miles before entering the sea at Dartmouth.

In the days when the tin mines were working, this area was extremely isolated, lacking even a burial ground of its own. Local people had to carry their dead across the moor to Lydford – "Eight miles in fair weather, and 15 in foul". In good weather, this is grand walking country with a choice of exploring the higher moor, dotted with a wealth of prehistoric remains, or following the lovely riverside and woodland path that leads to the famous Clapper Bridge near Postbridge, about five miles upstream.

To the east of Dartmeet, and hidden among bracken and gorse, is the **Coffin Stone**, a large boulder on which it was customary for the bearers to rest the body while making the moorland crossing. A cross and the deceased's initials were carved into the stone while the bearers had some liquid refreshment and got back their breath before continuing on their journey.

To the south-east of Dartmeet, on the southern edge of the National Park, is **Vensford Reservoir.** There's free fishing here, picnic tables and a footpath around the man-made lake.

YELVERTON

5 miles SE of Tavistock on the A386

In prehistoric times, the area around Yelverton must have been quite heavily populated to judge by the extraordinary concentration of stone circles and rows, hut and cairn circles, and burial chambers. The B3212 to Princetown passes through this once-populous stretch of moorland, part of which is now submerged beneath Burrator Reservoir.

This attractive large village stands on the very edge of Dartmoor and it enjoys grand views out across the Walkham Valley to the north with Brent Tor church, perched on its 1100 feet summit some ten miles away, clearly visible on a good day.

Yelverton itself has broad-verged streets, a feature which has caused it to be described as "rather like a thriving racecourse". The village is one of very few in the country to have had its name bestowed by the Board of Directors of a railway company. When the **Great Western Railway** opened a station here in 1859 the village was officially known as Elfordtown. The story goes that the London-based surveyors interpreted the Devon pronunciation of Elfordtown as Yelverton. So that was the name blazoned on the station signboard, and the name by which the village has been known ever since.

A rather unusual attraction here is the **Yelverton Paperweight Centre** which has a display of some 800 glass paperweights, including the work of artists from such renowned studios as Caithness and Whitefriars as well as work by individual artists. Along with the extensive range of paperweights for sale, the centre also displays a range of oil and watercolour paintings by artists who specialise in Dartmoor and moorland wildlife subjects.

BUCKLAND MONACHORUM

5 miles S of Tavistock off the A386

Tucked away in a secluded valley above the River Tavy, **Buckland Abbey** (National Trust) was founded in 1278 by Amicia, Countess of Devon, but became better known as the home of Sir Francis Drake. Drake purchased the former abbey in 1581 from his fellow-warrior (and part-time pirate), Sir Richard Grenville, whose exploits in his little ship, *Revenge* were almost as colourful as those of Drake himself. The house

remained in the Drake family until 1947 when it was acquired by the National Trust. Of the many exhibits at the abbey, Drake's Drum takes pride of place – according to legend, the drum will sound whenever England is in peril. The drum was brought back to England by Drake's brother, Thomas, who was with the great seafarer when he died on the Spanish Main in 1596. (Rather ignominiously, of dysentery). Elsewhere at the abbey, visitors can see a magnificent 14th century tithe barn, 154 feet long, housing an interesting collection of carts and carriages; a craft workshop and a herb garden.

In the village itself, on the site of a medieval vicarage, **The Garden House** is surrounded by a delightful garden created after World War II by Lionel Fortescue, a retired schoolmaster.

The village's church of St Andrew contains a tribute to the generations of Drakes who lived at

74 WHO'D HAVE THOUGHT IT INN

Milton Combe

With award winning ambience, fresh local produce and a bar frequented by Sir Francis Drake, the Who'd Have Thought It Inn is well worth a visit.

see page 195

The Garden House, Buckland Monachorum

River Tamar, Bere Alston

Buckland Abbey, and there is a carving of the *Golden Hind* on the family pew.

GULWORTHY

2 miles SW of Tavistock on the A390

This little village lies at the heart of an area that, in the mid-1880s, had a world wide reputation. A quarter of the world's supply of copper was extracted from this part of Devon and, more alarmingly, so was half of the world's requirements for arsenic. Mining for copper in this area has long been abandoned, due to the discovery of cheaper sources around the world, particularly in South America. Gulworthy's arsenic has also gone out of fashion as an agent of murder.

BERE ALSTON

5 miles SW of Tavistock on the B3257

For centuries, Bere Alston was a thriving little port on the River Tamar from whence the products of Dartmoor's tin mines were transported around the world. All that commercial activity has long since gone but the river here is still busy with the to-ings and fro-ings of sleek pleasure craft. Just a few miles upstream from Bere Alston is one of the county's most popular visitor attractions, **Morwellham Quay**. The port fell into disuse following the arrival of the railway and by the 1980s it was a ghost harbour with the Tamar valley breezes whistling through its abandoned buildings. Now restored, this historic site faithfully re-creates the busy atmosphere of the 1860s when half the world's copper came through this tiny harbour. Visitors are greeted by costumed staff and can then journey through the mines on a tramway that runs beside the River Tamar before venturing deep underground in the George & Charlotte copper mine. Another highlight is the restored Tamar ketch *Garlandstone*. Although Morwellham lies some 20 miles upstream from Plymouth, the Tamar river at this point was deep enough for 300-ton ships to load up with the precious minerals. Once known as the Devon Klondyke, Morwellham suffered a catastrophic decline when cheaper sources of copper were discovered in South America.

The quayside inn has also been restored. It was here that the dockside labourers used to meet for ale, food and the latest news of the ships that sailed from Morwellham. In those days, the news was chalked up on a blackboard and it still is. Though out of date, the stories nonetheless remain intriguing.

BERE FERRERS

6 miles SW of Tavistock off the B3257

The church in Bere Ferrers has the oldest Stained-glass window in Devon - excepting Exeter Cathedral - it is 600 years old. Whilst attempting to make a tracing of the window, the antiquarian draughtsman Charles Alfred Stothard fell and was killed.

At the nearby Bere Ferrers railway station the Tamar Belle vintage train comprises four carriages restored and converted to provide a dining coach, saloon/lounge and two uniquely arranged sleeping cars.

IVYBRIDGE

The original bridge over the Erme at Ivybridge was just wide enough for a single packhorse and the 13th century crossing that replaced it is still very narrow. It remains in use however. When the railway arrived here in 1848, Brunel constructed an impressive viaduct over the Erme valley. It was made of wood, however, so that too was replaced in 1895 by an equally imposing stone structure. The town grew rapidly in the 1860s when a quality paper-making mill was established to make good use of the waters of the Erme and more recently Ivybridge has continued to grow as a commuter town for Plymouth.

Serious walkers will know Ivybridge as the southern starting point of the **Two Moors Way**, the spectacular but gruelling 103-mile path across both Dartmoor and

Exmoor, finishing at Barnstaple. The trek begins with a stiff 1000 feet climb up Butterdon Hill, just outside Ivybridge – and that's the easy bit!

AROUND IVYBRIDGE

SOUTH BRENT

5 miles NE of Ivybridge off the A38

Standing on the southern flank of Dartmoor, just within the National Park, South Brent is a sizeable village of some 3000 souls. It has some brightly painted cottages and a 13th century church with a massive Norman tower, set beside the River Avon. This was once the main church for a large part of the South Hams as well as a considerable area of Dartmoor. Alongside the River Avon are some attractive old textile mills recalling the days when South Brent was an important centre for the production of woollens. In Victorian times, one of the mills was managed by William Crossing whose famous *Crossing's Guide to Dartmoor* provides a fascinating picture of life on the moor in the late 1800s.

In the days of stagecoach travel the town was a lively place with two "posting houses" servicing the competing coaches. It was said that four horses could be changed in 45 seconds and a full-course meal served in 20 minutes. The most famous of the coaches, the *Quicksilver*, left Plymouth at 8.30 in the evening and arrived in

75 THE OLDE PLOUGH INN

Bere Ferrers (nr Yelverton)
The Olde Plough Inn is in a beautiful location overlooking the river Tavy and is perfect for a refreshing pint of local ale.
see page 196

76 TAMAR BELLE

Bere Ferrers (nr Yelverton)
Uniquely converted 1930's train carriages; eat and sleep in all the elegance of a by-gone era.
 see page 197

77 SOUTH DEVON RAILWAY

Buckfastleigh

One of the most delightful ways of exploring the Dart river valley is by taking a journey on the nostalgic **South Devon Railway.**

 see page 196

78 THE WHITE HART

Buckfastleigh

This 17th century pub is full of tradition and character; the perfect place to relax after a day's walking.

 see page 198

79 DARTMOOR OTTERS & BUCKFAST BUTTERFLIES

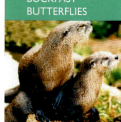

Buckfastleigh

Tropical gardens are home to a wide variety of exotic butterflies, whilst otters can be seen in a specially designed landscape.

 see page 198

London at 4 o'clock the following afternoon – a remarkable average speed of 11 mph, *including* stops.

BUCKFASTLEIGH

9 miles NE of Ivybridge off the A38

Buckfastleigh is a former wool town set on the banks of the River Mardle. Several old mill buildings still stand and the large houses of their former owners lie on the outskirts. A unique insight into the lives of local folk is provided by an old inn that has been restored and now houses the **Valiant Soldier Museum and Heritage Centre**. When the Valiant Soldier pub was closed in the 1960s, everything was left in place – even the money in the till. Rediscovered years later, this life-size time capsule features period public and lounge bars as well as domestic rooms including the kitchen, scullery, parlour and bedrooms.

Buckfastleigh is the western terminus and headquarters of the **South Devon Railway**, (formerly known as the Primrose Line), whose steam trains ply the seven-mile route along the lovely Dart Valley to and from Totnes. The Dart is a fast flowing salmon river and its banks abound with herons, swans, kingfishers, badgers and foxes. The company also offers a combined River Rail ticket so that visitors can travel in one direction by train and return by boat. The railway runs regular services during the season with the journey taking about 25 minutes each way. At Buckfastleigh station, there is a railway museum, railway

workshops, a café, model railway and a gift shop, as well as ample room for picnics and to visit.

Modes of transport seem to be something of a theme in Buckfastleigh. The town is also the base of the **Buckfastleigh Vintage Bus Service** which operates a fleet of historic old single- and double-decker buses that run between the town and various local attractions, such as Buckfast Abbey, on selected days throughout the season.

Another popular attraction close to the town is the **Buckfast Butterflies & Dartmoor Otter Sanctuary** where a specially designed tropical rain forest habitat has been created for the exotic butterflies. There's an underwater viewing area and both the butterflies and otters can be photographed, with the otters' thrice-daily feeding times providing some excellent photo-opportunities.

A couple of miles south of Buckfastleigh, **Pennywell** is a spacious all-weather family attraction which offers a wide variety of entertainments and activities. Pennywell boasts the UK's longest gravity go-kart ride and promises that their hands-on activities provide something new every half hour.

Another mile or so south, the little church of Dean Prior stands beside the A38. The vicar here at the time of the Restoration was the poet and staunch royalist, **Robert Herrick** (1591-1674). Herrick's best known lines are probably the opening stanza of *To the Virgins, to* make *Much of Time*:

Gather ye rosebuds while ye may,
Old Time is still a-flying
And this same flower that smiles today
Tomorrow will be dying.

Herrick apparently found rural Devon rather dull and much preferred London where he had a mistress 27 years his junior. Perhaps to brighten up the monotony of his Devonshire existence, he had a pet pig which he took for walks and trained to drink beer from a tankard. Herrick died in 1674 and was buried in the churchyard where a simple stone marks his assumed last resting place.

BUCKFAST

10 miles NE of Ivybridge off the A38

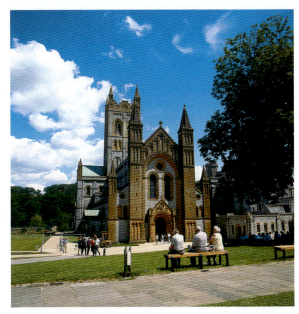

Buckfast Abbey

Dominating this small market town is **Buckfast Abbey**, a Benedictine monastery built in the Norman and Gothic style between 1907 and 1938. If you've ever wondered how many people it takes to construct an abbey, the astonishing answer, at Buckfast at least, is just six. Only one of the monks, Brother Peter, had any knowledge of building so he had to check every stone that went into the fabric. A photographic exhibition at the abbey records the painstaking process that stretched over 30 years. Another monk, Brother Adam, became celebrated as the bee-keeper whose busy charges produced the renowned Buckfast Abbey honey. The abbey gift shop also sells the famous Buckfast Tonic Wine, recordings of the abbey choristers and a wide range of religious items, pottery, cards and gifts. Within the tranquil abbey grounds are a sensory garden and a Physic Garden where both medicinal and culinary herbs are grown. The gardens are also home to the fragrant National Lavender Collection.

UGBOROUGH

3 miles E of Ivybridge off the A3121

This attractive village, which has regularly won awards in 'Best Kept Village' competitions, has an imposing church more than 130 feet long that stands on top of a substantial prehistoric earthwork. Inside, there are some exceptional features, including a rood screen with a set of 32 painted panels, an unusual monumental brass of an unknown 15th century woman and a carved roof boss in the north aisle depicting a sow and her litter.

SPARKWELL

3 miles NW of Ivybridge off the A38

Just to the north of this village are the **Dartmoor Wildlife Park and West Country Falconry Centre**. The Park occupies some 30 acres of beautiful Devon countryside and contains more than 150 species of animals including a comprehensive big cat collection. It also houses the Westcountry Falconry Centre and features falconry displays daily.

Dartmoor Wildlife Park, Sparkwell

CORNWOOD

3 miles NW of Ivybridge off the A38

Cornwood is a pleasant village on the River Yealm, a good base from which to seek out the many Bronze Age and industrial remains scattered across the moor. One of the most remarkable sights in Dartmoor is the double line of stones set up on Stall Moor during the Bronze Age. One line is almost 550 yards long; the other begins with a stone circle and crosses the River Erme before ending at a burial chamber some two miles distant. There are no roads to these extraordinary constructions, they can only be reached on foot.

If you approach Dartmoor from the south, off the A38, Cornwood is the last village you will find before the moors begin in earnest. Strike due north from here and you will have to cross some 15 miles of spectacular moorland before you see another inhabited place. (Her Majesty's Prison at Princetown, as it happens.)

BOVEY TRACEY

This ancient market town takes its name from the River Bovey and the de Tracy family who received the manor from William the Conqueror. The best-known member of the family is Sir William Tracy, one of the four knights who murdered Thomas à Becket in Canterbury Cathedral. To expiate his crime, Sir William is said to have endowed a church here, dedicated to St Thomas. That building was destroyed by fire and the present church is 15th century with a 14th century tower. Its most glorious possession is a beautifully carved screen of 1427, a gift to the church from Lady Margaret Beaufort, the new owner of the manor and the mother of King Henry VII.

Bovey Tracey, unlike so many Devon towns and villages, has never suffered a major fire. This is perhaps just as well since its fire-fighting facilities until recent times were decidedly limited. In 1920, for example, the town did have an engine, and five volunteers to man it, but no horses to draw it. The parish council in that year issued a notice advising "all or any persons requiring the Fire Brigade with Engine that they must take the responsibility of sending a Pair of Horses for the purpose of conveying the Engine to and from the Scene of the Fire".

For such a small town, Bovey Tracey is remarkably well-supplied with shops as well as the **Riverside Mill** which is run by the Devon Guild of Craftsmen. This is also the South West's leading gallery and craft showroom with work selected from around 240 makers, many with national and international reputations. The Guild presents changing craft exhibitions and demonstrations and the mill also contains a study centre, gallery and a café with roof terrace.

Another of the town's historic buildings, a former pottery, is now home to the **House of Marbles**

and **Teign Valley Glass**, where an unusual range of games, toys, marbles and glassware has been manufactured for many years. After wandering through the old pottery buildings and seeing the listed kilns, visitors can browse through the exhibitions in the museum of glass, games, marbles and Bovey Pottery as well as watch glass blowing when work is in progress. The shop sells all manner of glass items, from wine glasses and paperweights to marbles.

Set in some 10 acres of glorious woodland through which there are footpaths, **Cardew Teapottery** is where the world's most collectable teapots can be seen being made. During the week there are tours of the factory and visitors are invited to try their hand at decorating and personalising their own plate, mug or eggcup. The gift shop stocks a vast selection of pottery and other gift items, including one of the largest displays of teapots in the world.

Walkers will enjoy the footpath that passes through the town and follows the track bed of the former railway from Moretonhampstead to Newton Abbot, which runs alongside the River Bovey for part of its length.

AROUND BOVEY TRACEY

ILSINGTON

3 miles SW of Bovey Tracey off the B3387

Like so many Dartmoor communities, Ilsington was once an important centre of the wool

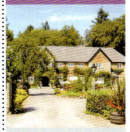

80 THE EDGEMOOR

Bovey Tracey

This opulent hotel treats its guests like royalty, close to Dartmoor and Devon's south coast, The Edgemoor makes a perfect getaway.

see page 199

Just to the north of Bovey Tracey is Parke, formerly the estate of the Tracy family but now owned by the National Trust and leased to the Dartmoor National Park as its headquarters. There are interpretive displays on all aspects of the moor, copious information about the area, and within the attractive grounds is a Rare Breeds Farm. The centre can also provide details of the many nature trails, and woodland and riverside walks, including one to the famous Becky Falls where the Becka Brook makes a sudden 70 feet drop.

Ilsington is a sizeable parish and includes the three well-known tors of Rippon, Saddle and Haytor Rocks. The latter is perhaps the most dramatic, especially when approached from the west along the B3387, and with a height of almost 1500 feet provides a popular challenge for rock climbers. In the early 1800s, the shallow valley to the north of Haytor Rocks was riddled with quarries which supplied granite for such well-known buildings as London Bridge, the National Gallery and the British Museum.

81 BAGTOR HOUSE

Ilsington

A stunning 15th century bed and breakfast manor house in the heart of Dartmoor that comes complete with its own ponds, ducks and tennis court.

 see page 200

is a characteristic trio of late medieval buildings – church, church house and inn. The interior of St Michael's Church is well worth seeing with its impressive array of arched beams and roof timbers which seem to hang in mid-air above the nave. The medieval pew ends are thought to be the only ones in Devon carved with the distinctive "poppy head" design; there's also a mid-14th century effigy of a woman; and an elaborately carved 16th century rood screen.

Entry to the churchyard is by way of an unusual lych gate with an upper storey which once served as the village schoolroom. The present structure is actually a replica of the original medieval gate which apparently collapsed when someone slammed the gate too energetically. The nearby church house, dating back to the 1500s, is now sub-divided into residential dwellings known as St Michael's Cottages.

This small village was the birthplace of the Jacobean dramatist John Ford (1586-1639) whose most successful play, *Tis Pity She's A Whore* (1633), is still occasionally revived.

ASHBURTON

7 miles SW of Bovey Tracey off the A38

This appealing little town lies just inside the boundary of the Dartmoor National Park, surrounded by lovely hills and with the River Ashburn splashing through the town centre. Municipal history goes back a long way here,

to AD821..AD in fact, when the town elected its first Portreeve, the Saxon equivalent of a mayor. The traditional office continues to the present day, although its functions are now purely ceremonial. But each year, on the fourth Tuesday in November, officials gather to appoint not just their Portreeve but also the Ale Tasters, Bread Weighers, Pig Drovers and even a Viewer of Watercourses.

In medieval times, Ashburton's prosperity was based on tin. As one of Devon's four stannary towns, it benefited from the trade generated by the Dartmoor tinners who were obliged to come here to have their metal weighed and stamped, and to pay the duty. Later, the cloth industry was the town's main money-spinner, with several fulling mills along the banks of the Ashburn producing cloth which the East India Company exported to China.

The town is characterised by its many attractive houses and shops, with distinctive slate hung frontages. Housed in the former home and workshop of a brushmaker, **Ashburton Museum** offers a fascinating insight into the history of this stannary town as well as the domestic and rural life of Dartmoor down the centuries. The collections include old farming implements, Victorian toys, a model of the old Market Hall and Native American artefacts donated by Paul Endicott, whose parents had left Ashburton for Oklahoma at the beginning of the 1900s.

The Card House, now a small

supermarket, was formerly a gaming house and its slate hung frontage is carved with the different suits of a pack of cards.

WIDECOMBE IN THE MOOR

6 miles W of Bovey Tracey off the B3212

This pleasing village enjoys a lovely setting in the valley of the East Webburn river and its grand old church, with a massive 120 feet high granite tower rising against a backdrop of high moorland, has understandably been dubbed the **"Cathedral of the Moors"**. Dedicated to St Pancras, the church was built with funds raised by tin miners in the 14th century, and enlarged during the next two centuries. A panel inside the church records the disastrous events of 21st October 1638. A sizeable congregation had gathered for a service when a bolt of lightning struck the tower, dislodging huge blocks of masonry on to the worshippers. Four were killed and a further 60 badly injured. (Local legend maintains that the Devil had been spotted earlier that day spitting fire and riding an ebony stallion across the moor).

In addition to the church, two other buildings are worth mentioning. Glebe House is a handsome 16th century residence which has since been converted to a shop, and **Church House** is an exceptional colonnaded building which was originally built around 1500 to accommodate those travelling large distances across the moor to attend church services. It was later divided into almshouses then served in succession as a brewery and a school. It is now a National Trust shop and information centre.

From Widecombe, a country lane leads to **Grimspound** which is perhaps the most impressive of all Dartmoor's Bronze Age survivals. This settlement was occupied between 1800BC and 500BC and is remarkably well-preserved. There are 24 hut circles here, some of them reconstructed, and it's still possible to make out the positions of door lintels and stone sleeping shelves. Today, the area around Grimspound is bleak and moody, an atmosphere which recommended itself to Sir Arthur Conan Doyle who had Sherlock Holmes send Dr Watson into hiding here to help solve the case of *The Hound of the Baskervilles*.

LUSTLEIGH

3 miles NW of Bovey Tracey off the A382

Lustleigh is one of Dartmoor's most popular and most photographed villages. Placed at all angles on the hillside is a ravishing assortment of 15th and 16th century deeply-thatched, colour-washed cottages, picturesquely grouped around the church. Appropriately for such a genuinely olde-worlde village, Lustleigh keeps alive some of the time-honoured traditions of country life, enthusiastically celebrating May Day each year with a procession through the village, dancing round the maypole, and the coronation of a May Queen. From the village

82 CAFÉ ON THE GREEN

Widecombe in the Moor

Just 100 yards from the famous 'Cathedral of the Moor', this fine eatery has a great location in the heart of Dartmoor with views over the village green and the church

 see page 201

The famous Widecombe Fair to which Uncle Tom Cobleigh, his boisterous crew and the old grey mare, were making their way is still held here on the second Tuesday in September and although it is no longer an agricultural event, remains a jolly affair. A succession of real-life Tom Cobleighs have lived around Widecombe over the centuries but the song probably refers to a gentleman who died in 1794. An amorous bachelor, this Uncle Tom Cobleigh had a mane of red hair and he refused to maintain any babies that did not display the same characteristic.

Becky Falls Woodland Park, Lustleigh

83 PRIMROSE TEAROOMS

Lustleigh

Pretty, thatched tearooms offering a wide variety of teas and delicious home made cakes and snacks.

 see page 200

there are some delightful walks, especially one that passes through Lustleigh Cleave, a wooded section of the steep-sided Bovey valley. Also close by is the **Becky Falls Woodland Park**, with its waterfalls, rugged landscape and attractions for all the family. Here, too, is **Yarner Wood Nature Reserve**, home to pied flycatchers, wood warblers and redstarts.

NORTH BOVEY

6 miles NW of Bovey Tracey off the B3212

In any discussion about which is the "loveliest village in Devon", North Bovey has to be one of the leading contenders. Set beside the River Bovey, it is quite unspoiled, with thatched cottages grouped around the green, a 15th century church and a delightful old inn, the Ring of Bells, which like many Devon hostelries was originally built, back in the 13th century, as a lodging house for the stonemasons building the church.

MORETONHAMPSTEAD

7 miles NW of Bovey Tracey on the A382

Moreton, as this little town is known locally, has long claimed the title of "Gateway to east Dartmoor", a rôle in which it was greatly helped by the branch railway from Newton Abbot which operated between 1866 and 1964. This is the gentler part of Dartmoor, with many woods and plantations, and steep-sided river valleys. Within easy reach are picture-postcard villages such as Widecombe in the Moor, striking natural features like Haytor, and the remarkable Bronze Age stone hut-circle at Grimspound.

The best approach to Moreton is by way of the B3212 from the southwest. From this direction you are greeted with splendid views of the little hilltop town surrounded by fields and with the tower of **St Andrew's Church** piercing the skyline. Built in Dartmoor granite during the early 1400s, the church overlooks the Sentry, or Sanctuary Field, an attractive public park. In the south porch are the tombstones of two French officers who died here as prisoners of war in 1807. At one point during those years of the Napoleonic Wars, no fewer than 379 French officers were living in Moreton, on parole from the military prison at Princetown. One of them, General Rochambeau, must have sorely tested the patience of local people. Whenever news arrived of a French success, he would don his full-dress uniform and parade through the streets.

One of the most interesting buildings in Moreton is the row of **Almshouses** in Cross Street. Built in 1637, it is thatched and has a striking arcade supported by sturdy granite columns. The almshouses are now owned by the National Trust but are not open to the public. Just across the road from the almshouses is **Mearsdon Manor Galleries,** the oldest house in Moreton, dating back to the 14th century. The ground floor of the manor is now a very pleasant traditional English tea room. In total contrast, the remaining rooms contain an astonishing array of colourful, exotic artefacts collected by the owner, Elizabeth Prince, on her trips to the Far East. There are Dartmoor-pony-sized wooden horses, Turkish rugs, Chinese lacquered furniture, finely-carved jade – a veritable treasury of Oriental craftsmanship.

Almshouses, Moretonhampstead

Two miles west of Moretonhampstead on the B3212, the **Miniature Pony Centre** is home to miniature ponies, donkeys and other horse breeds, as well as pygmy goats, pigs, lambs and many other animals. There are pony rides for children aged nine and under, a daily birds of prey display, indoor and outdoor play areas and a cafeteria.

Hayne
Budleigh Salterton
Bovey Tracey
102
103
Exmouth
Widecombe in the Moor
Kingsteignton
101
92
93 Teignmouth
Ashburton
Newton Abbot
91
Holne
100
Maidencombe
Buckfastleigh
Kingskerswell
90 Babbacombe
Staverton
99
Torquay
Dean
94 **95**
96
84 **85**
South Brent
Tigley
Totnes
Paignton
86 **87**
88 **89**
Luscombe
Brixham
Curtisknowle
97
98
Dartmouth
Halwell
Kingswear
Warfleet

The English Riviera

The most extensive conurbation in Devon, Torbay includes the three major towns of Torquay, Paignton and Brixham, strung around the deep indentation of Tor Bay. The excellent beaches and leisure facilities here have made it the county's busiest resort area with a host of indoor and outdoor attractions on offer. Torquay is the more sophisticated of the three, with elegant gardens, excellent shops and a varied nightlife. Paignton prides itself as being "unbeatable for family fun", and Brixham is a completely enchanting fishing town where life revolves around its busy harbour.

If you think Torbay's claim to be "The English Riviera" is a mite presumptuous, just take a look at all those palm trees. You see them everywhere here: not just in public parks and expensively maintained hotel gardens, but also giving a Mediterranean character to town house gardens, and even growing wild. They have become a symbol of the area's identity, blazoned on tourism leaflets, brochures, T-shirts, shop fronts, key-rings and hats.

The first specimen palm trees arrived in Britain in the 1820s and it was soon discovered that this sub-tropical species took kindly to the genial climate of South Devon. Today, there are literally thousands of them raising their spiky tufted heads above the more familiar foliage of English gardens. To the uninitiated, one palm tree may look much like another, but experts will point out that although the most common variety growing here is Cordyline Australis (imported from New Zealand), there are also Mediterranean Fan Palms, Trachycarpus Fortunei from the Chusan Islands in the East China Sea, and Date Palms from the Canary Islands. The oldest palm tree on record in the area is now over 80 years old and more than 40 feet high.

The Mediterranean similarities don't end there. Torquay, like Rome, is set on seven hills and the red-tiled roofs of its Italianate villas, set amongst dark green trees, would look equally at home in some Adriatic resort. The resemblance is so close that in one film in the Roger Moore TV series, *The Saint,* a budget-conscious producer made Torquay double for Monte Carlo.

Oddicombe Beach, Torquay

103

84 THE WESTBANK

Torquay

Victorian guest house, a few minutes walk from the seafront and beautiful beaches of Torquay.

 see page 202

85 KINGSHOLM

Torquay

Excellent value AA 4-star guest accommodation with delightful views overlooking Torwood Gardens.

 see page 202

86 BARCLAY COURT

Torquay

A quality guest house offering wonderful accommodation in the heart of the English Riviera.

 see page 203

TORQUAY

In Victorian times, Torquay liked to be known as "The English Naples", a genteel resort of shimmering white villas set amongst dark green trees and spread, like Rome, across seven hills. It was indisputably the West of England's premier resort with imposing hotels like the Imperial and the Grand catering for "people of condition" from across Europe. At one time, the town could boast more royal visitors to the square mile than any other resort in the world. **Edward VII** came here on the royal yacht *Britannia* and anchored in the bay. Each evening he would be discreetly ferried across to a bay beneath the Imperial Hotel and then conducted to the first floor suite where his mistress, Lily Langtry, was waiting.

The town's oldest building is **Torre Abbey,** founded in 1195 but largely remodelled as a Georgian mansion by the Cary family between 1700 and 1750. Within its grounds stand the abbey ruins and the Spanish Barn, a medieval tithe barn so named because 397 prisoners from the Spanish Armada's flagship *Nuestra Señora del Rosario* were detained here in 1588. Torre Abbey was sold to Torbay Council in 1930 and, together with its extensive gardens, was open to the public until 2004 when the building was closed for major refurbishment. It re-opened in the summer of 2008. The Abbey owns some 600 oils and water-colours from the 18th to the mid-20th centuries, including Pre-Raphaelite works such as Holman Hunt's *The Children's Holiday* and Burne-Jones' drawings of The Planets.

One of the abbey's most popular attractions was the **Agatha Christie Memorial Room** in the Abbot's Tower, which contained fascinating memorabilia loaned by her daughter - Agatha's favourite armchair, her 1937 Remington Portable Typewriter and her plotting notebook containing the handwritten manuscript of the best seller 'A Caribbean Mystery'.

Dame Agatha was born in Torquay in 1890 and the town has created an **Agatha Christie Mile** which guides visitors to places of interest that she knew as a girl and young woman growing up in the town.

Torquay Museum also has an interesting exhibition of photographs recording her life, as well as a pictorial record of Torquay over the last 150 years, and displays chronicling the social and natural history of the area. Amongst the museum's other treasures are many items discovered at **Kents Cavern**, an astonishing complex of caves regarded as "one of the most important archaeological sites in Britain". Excavations here in the 1820s revealed a remarkable collection of animal bones – the remains of mammoths, sabre-toothed tigers, grizzly bears, bison, and cave lions. These bones proved to be the dining-room debris of cave dwellers who lived here some 30,000 years ago, the oldest known residents of Europe. The caves are open daily, all year, offering guided tours, a sound and light show, a gift shop and refreshment room. The cavern has attracted the attentions of writers over the years and Agatha Christie refers to it in her novel *The Man in the Brown Suit,* where she describes the mammoth and woolly rhino bones found here during the 1870s; Beatrix Potter visited the cave in 1893 and described it as "very easy to explore and only moderately damp."

Another popular attraction is **Bygones** in Fore Street where visitors can wander back in time through a real olde worlde street complete with ironmongers, sweet shop, apothecary's shop, forge – and pub. There are many original

Victorian artefacts and other attractions include a giant model railway and railwayana collections; a children's fantasy land; a World War I exhibit, tearoom and shop.

Located on Beacon Quay, **Living Coasts** is operated by the same wildlife trust that runs Paignton Zoo. It is best described as a coastal zoo which provides a natural habitat for seals, penguins, puffins, auks and sea ducks with the emphasis on the coast and environmental issues. There's a café and a restaurant with grand views across Tor Bay.

A recent attraction is the visually striking 45 metres long moving footbridge, which links the north and south piers and allows pedestrians to walk all around the

87 RAVENSWOOD

Torquay

Great hotel in a central location offering good value for money accommodation.

 see page 204

88 RICHWOOD SPA GUEST ACCOMMODATION

Torquay

This great hotel boasts an outdoor heated swimming pool and two bars.

 see page 205

89 AVENUE PARK GUEST HOUSE

Torquay

Where comfort and warm, friendly hospitality awaits you.

 see page 206

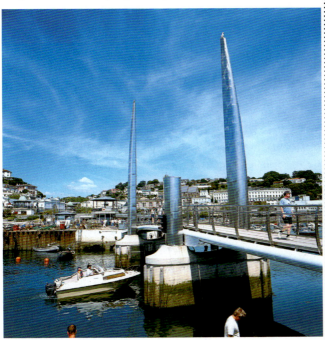

Pedestrian Lift Bridge, Torquay

90 BABBACOMBE MODEL VILLAGE

Babbacombe, Torquay

See thousands of miniature buildings, people and vehicles, in a variety of settings, including a medieval castle and a circus.

 see page 207

91 POTTERS MOORING HOUSE

Shaldon

Potters Mooring takes pride in offering the highest standards of comfort and hospitality.

 see page 207

harbour for the first time. The centre section of the footbridge hydraulically lifts in two giving a 10m opening, the underwater gate drops to allow safe passage of vessels into the harbour.

About a mile north of Torquay is another attraction but this village is one-twelfth life size. **Babbacombe Model Village** contains some 400 models, many with sound and animation. Created by Tom Dobbins, a large number of the beautifully crafted models have been given entertaining names: "Shortback & Sydes", the gents' hairdresser, for example, "Walter Wall Carpets" and "Jim Nastik's Health Farm". The site also contains some delightful gardens, including a collection of more than 500 types of dwarf conifer, a 1000 feet model railway, an ornamental lake stocked with koi carp and much more.

AROUND TORQUAY

COMBETEIGNHEAD

3 miles N of Torquay off the A380 or A379

Standing across the river from Bishopsteignton, Combeteignhead is a charming village which **John Keats** came to know well when he was staying with his consumptive brother Tom at nearby Teignmouth in 1818. In a letter to his family he often enclosed scraps of "happy doggerel" like this:

Here all the summer I could stay,
For there's Bishop's Teign
And King's Teign
And Coomb at the clear Teign head -
Where close by the stream

You may have your cream
All spread upon Barley bread.

SHALDON

7 miles N of Torquay on the A379

Set on the southern bank of the Teign estuary, Shaldon's Marine Parade provides a grand viewpoint for watching the busy traffic sailing in and out of the river. A goodly number of Regency houses add architectural dignity to the town, a reminder of the era when affluent Londoners, unable to holiday in a Europe dominated by Napoleon, began to discover the gentle charms of south-western England. A more recent attraction for visitors is the **Shaldon Wildlife Trust's** breeding centre for rare small mammals, reptiles and exotic birds, just to the north of the town.

Popular with families, the beach at **Ness Cove** lies at the foot of the imposing Ness Foreland and is reached by way of a genuine smugglers' tunnel.

TEIGNMOUTH

9 miles N of Torquay on the A381 & A379

Teignmouth has something of a split personality. On the coastal side is the popular holiday resort with its two miles of sandy beaches, a splendid promenade almost as long, and a pier. There's also a 25 feet-high lighthouse which serves no apparent purpose apart from looking rather fetching. The residential area contains much fine Regency and Georgian building. Particularly noteworthy are the **Church of St James** with its striking octagonal tower of 1820, and the former **Assembly Rooms**, a dignified colonnaded building which now houses the Riviera Cinema. Teignmouth's Georgian past is recalled on Wednesdays during the season when local people dress up in 18th century costume.

On the river side of the town is the working port, approached by the narrowest of channels. The currents here are so fast and powerful that no ship enters the harbour without a Trinity House pilot on board. **The Quay** was built in 1821 with granite from the quarries on Haytor Down. This durable stone was in great demand at the time. Amongst the many buildings constructed in Haytor granite were London Bridge, (the one now relocated to Lake Tahoe in California), and the British Museum. Teignmouth's main export nowadays is potter's clay, extracted from pits beside the River Teign, but boat building also continues, albeit on a small scale.

Close to the railway station and occupying a handsome 18th century building, **Teignmouth Museum** is dedicated to the history of the town and its people. Among the fascinating exhibits here can be seen a collection of artefacts rescued from a Spanish Armada ship wrecked near here and there are also displays on local railway history, the town's boatyards and local lace-making.

DAWLISH

12 miles N of Torquay on the A379

This pretty seaside resort, which boasts one of the safest beaches in England, has the unusual feature of a main railway line separating the town from its sea front. The result is, in fact, much more appealing than it sounds. For one thing, the railway keeps motor traffic away from the beachside, and for another, the low granite viaduct which carries the track has weathered attractively in the century and a half since it was built. The arches under which beach-goers pass create a kind of formal entrance to the beach and the Victorian station has become a visitor attraction in its own right.

By the time Brunel's railway arrived here in 1846, Dawlish was already well-known as a fashionable resort. John Keats, with his convalescent brother, Tom, had visited the town in 1818. The great poet was inspired to pen the less-than-immortal lines:

Over the hill and over the Dale
And over the bourne to Dawlish
Where Gingerbread wives
have a scanty sale
And gingerbread nuts are smallish.

Other distinguished visitors included Jane Austen, (one of whose characters cannot understand how one could live anywhere else in Devon but here), and Charles Dickens, who, in his novel of the same name has Nicholas Nickleby born at a farm nearby. All of these great literary figures arrived not long after the first houses were built along the Strand. That had happened in 1803. Up until then, Dawlish was just a small settlement beside the River Daw, located about a mile inland in

92 LYNTON HOUSE

Teignmouth

A friendly and welcoming family run hotel offering great views over the sea and the river Teign.

see page 208

93 OYSTERCATCHER CAFÉ

Teignmouth

Quaint little nautically themed café serving great home cooked meals.

see page 209

A couple of miles northeast of the town of Dawlish is Dawlish Warren, a mile-long sand spit which almost blocks the mouth of the River Exe. There's a golf course here and also a 55-acre Nature Reserve, home to more than 450 species of flowering plants. For one of them, the Jersey lily, this is its only habitat in mainland England. Guided tours of the Reserve, led by the warden, are available during the season.

94 BRISTOL HOUSE

Paignton

Value for money accommodation 100 yards from the seafront and close to the town centre.

 see page 209

order to be safe from raiders. This is where the 700-year-old church stands, surrounded by a small group of thatched cottages.

At the time of John Keats' visit, the town was being transformed with scores of new villas springing up along the Strand. Earlier improvers had already "beautified" the River Daw, which flows right through the town, by landscaping the stream into a series of shallow waterfalls and surrounding it with attractive gardens like **The Lawn.** Until Regency times, The Lawn had been a swamp populated by herons, kingfishers and otters. Then in 1808, the developer John Manning filled in the marshy land with earth removed during the construction of Queen Street. Today, both The Lawn and Queen Street still retain the elegance of those early-19th century days.

Housed in an elegant Georgian residence, which is itself an important part of the town's heritage, is the **Dawlish Museum**, where visitors can see a Victorian parlour and rooms displaying collections of china, prints, industrial tools, historically dressed dolls and by-gone toys. However, the most unusual collection here is undoubtedly that of early surgical instruments that was donated to the museum by a retired local doctor.

Railway enthusiasts will want to travel four miles north to the village of Starcross to see the last surviving relic of Isambard Kingdom Brunel's **Atmospheric Railway**. The great engineer had intended that the stretch of railway between Exeter and Totnes should be powered by a revolutionary new system. The train would be attached to a third rail which in fact was a long vacuum chamber, drawing the carriages along by the effects of air pressure. His visionary plan involved the building of 10 great Italianate engine houses at three mile intervals along the line. Sadly, the project was a failure, partly for financial reasons, but also because the leather seals on the vacuum pipe were quickly eaten away by the combined forces of rain, salt and hungry rats. The exhibition at Starcross displays a working model, using vacuum cleaners to represent the pumping houses, and volunteers are even propelled up and down the track to demonstrate the viability of the original idea.

Brunel had to fall back on conventional steam engines but the route he engineered from Exeter to Newton Abbot is one of the most scenic in the country, following first the western side of the Exe estuary, then hugging the seaboard from Dawlish Warren to Teignmouth before turning inland along the north bank of the River Teign.

PAIGNTON

3 miles SW of Torquay on the A379

Today, Torquay merges imperceptibly into Paignton, but in early Victorian times Paignton was just a small farming village, about half a mile inland, noted for its cider and its "very large and sweet flatpole cabbages". The town's two superb sandy beaches, ideal for families with young children, were to change all that. A pier and promenade add to the town's appeal, and throughout the summer season there's a packed programme of specials events, including a Children's Festival in August, fun fairs and various firework displays.

The most interesting building in Paignton is undoubtedly **Oldway Mansion,** built in 1874 for Isaac Singer, the millionaire sewing-machine manufacturer. Isaac died the following year and it was his son, Paris, who gave the great mansion its present exuberant form. Paris added a south side mimicking a music pavilion in the grounds of Versailles, a hallway modelled on the Versailles hall of mirrors, and a sumptuous ballroom where his mistress Isadora Duncan would display the new, fluid kind of dance she had created based on classical mythology. Paris Singer sold the mansion to Paignton Borough Council in 1946 and it is now used as a Civic Centre, but many of the splendid rooms (and the extensive gardens) are open to the public free of charge and guided tours are available.

An experience not to be missed in Paignton is a trip on the **Paignton and Dartmouth Steam Railway,** a seven mile journey along the lovely Torbay coast and through the wooded slopes bordering the Dart estuary to Kingswear where travellers board a ferry for the ten-minute crossing to Dartmouth. The locomotives and

rolling stock all bear the proud chocolate and gold livery of the Great Western Railway, and on certain services you can wine and dine in Pullman style luxury in the "Riviera Belle Dining Train". During the peak season, trains leave every 45 minutes or so.

Another major attraction in the town is **Paignton Zoo**, set in 75 acres of attractive botanical gardens and home to some 300 species of world animals. A registered charity dedicated to protecting the global wildlife heritage, the zoo is particularly concerned with endangered species such as the Asiatic lions and Sumatran tigers which are now provided with their own forest habitat area. Orang utans and gorillas roam freely on large outdoor islands, free from cages. The route of the Jungle Express miniature railway provides good views of these and many other animals.

Located on Goodrington Sands, **Quaywest** claims to be

95 THE CLIFTON AT PAIGNTON

Paignton
A high quality B & B providing comfortable accommodation and outstanding food.
see page 210

96 THE BLACK TULIP

Paignton
A small family run café serving a huge selection of tasty homemade dishes, just 5 minutes from the seafront.
see page 210

Paignton and Dartmouth Steam Railway

97 THE BREAKWATER

Brixham

This excellent family run business offers great views of Torbay and quality food in relaxed surroundings.

see page 211

Britain's "biggest, best, wildest and wettest waterpark", with the highest water slides in the country. Other amusements include go-karts, bumper boats, and crazy golf and the site also offers a choice of bars, restaurants and cafés.

BRIXHAM

8 miles S of Torquay on the A3022

In the 18th century, Brixham was the most profitable fishing port in Britain and fishing is still the most important activity in this engaging little town, although the trawlers now have to pick their way between flotillas of yachts and tour boats. On the quay there are stalls selling freshly caught seafood and around the harbour a maze of narrow streets where you'll find a host of small shops, tearooms and galleries. From the busy harbour, there are regular passenger ferries to Torquay and coastal cruises in the 80-year-old Brixham-built yacht *Vigilance* and other craft.

It was at Brixham that the Prince of Orange landed in 1688 to claim the British throne as William III; an imposing statue of him looks inland from the harbour. And in 1815, all eyes were focussed on the *Bellerophon*, anchored in the bay. On board was Napoleon Bonaparte, getting his only close look at England before transferring to the *Northumberland* and sailing off to his final exile on St Helena.

A short walk from the quay brings you to **Battery Gardens,** so named because an Emergency Coastal Defence Battery was established here in World War II. It is now a Scheduled Monument with many of the buildings and structures from that time still standing. A museum on site tells their story.

Also close to the harbour is All Saints' Church where the **Revd Henry Francis Lyte** was Vicar from 1823 until his death in 1847. During his last illness, the Revd Lyte composed what is perhaps the best known and best loved English hymn – *Abide with me*. The church bells play the tune each evening.

To the west of the town is **Berry Head Country Park** which is noted for its incredible views (on a good day as far as Portland Bill, 46 miles away), its rare plants, (like the white rock-rose), and its colonies of sea birds such as fulmars and kittiwakes nesting in the cliffs. The park also boasts the largest breeding colony of guillemots along the entire Channel coast. A video camera has been installed on the cliffs to relay live close-up pictures of the guillemots and other seabirds. Within the park

Brixham Harbour

Greenway Gardens, nr Brixham

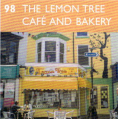

98 THE LEMON TREE
CAFÉ AND BAKERY

Brixham

A delightful café and bakery,
spread over two floors, just a
few minutes walk from
Brixham's picturesque
harbour.

 see page 212

is a lighthouse which has been called "the highest and lowest lighthouse in Britain". The structure is only 15 feet high, but it stands on a 200 feet high cliff rising at the most easterly point of Berry Head.

In the town itself, the **Strand Art Gallery** was founded in 1972 and showcases the work of internationally famous local artists. It is the largest art gallery in the West Country and has more than 400 original paintings on display. Visitors can see the artists at work, either in the gallery or on the slipway outside.

GALMPTON

8 miles S of Torquay on the A3022

The major attraction here is **Greenway**, the home of Dame Agatha Christie for the last 30 years of her life. Her daughter now lives there and the house is currently not open to the public, but the lovely gardens overlooking the river are open Wednesday to Sunday inclusive, with gardener's guided walks every Friday. Parts of the house itself are expected to open to the public in the summer of 2009. Also within the grounds is the **Barn Gallery** which mounts exhibitions of contemporary art by local artists. Parking is extremely limited but cruises and ferries are available from Dartmouth, Torquay and Brixham.

KINGSWEAR

10 miles S of Torquay off the A379

Kingswear sits on the steeply rising east bank of the River Dart, looking across to the picturesque panorama of Dartmouth stretched

Cockington Village

99 LANSCOMBE HOUSE

Cockington

This warm and convivial hotel is the perfect base from which to explore South Devon.

see page 213

Rupert and Lady Dorothy D'Oyly Carte. (Lady Dorothy's grandfather, Richard, had produced the Gilbert and Sullivan comic operas). The garden was created between 1925 and 1940 by Lady Dorothy who introduced a wonderfully imaginative variety of plants. The 20-acre site, protected by a deep combe, contains formal gardens, wooded areas with wild flowers, tranquil pools and secret paths weaving in and out of glades.

COCKINGTON VILLAGE

2 miles W of Torquay off the A380

Just a mile or so from Torquay town centre is Cockington Village, a phenomenally picturesque rural oasis of thatched cottages, a working forge, and the Drum Inn which was designed by Sir Edward Lutyens and completed in 1930. From the village there's a pleasant walk through the park to **Cockington Court**, now a Craft Centre and Gallery. Partly Tudor, this stately old manor was for almost three centuries the home of the Mallock family. In the 1930s they formed a trust to preserve "entire and unchanged the ancient amenities and character of the place, and in developing its surroundings to do nothing which may not rather enhance than diminish its attractiveness". The Trust has been spectacularly successful in carrying out their wishes.

COMPTON

4 miles W of Torquay off the A381

Dominating this small village, **Compton Castle** (NT) dates back

across the hillside on the opposite bank. The town is the terminus for the Paignton and Kingswear steam railway and passengers then join the ferry for the 10-minute crossing to Dartmouth. There's also a vehicle ferry. Above the town stand the impressive remains of Kingswear Castle which is now owned by the Landmark Trust and has been converted to holiday flats. Together with its twin across the river, Dartmouth Castle, the fortresses guarded the wide estuary of the Dart. If an invasion seemed imminent, a huge chain was strung across the river from Dartmouth as an additional deterrent.

About three miles to the east of Kingswear, **Coleton Fishacre House & Garden** (NT) is a delightful coastal garden basking in a mild climate that favours the cultivation of exotic trees and shrubs. Reflecting the Arts and Crafts style from outside but with Art Deco features within, the house was built in the 1920s for

Compton Castle

100 THE BUTCHERS ARMS

Abbotskerswell

Beautiful stone built former smithy, with all the friendly atmosphere and excellent food expected of a traditional Devonshire pub.

see page 213

to the 1300s. In Elizabethan times it was the home of Sir Humphrey Gilbert, Walter Raleigh's half brother and the coloniser of Newfoundland in 1583. Complete with battlements, towers and portcullis, the castle also boasts an impressive Great Hall, a solar and an ancient kitchen. The castle is still occupied by the Gilbert family although owned by the National Trust.

NEWTON ABBOT

7 miles NW of Torquay on the A380

An ancient market town, Newton Abbot took on a quite different character in the 1850s when the Great Western Railway established its locomotive and carriage repair works here. Neat terraces of artisans' houses were built on the steep hillsides to the south; the more well-to-do lived a little further to the north in Italianate villas around Devon Square and Courtenay Park.

The town's greatest moment of glory was on November 5th, 1688 when William, Prince of Orange, "the glorious defender of the Protestant religion and the liberties of England" was first proclaimed king as **William III.** This climactic moment of the "Glorious Revolution" took place in front of St Leonard's Church of which only the medieval tower now remains. The new king had landed at Brixham and was on his way to London. Stopping off in Newton Abbot, he stayed at the handsome Jacobean manor, Forde House, which is now used as offices by the District Council.

To the south of the town is a delightful attraction in the shape of the Hedgehog Hospital at Prickly Hill Farm – where else? As well as caring for injured hedgehogs, the hospital has a hedgehog village and a hedgehog friendly garden. Visitors are encouraged to help feed the little creatures and to hold

101 THE SANDYGATE INN

Kingsteignton

16th century inn offering home cooked food, real ales and a great atmosphere.

see page 214

Bradley Manor, Newton Abbot

Maltings has been malting in Newton Abbot for more than 100 years and claims to offer the finest selection of bottled beers to be found in Devon. The speciality beer shop is open throughout the year and guided tours of the maltings are available during the summer months.

CHUDLEIGH

14 miles NW of Torquay off the A38

Activists who oppose the building of new roads will find little sympathy in this former coaching town on what used to be the main thoroughfare between Exeter and Plymouth. By the 1960s, the volume of traffic had reached unbearable levels, especially during the holiday season. Mercifully, the dual carriageway A38 now bypasses the little town and it is once again possible to enjoy Chudleigh's 14th century church, containing some fine memorials to the Courtenay family, and its former Grammar School nearby which was founded in 1668. (It is now a private house). It was at the coaching inn here that William of Orange stayed after his landing at Torbay. From one of its windows, the new king addressed the good people of Chudleigh. The Dutchman's English was so bad however they were unable to understand what he was saying. They cheered him anyway.

Clifford Street is named after Sir Thomas Clifford, Lord Treasurer to Charles II and a member of the king's notorious Cabal, his secretive inner Cabinet. As was the custom then, Sir

---

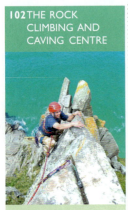

102 THE ROCK CLIMBING AND CAVING CENTRE

Chudleigh

A thrill-seekers heaven located in South Devon's area of outstanding natural beauty.

 see page 215

---

them – carefully, of course! Other animals here include lambs, goats and sheep, and there's also a café.

On the northern outskirts of the town is **Newton Abbot Racecourse** where National Hunt racing takes place from the spring through to the autumn. For the rest of the year, the site is used for country fairs and other events.

On the western edge of the town stands **Bradley Manor** (NT), a notable example of medieval domestic architecture. Most of it dates from around 1420 and includes a chapel, Solar, Great Hall and porch. By the mid-1750s this quaint style of architecture was decidedly out of fashion and the building became a farmhouse with poultry occupying the chapel. The house was given to the National Trust in 1938 by the then owner, Mrs AH Woolner. Her family continue to live here and manage the property.

Newton Abbot also boasts the only traditional working malthouse open to the public. **Tuckers**

Ugbrooke House, Chudleigh

103 THE HIGHWAYMAN'S HAUNT

Chudleigh

Enjoy a fresh locally sourced menu in this 13th century thatched inn, while enjoying the friendly rustic atmosphere.

 see page 216

Thomas used his official position to amass a considerable fortune. This was later put to good use by his grandson who employed Robert Adam and 'Capability Brown' to design **Ugbrooke House and Park,** a couple of miles southwest of Chudleigh and well worth visiting. Dating from the mid-1700s and replacing an early Tudor manor house, Ugbrooke is named after the Ug Brook that flows through the estate and was dammed to create three lakes in the beautifully landscaped grounds. In the 1930s, the 11th Lord Clifford abandoned the estate as he could not afford to live there. During World War II, Ugbrooke was used as a school for evacuated children and as a hostel for Polish soldiers. In the 1950s, some of the ground floor rooms were used to store grain but today the house has been beautifully restored by the present Lord and Lady Clifford. It is noted for its portraits by Lely, collections of Chinese porcelain, dolls, military uniforms and Chippendale furniture.

Plymouth and the South Hams

With around a quarter of a million inhabitants, Plymouth is now the largest centre of population in the south west peninsula but its development has been comparatively recent. It wasn't until the late 1100s that the harbour was recognised as having any potential as a military and commercial port. Another 300 years passed before it was established as the main base for the English fleet guarding the western channel against a seaborne attack from Spain. Plymouth is still the Royal Navy's principal home base and the Navy has another major presence in this area, the Britannia Royal Naval College in the delightful little port of Dartmouth.

Dartmouth lies within the area known as the South Hams, the 'hamlets south of Dartmoor'. Described by one ancient writer as "the frutefullest part of all Devonshire", this favoured tract of land enjoys an exceptionally mild climate, fertile soil and well-watered pastures. The coastline here is very varied - it boasts some of the most spectacular cliff scenery in Devon along with some fine, sandy beaches, most notably at Blackpool Sands

Smeaton's Tower, Plymouth Hoe

Plymouth Breakwater and Great Mew Stone

PLYMOUTH

• Two miles from the Hoe, Plymouth's remarkable Breakwater protects the Sound from the destructive effects of the prevailing south-westerly winds. Built by prisoners between 1812 and 1840, this massive mile-long construction required around four million tons of limestone. The surface was finished with enormous dovetailed blocks of stone, and the structure rounded off with a lighthouse at one end. •

Perhaps the best way of getting to know this historic city is to approach **Plymouth Hoe** on foot from the main shopping area, along the now-pedestrianised Armada Way. It was on the Hoe on Friday, July 19th, 1588, that one of the most iconic moments in English history took place. Commander of the Fleet, and erstwhile pirate, Sir Francis Drake was playing bowls here when he was informed of the approach of the Spanish Armada. With true British phlegm, Sir Francis completed his game before boarding *The Golden Hind* and sailing off to harass the Spanish fleet. A statue of Sir Francis, striking a splendidly belligerent pose and looking proudly to the horizon, stands on the Hoe which is still an open space, combining the functions of promenade, public park and parade ground.

Just offshore, the striking shape of **Drake's Island** rises like Alcatraz from the deep swirling waters at the mouth of the River Tamar. In medieval times it was known as St Nicholas' Island. The name was changed when Sir Francis Drake was appointed governor and began to fortify the island. In its time, this stark fortified islet has been used as a gunpowder repository, (it is said to be riddled with underground tunnels where the powder was stored), a prison, and a youth adventure centre.

On a clear day, it's possible to see the famous **Eddystone Lighthouse**, 12 miles out in the Channel. The present lighthouse is the fourth to be built here. The first, made of timber, was swept away in a huge storm in 1703 taking with it the man who had built the lighthouse, the ship-owner Winstanley. In 1759, a much more substantial structure of dovetailed granite blacks was built by John Smeaton. It stood for 120 years and even then it was not the lighthouse but the rocks on which it stood which began to collapse. The lighthouse was dismantled and re-erected on the Hoe where, as **Smeaton's Tower**, it is one of the city's most popular tourist attractions. From the top, there are good views of Millbay Docks, Plymouth's busy commercial port which was once thronged with transatlantic passenger liners. Today, the docks handle a variety of merchant shipping, as well as the continental ferry services to Brittany and northern Spain. To the east, the view is dominated by **The Citadel**, a massive fortification built by Charles II, ostensibly as a defence against seaborne attack. Perhaps bearing in mind that Plymouth had resisted a four-year siege by his father's troops during the Civil War, Charles's Citadel has a number of gun ports bearing directly on the city. The Citadel is still a military base, but there are guided tours every afternoon from May to September.

Close by the Citadel is Plymouth's oldest quarter, the **Barbican.** Now a lively entertainment area filled with restaurants, pubs, and an innovative small theatre, it was once the main trading area for merchants exporting wool and importing wine.

A few yards away are the **Mayflower Steps** where the Pilgrim Fathers boarded ship for their historic voyage to Massachusetts. The names of the Mayflower's company are listed on a board on nearby Island House, now the tourist information office. Many other emigrants were to follow in the Pilgrim Fathers' wake, with the result that there are now more than 40 communities named Plymouth scattered across the English-speaking world.

A number of interesting old buildings around the Barbican have survived the ravages of time and the terrible pasting the city received during World War II. **Prysten House**, behind St Andrew's Church, is a 15th century priest's house; the **Elizabethan House** in New Street has a rich display of Elizabethan furniture and furnishings, and the **Merchant's House** in St Andrew's Street, generally regarded as Devon's finest Jacobean building, is crammed full of interesting objects relating to Plymouth's past. A particularly fascinating exhibit in the Merchant's House is the **Park Pharmacy**, a genuine Victorian pharmacy complete with its 1864 fittings and stocked with such preparations as Ipecacuanha Wine ("one to two tablespoonfuls as an emetic") and Tincture of Myrrh and Borax, "for the teeth and gums". Another vintage shop is **Jacka's Bakery** which claims to be the oldest commercial bakery in the country and is reputed to have supplied the *Mayflower* with ship's biscuits.

Also in the Barbican area is the **National Marine Aquarium**, located on the Fish Quay. The Aquarium experience comprises a total of 50 live exhibits including

National Marine Aquarium, Plymouth

104 THEATRE ROYAL PLYMOUTH

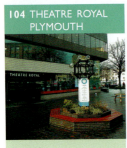

Plymouth

A wide range of performances, catering for all tastes, are included in the programme at this exciting venue.

see page 217

•

Plymouth's best-known export has to be Plymouth Gin which has been produced in the city since 1793. At the company's Black Friars Distillery visitors can take a guided tour and learn about the art of making this famous tipple. In the Refectory Bar here, it is said, the Pilgrim Fathers spent their last night before setting sail in the Mayflower. A favourite of Churchill, Roosevelt, Ian Fleming and Alfred Hitchcock, Plymouth Gin is considered to be the original base for a Dry Martini and it holds a hallowed place in the Savoy Cocktail book – the bible of mixed drinks.

•

three massive tanks, the largest of which – Britain's deepest tank – holds 2.5 million litres of water. More than 4000 animals from 400 species are displayed in realistic habitats from local shorelines to coral reefs. The virtual reality tour includes encounters with brilliantly coloured fish, seahorses and even Caribbean sharks. Another zone, Explorocean, focuses on ocean exploration and sustainability through innovative, interactive exhibits. The most recent addition to the aquarium's attractions is its 4D Screen on the Sea which presents "Turtle Vision", the story of a turtle's encounter with a man-made disaster told in vivid animation and special effects. As the aquarium points out, "The 4th dimension includes effects that will leave you slightly damp".

Close to Smeaton's Tower is the **Plymouth Dome**, a stunning attraction that brilliantly captures Plymouth's long history. The imaginative exhibitions here allow visitors to experience the stench and grime of an Elizabethan street, brave the seas with Drake and Cook and witness the devastation of Plymouth's port by the Luftwaffe. One gallery features the four lighthouses of Eddystone Rock.

Locally, the Tamar estuary is known as the Hamoaze, (pronounced ham-oys), and it's well worth taking one of the boat trips that leave from the Mayflower Steps. This is certainly the best way to see Devonport Dockyard, while the ferry to Cremyll on the Cornish

bank of the Tamar drops off passengers close to Mount Edgcumbe Country Park and the old smuggling village of Cawsand.

The blackest date in Plymouth's history is undoubtedly March 21st, 1941. On that night, the entire centre of the city was razed to the ground by the combined effects of high-explosive and incendiary bombs. More than 1000 people were killed; another 5000 injured. After the war, the renowned town planner Sir Patrick Abercrombie was commissioned to design a completely new town centre. Much of the rebuilding was carried out in the 1950s, which was not British architecture's golden age, but half a century later the scheme has acquired something of a period charm. Abercrombie's plan included some excellent facilities, like the first-rate **Museum and Art Gallery**, the **Theatre Royal** with its two auditoria, the **Arts Centre**, and the **Pavilions** complex of concert hall, leisure pool and skating rink.

In August each year Plymouth hosts the **British Fireworks Championships** when thousands of people throng The Hoe to watch six different fireworks companies let off displays over Plymouth Sound.

A few miles north of the city stands **Crownhill Fort**, one of the largest and best-preserved of Plymouth's many fortifications. The fort was built between 1863 and 1872 and was the most advanced of Lord Palmerston's series of fortresses built to defend the country from a French invasion. It's a wonderful place to explore, especially if you visit on one of the days when the fort comes alive again as the original Victorian drill is followed and a wide range of cannon fired.

AROUND PLYMOUTH

TAMERTON FOLIOT

3 miles N of Plymouth off the B3373

Set on a hillside overlooking a large creek that runs into the River Tamar, Tamerton Foliot was the birthplace of Gilbert Foliot who was to hold the position of Bishop of London for 35 years, from 1153 to 1188. He was an arch-adversary of Thomas à Becket who excommunicated him, a punishment that was overturned by the Pope. The village has a 15th century church with some outstanding monuments to the local landowners, the Copleston, Gorges and Radcliffe families, and an interesting Tudor pulpit with linen fold panelling.

Overlooking the Tavy and Tamar estuary, **Warleigh Point Nature Reserve** includes one of the finest examples of coastal oak woodland in Devon and, along with magnificent views, is home to a wealth of wildlife.

PLYMPTON

4 miles E of Plymouth on the B3416

Now more of a suburb of Plymouth than a town in its own right, in early medieval times Plympton was larger than its neighbour and the earthwork of a medieval castle can still be seen. The town boasts one of Devon's grandest mansions, **Saltram** (National Trust). Built during the reign of George II for the Parker family, this sumptuous house occupies a splendid site high above the Plym estuary. In the 1760s Robert Adam was called in, at enormous expense, to decorate the dining room and "double cube" saloon, which he accomplished with his usual panache. There are portraits of the Parkers by Sir Joshua Reynolds (who was born in the nearby village of Plympton St Maurice) and, amongst the fine furniture, a magnificent four-poster bed by Thomas Chippendale. Other attractions include the great kitchen with its fascinating assortment of period kitchenware, an orangery in the gardens, and the former chapel, now a gallery displaying the work of West Country artists. Saltram House appeared as Norland House in the 1995 feature film of Jane

105 PLYM VALLEY RAILWAY

Plympton

The Plym Valley Railway is in the process of restoring the line between Plymouth and Launceston. Trains run on Sundays.

 see page 217

Plym Valley Railway, Plympton

Austen's *Sense and Sensibility* starring Emma Thompson and Hugh Grant.

The garden at Saltram is mainly 19th century and contains several follies as well as some beautiful shrubberies and imposing specimen trees. The shop and gallery offer work for sale by contemporary local artists.

From the village, the **Plym Valley Railway** carries passengers on a short length of restored track, part of a GWR branch line that ran from Plymouth to Launceston via Tavistock. Travelling in rolling-stock redolent of the 1950s and '60s, passengers are conveyed to the local beauty spot, Plym Bridge.

To the north of Plympton is a fine Georgian mansion that is often overlooked. **Hemerdon House**, which is still occupied by the original family, contains family and other portraits, silver, books and period furniture and is open on a limited basis.

TURNCHAPEL

1 mile SE of Plymouth off the A379

Enjoying views across Cattewater to Plymouth, the village of Turnchapel is strung along the waterside. The village was declared a Conservation Area in 1977 and, with its two pubs, church, and waterfront, is a pleasant place to wander around. Nearby, there are ex-RAF Catalina flying boats to admire; and from Mountbatten Peninsula grand vistas open up over to Plymouth Hoe and Drake's Island. It was at RAF Mountbatten that TE Lawrence, 'Lawrence of Arabia', served as a humble aircraftman for several years.

A short distance to the south is a stretch of coastline known as **Abraham's Garden**. The story goes that, during the fearful plague of 1665, a number of Spanish slaves were buried here. In their memory, it is said, the shrubbery always remains green, even in winter.

WEMBURY

6 miles SE of Plymouth off the A379

Wembury church provides a dramatic landmark as it stands isolated on the edge of the cliff, and the coastal path here provides spectacular views of the Yealm estuary to the east, and Plymouth Sound to the west. The path is occasionally closed to walkers when the firing range is in use, so look out for the red warning flags.

The Great Mew Stone stands a mile offshore in Wembury Bay. This lonely islet was inhabited until

Wembury Beach

Newton Ferrers

106 KITLEY HOUSE

Yealmpton

A simply stunning lakeside country house hotel, ideal for those special occasions.

 see page 218

the 1830s when its last residents, the part-time smuggler Sam Wakeham and his family, gave up the unequal struggle to make a living here. The Mew Stone is now the home of seabirds who surely couldn't have taken kindly to its use as a target from time to time by the HMS Cambridge gunnery school on Wembury Point. Fortunately, following complaints from local residents and conservationists, the shelling practice was ceased in the late 1970s.

NEWTON FERRERS

9 miles SE of Plymouth on the B3186

A picturesque fishing village of whitewashed cottages sloping down to the river, Newton Ferrers is beloved by artists. It is also one of the south coast's most popular yachting centres. Part of the village sits beside the River Yealm (pronounced "Yam"), the rest alongside a large creek. When the creek dries out at low tide, it is possible to walk across to Noss Mayo on the southern bank. (When the tide is in, a ferry operates, but only during the season.)

THE SOUTH HAMS

"The frutefullest part of all Devonshire." said an old writer of this favoured tract of land lying south of Dartmoor, bounded by the River Dart to the east and the River Erme to the west. The climate is exceptionally mild, the soil fertile and the pastures well-watered. But the rivers that run off Dartmoor to the sea, slicing north-south through the area, created burdensome barriers to communications until fairly recent times. This comparative isolation kept the region unspoilt but also kept it poor.

There are few towns of any size – only Totnes, Kingsbridge and Modbury really qualify, along with the picturesque ports of Dartmouth and Salcombe. For the rest, the South Hams is a charmed landscape of drowsy villages linked by narrow country lanes running between high banks on which wildflowers flourish: thanks to an enlightened County Council, the verges were never assaulted with massive quantities of herbicides as in other areas.

The area has been known as the South Hams, the 'homesteads south of Dartmoor', since Saxon times, but one town at least claims a history stretching much further back in time. We begin our exploration of the South Hams at Totnes which is the second oldest borough in England. The town sent its first Member of Parliament to London in 1295, and elected the first of its 630-odd Mayors in 1359.

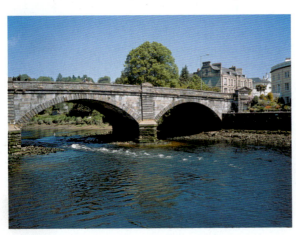

Bridge over River Dart, Totnes

TOTNES

This captivating little town claims to have been founded by an Ancient Trojan named Brutus in 1200BC. The grandfather of Aeneas, the hero of Virgil's epic poem *The Aeneid,* Brutus sailed up the River Dart, gazed at the fair prospect around him and decided to found the first town in this new country which would take its name, Britain, from his own. The **Brutus Stone**, set in the pavement of the main shopping street, Fore Street, commemorates this stirring incident when both the town and a nation were born.

The first recorded evidence of this town, set on a hill above the highest navigable point on the River Dart, doesn't appear until the mid-10th century when King Edgar established a mint at Totnes. The Saxons already had a castle of sorts here, but the impressive remains of **Totnes Castle** are Norman, built between the 1100s and early 1300s. Towering over the town, it is generally reckoned to be the best-preserved motte and bailey castle in Devon.

A substantial section of Totnes' medieval town wall has also survived. The superb **East Gate**, which straddles the steep main street is part of that wall.

Just a little way down the hill from East Gate is the charming **Guildhall** of 1553, a remarkable little building with a granite colonnade. It houses both the Council Chamber (which is still in use) and the underground Town

Gaol (which is not). The cells can be visited, as can the elegant Council Chamber with its plaster frieze and the table where Oliver Cromwell sat in 1646.

Almost opposite the Guildhall is another magnificent Elizabethan building, currently occupied by Barclays Bank. It was built in 1585 for Nicholas Ball who had made his fortune from the local pilchard fishery. When he died, his wife Anne married Sir Thomas Bodley and it was the profit from pilchards that funded the world-famous Bodleian Library at Oxford University.

The town's Elizabethan heritage really comes alive if you are visiting on a Tuesday in summer. You will find yourself stepping into a pageant of Elizabethan colour, for this is when the people of Totnes array themselves in crisp, white ruffs and velvet gowns for a charity market which has raised thousands of pounds for good causes since it began in 1970. In August, the Elizabethan Society organises the **Orange Race** which commemorates a visit to the town by Sir Francis Drake during which he presented "a fair red orange" to a small boy in the street. Today, contestants chase their oranges down the hill.

The parish church of Totnes is **St Mary's.** It was entirely rebuilt in the 15th century when the town's cloth industry was booming – at that time Totnes was second in importance only to Exeter. The church's most glorious possession is a rood-screen delicately carved in stone from the quarry at Beer.

Close by at 70 Fore Street is the **Totnes Elizabethan House Museum**, housed in an attractive half-timbered Elizabethan building whose upper floors overhang the street. Built in around 1575 for Walter Kellond, a cloth merchant, the three floors of his former home contain a wide range of exhibits that illustrate local social history from industry and archaeology to costumes and toys. One of the fascinating exhibits here honours a distinguished son of Totnes, Charles Babbage (1791-1871) whose 'Analytical Machine' is universally acknowledged as the forerunner of the electronic computer. The museum display records his doomed struggle to perfect such a calculator using only mechanical parts. A little further up the hill, in High Street, the **Butterwalk** and **Poultrywalk** are two ancient covered shopping arcades whose upper storeys rest on pillars of granite, timber or cast iron.

In recent years, Totnes has earned the title of 'Natural Health Capital of the West Country'. The first Natural Health Centre was established here in 1989. In subsequent years, other practitioners have also arrived, offering a huge range of alternative medicine therapies. In alphabetical order they include acupuncture, the Alexander technique, aromatherapy, chiropractic, homoeopathy, genuine non-sexual massage, osteopathy and reflexology. Visitors will also find specialist shops stocked with natural medicines, organic food, aromatherapy products, relaxation

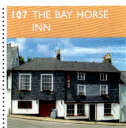

107 THE BAY HORSE INN

Totnes

This CAMRA award winning pub supplies wonderful accommodation as well as a great pint.

 see page 219

One excursion from Totnes not to be missed is the breathtakingly beautiful river trip to Dartmouth, 12 miles downstream. This stretch of the river has been called the "English Rhine" and the comparison is no exaggeration. The river here is well away from roads, making it an ideal location for seeing wading-birds, herons, cormorants, and even seals. During the summer, there are frequent departures from the quay by the bridge. Another memorable journey is by steam train along the seven-mile stretch of the South Devon Railway, also known as the Primrose Line, which runs through the glorious scenery of the Dart Valley to Buckfastleigh. Most of the locomotives and carriages are genuine Great Western Railway stock and are painted in the GWR's famous chocolate and cream livery.

tapes and books on spiritual healing.

For centuries, Totnes was a busy river port and down by **Totnes Bridge**, an elegant stone structure of 1828, the quay was lined with warehouses, some of which have survived and been converted into highly desirable flats. Nearby, on the Plains, stands a granite obelisk to the famous explorer William Wills, a native of the town who perished from starvation when attempting to re-cross the Australian desert with Robert Burke in 1861.

On nearby Coronation Road, **Totnes Town Mill**, a restored Victorian water wheel and mill, has a display on mill technology and an excellent exhibition showing the development of the town. It also houses Totnes Image Bank & Rural Archive, a collection of photographic images of the town, and the Tourist Information Centre.

Next door to the railway, the **Rare Breeds Farm** includes a hedgehog rescue centre, some spectacular owls, red squirrels, goats, sheep, birds and much more. It also has a Garden Café with views of working steam trains and Totnes Castle.

Even that list of attractions isn't exhaustive. The **Devonshire Collection of Period Costume** is housed in one of the town's most interesting 16th century houses.

AROUND TOTNES

DARTINGTON

2 miles NW of Totnes on the A384

When Leonard and Dorothy Elmhirst bought **Dartington Hall**

and its estate in 1925 the superb Great Hall had stood roofless for more than a century. The buildings surrounding the two large quadrangles laid out in the 1390s by John Holand, Earl of Exeter, were being used as stables, cow houses and hay lofts. The Elmhirsts were idealists and since Dorothy (*née* Whitney) was one of the richest American women of her time, they possessed the resources to put their ideals into practice. They restored the Hall, re-opened it as a progressive school, and set about reviving the local rural economy in line with the ideology of the Indian philosopher, Rabindranath Tagore. The Elmhirsts were closely involved in the creation of the famed Dartington Glass. Sadly, long after their deaths, their school closed in 1995 as a consequence of financial problems and a pornography scandal. But the headmaster's residence, **High Cross House**, a classic Modernist building of the early 1930s has now been converted into an art gallery. Visitors are welcome here and also to wander around the 26-acre gardens surrounding the Hall. There is no charge for entry to the quadrangle and Great Hall, but donations for its upkeep are welcomed. Guided tours are available by appointment.

Dartington Hall hosts more than 100 music performances each year during its International Summer School, a season which attracts musicians and artistes of the highest calibre from all over the

Crocuses at Dartington Hall, Dartington

world. All year round, even more visitors are attracted to the **Dartington Cider Press Centre**, a huge gallery on the edge of the estate which displays a vast range of craft products – anything from a delicate handmade Christmas or birthday card to a beautifully modelled item of pottery.

STAVERTON

3 miles N of Totnes off the A384

Just a short walk down the road from the village, with its riverside walks and famous inn, is a particularly pretty station on the South Devon Railway that is frequently used in film and television productions.

BERRY POMEROY

2 miles E of Totnes off the A385 or A381

For the last 1000 years this small village has been owned by just two families. The de la Pomerais dynasty arrived with William the Conqueror and held the land for

Berry Pomeroy Castle

127

almost 500 years. In the early 1300s they built **Berry Pomeroy Castle** in a superb position on a wooded promontory above the Gatcombe Brook. Substantial remains of the castle still stand, including sections of the curtain wall and the 14th century gatehouse. In 1548 the Pomeroys, as they were now known, sold the estate to Sir Edward Seymour whose sister, Jane, had been the third wife of Henry VIII. Sir Edward built a three-storey Tudor mansion within the medieval fortifications but this too is now a shell. Although the castle is still owned by Sir Edward's descendant, the Duke of Somerset, it is administered by English Heritage and open to the public daily during the season. In the village itself, St Mary's Church contains some interesting monuments to the Pomeroys and Seymours, as well as an outstanding rood screen.

ASHPRINGTON

2 miles SE of Totnes off the A381

Set in a stunning location above the River Dart, **Sharpham Vineyard and Cheese Dairy** offers two gastronomic experiences. Visitors can sample the international award-winning red and white wines, and watch the dairy cheese being made. The entrance fee includes complimentary tastings. During the summer months, the shop and the Vineyard Café are open. An attractive way of visiting the vineyard is by taking one of the ferry boats along the River Dart which will stop at Sharpham on request.

STOKE GABRIEL

5 miles SE of Totnes off the A385

A charming village of narrow lanes and alleys, Stoke Gabriel stands on a hillside above a tidal spur of the River Dart. A weir was built across the neck of the creek in Edwardian times and this traps the water at low tide, giving the village a pleasant lakeside atmosphere. The part-13th century church of St Gabriel has a restored late-medieval pulpit and a truncated screen with some good wainscot paintings. In the churchyard are the rather forlorn remains of an oak tree reputed to be more than 1500 years old. To the west of the village, a lane leads to the riverside hamlet of Duncannon where, by general consent, the River Dart is at its most lovely.

DITTISHAM

11 miles SE of Totnes off the A3122

The best way to reach the pretty yachting village of Dittisham is by passenger ferry from Dartmouth. This village of atmospheric cottages, whose narrow streets drop down to the River Dart, is in an area renowned for its fruit farming; Dittisham plums were especially famous and are still grown on a small scale.

Dittisham's Church of St George has many interesting features, including the Royal Coat of Arms of Charles II hanging over a door (granted at the time of the Restoration in gratitude to the townspeople for their loyalty to the Royalist cause), a beautiful 15th century carved stone 'wineglass' pulpit, and windows in the north aisle inserted in about 1846 under the direction of Augustus Pugin.

DARTMOUTH

14 miles SE of Totnes on the A3122

For centuries, this entrancing little town clinging to the sides of a precipitous hill was one of England's principal ports. Millions of casks of French and Spanish wine have been offloaded onto its narrow quays. During the 1100s Crusaders on both the Second and Third Crusades mustered here, and from here they set sail. In its sheltered harbour, Elizabeth's men o'war lay in wait to pick off the stragglers from the Spanish Armada. In 1620, the *Mayflower* put in here for a few days for repairs before hoisting sail on August 20th for Plymouth and then on to the New World where the pilgrims arrived three months later. The quay from which they embarked later became the major location for the BBC-TV series, *The Onedin Line,* and was also seen in the 1995 feature film *Sense and Sensibility* starring Emma Thompson and Hugh Grant.

Geoffrey Chaucer visited the town in 1373 in his capacity as Inspector of Customs and is believed to have modelled the 'Schipman of Dertemouthe' in his *Canterbury Tales* on the character of the then Mayor of Dartmouth, John Hawley. Hawley was an enterprising merchant and seafarer who was also responsible for building the first **Dartmouth**

Dartmouth

Castle (English Heritage). Dramatically sited, it guards the entrance to the Dart estuary and was one of the first castles specifically designed to make effective use of artillery. In case the castle should prove to be an inadequate deterrent, in times of danger a heavy chain was strung across the harbour to Kingswear Castle on the opposite bank. (Kingswear Castle is now owned by the Landmark Trust and available for holiday rentals.)

There's a striking monumental brass to John Hawley and his two wives in the **Church of St Saviour's**, a part-14th century building against whose wall ships used to tie up before the New Quay was constructed in the late 1500s. Nearby is the **Custom House**, a handsome building of 1739 which has some fine internal plasterwork ceilings.

Also worth seeking out are **The Butterwalk**, a delightful timber-framed arcade dating from 1640 in which the **Dartmouth**

The Butterwalk, Dartmouth

the Great Western Railway as the terminus of their line from Torbay and passengers were ferried across to Kingswear where the railway actually ended. The station at Dartmouth is now a restaurant. The other building of note is the **Britannia Royal Naval College** (guided tours during the season). This sprawling red and white building, built between 1899 and 1905, dominates the northern part of the town as you leave by the A379 towards Kingsbridge. Though on land, the jargon of a ship is still used throughout the building. Several members of the Royal family have received their training here, including Princes Charles and Andrew, Prince Philip, George VI and Edward VIII. Earlier, King George V and his brother lived in the old sailing ships, which were known as 'wooden-wallers'. The **Britannia Museum** tells the history of the college, from its beginnings in the mid 19th century and through the building of the college to the present day, and a gift shop sells memorabilia.

Museum occupies the ground floor. The museum has an excellent collection of model ships, ships in bottles and a nostalgic selection of vintage photographs of the town. In one of the galleries King Charles II held court whilst stormbound in Dartmouth in 1671. Some of the unique features of this magnificent room are the original panelling and the superb plaster ceiling.

Two other buildings in Dartmouth should be mentioned. One is the railway station, possibly the only one in the world which has never seen a train. It was built by

Near the eastern boundary of the South Hams flows the enchanting River Dart, surely one of the loveliest of English rivers. Rising in the great blanket bog of the moor, the Dart flows for 46 miles and together with its tributaries drains the greater part of Dartmoor. Queen Victoria called the Dart the "English Rhine", perhaps thinking of the twin castles of Dartmouth and Kingswear that guard its estuary. It was her ancestor, Alfred the Great who developed Dartmouth as a strategic base and the town's long connection with the senior service is reflected in the presence here of the Royal Naval College. The spectacular harbour is still busy with naval vessels, pleasure boats and ferries, and particularly colourful during the June **Carnival** and the **Dartmouth Regatta** in late August.

The most picturesque approach to the town is to drive to Kingswear and then take one of the two car ferries for the 10 minute trip across the river. Parking space in Dartmouth is severely restricted and it is strongly recommended that you make use of the Park & Ride facility located just outside the town on the A3122.

STOKE FLEMING

16 miles SE of Totnes on the A379

Stoke Fleming is one of the most delightful villages in the South Hams, perched high on the cliffs 300 feet above Start Bay and with a prominent church that has served generations of mariners as a reassuring landmark. Inside is a brass of 1351 which is reckoned to be one of the oldest in Devon and another which commemorates the great-grandfather of the celebrated engineer, Thomas Newcomen. Less than a mile from the village are the misleadingly-named **Blackpool Sands**, a broad crescent of sandy beach overhung by Monterey pines. Set in an unspoilt and sheltered bay, the sands are an ideal family beach as there is swimming in clean water, sandpits, a boating pond, a bathing

raft and a beach café along with beachside shops.

HARBERTON

2 miles SW of Totnes off the A2381

This delightful village is regarded as absolutely typical of the South Hams, a place where those two traditional centres of English village life, church and inn, sit comfortably almost side by side. **St Andrew's Church**, which is famous for its amazing, fantastically-carved, 15th century altar screen, has been closely linked to the village hostelry for almost 900 years. Church House Inn, as the name suggests, was originally built to house the masons working on the church around AD1100. Harberton was then a major centre for church administration and a much more important place than Totnes. The inn became the Chantry House for the monks, the civil servants of their time, and what is now the bar comprised their Great Hall, chapel and workshop where they would congregate for a glass of wine.

Blackpool Sands, Stoke Fleming

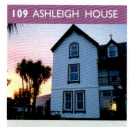

109 ASHLEIGH HOUSE

Kingsbridge

This beautiful Victorian house provides an excellent base from which to explore the South of Devon.

 see page 219

During the season, a popular excursion from Kingsbridge is the river cruise to Salcombe. Coastal cruises and private charter boats are also available.

In 1327 the Abbot handed the property over to the poor of the parish but it was not until 1950 that it passed out of the Church's hands altogether. During restoration work ancient plaster was removed to reveal massive beams of fluted mellow oak and a fine medieval screen. Other treasures discovered then were a Tudor window frame and a latticed window containing priceless panes of 13th century handmade glass. The inn's ecclesiastical connections are enhanced even more by the old pews from redundant churches which provide some of the seating.

KINGSBRIDGE

The broad body of water to the south of Kingsbridge is officially known as **Kingsbridge Estuary**, although strictly speaking it is not an estuary at all – no river runs into it – but a ria, or drowned valley. Whatever the correct name, it provides an attractive setting for this busy little town, an agreeable spot in which to spend an hour or two strolling along the quayside or through the narrow alleys off Fore Street bearing such graphic names as Squeezebelly Lane.

In Fore Street is St Edmund's parish church, mostly 13th century, and well known for the rather cynical verse inscribed on the gravestone of Roger Phillips who died in 1798:

> *Here lie I at the chancel door*
> *Here lie I because I'm poor*
> *The further in the more you pay*
> *Here lie I as warm as they.*

Nearby is **The Shambles**, an Elizabethan market arcade whose late-18th century upper floor is supported on six sturdy granite pillars. The town's rather modest Victorian Town Hall has an unusual onion-shaped clock tower that adds a touch of glamour to the building. Beyond the church, the former Kingsbridge Grammar School, founded in 1670, now houses the **Cookworthy Museum of Rural Life**, named after William Cookworthy who was born at Kingsbridge in 1705. Working as an apothecary at Plymouth, William encountered traders from the Far East who had brought back porcelain from China. English pottery makers despaired of ever producing such delicate cups and plates, but Cookworthy identified the basic ingredient of porcelain as kaolin, huge deposits of which lay in the hills just north of Plymouth. Ever since then, the more common name for kaolin has been China clay. The museum tells the story of the town along with re-creations of a 17th century schoolroom, a Victorian kitchen and an Edwardian pharmacy.

AROUND KINGSBRIDGE

TORCROSS

7 miles E of Kingsbridge on the A379

Normally, the four-mile stretch of sand and shingle beach near Torcross is too extensive to ever become crowded but back in 1943 things were very different. The beach had been selected by the Allied Commanders for a "dress rehearsal" of the impending D-Day invasion of Normandy. The area was swarming with troops and because live ammunition was being used in the training exercise, all the local people were evacuated, more than 3000 of them from seven coastal villages.

Those D-Day preparations are recalled at Torcross where a Sherman tank recovered from the sea in 1984 is on display in the car park. While the exercises were in progress, an enemy E-boat attacked the landing forces and more than 600 Allied servicemen lost their lives. Beside the tank are memorial tablets to the men who died during this little-publicised military tragedy, and to the many who later perished on the Normandy beaches.

SLAPTON

8 miles E of Kingsbridge off the A379

To the south of Slapton, the A379 runs for 2.5 miles along the top of a remarkable sand and shingle bank which divides the salt water of Start Bay from the fresh water of Slapton Ley, the largest natural lake in Devon. Continually replenished by three small rivers, this shallow body of water is a designated Nature Reserve and home to large numbers of freshwater fish, insects, water-loving plants and native and migrating birds. The **Slapton Ley Field Study Centre**, located in Slapton village, has leaflets detailing the delightful circular nature trails through this fascinating Site of Special Scientific Interest.

An obelisk on the beach near Slapton, presented in 1954 by the US Army authorities to the people of the South Hams, commemorates the period in 1943 when the beach was used by Allied troops as a "dress rehearsal" for the D-Day landings. The story is well told in Leslie Thomas's novel *The Magic Army*.

CHIVELSTONE

7 miles SE of Kingsbridge off the A379

Even in Devon it would be hard to find anywhere further away from the madding crowd than Chivelstone, an unassuming village hidden away in a maze of country lanes in the extreme southwest of the county and well worth seeking out. It's the tranquil rural surroundings that make Chivelstone so appealing but the village also has a fine parish church, the only one in England dedicated to the 4th century pope, St Sylvester. Historically, Sylvester is a misty figure but an old tradition claims that his saintly ministrations cured the Roman emperor, Constantine, of leprosy. Chivelstone church was built at a time (the 15th century) when this disfiguring disease was still common in England: it seems likely the parishioners hoped that by dedicating their church to him, St Sylvester would protect them from the ravages of a deeply feared illness which, once contracted, imposed total social exclusion on its innocent victims.

110 PORT LIGHT

Bolberry Down

Beautifully located hotel, restaurant and bar offering excellent home-cooked food and comfortable en suite rooms.

 see page 221

111 THE LODGE HOTEL & SAINTS RESTAURANT

Malborough

This fresh and comfortable hotel is the ideal holiday destination.

  see page 222

134

BEESANDS

8 miles SE of Kingsbridge off the A379

Beesands lies little more than a mile due south of Torcross and can easily be reached on foot along the coast path. By car, a four mile detour is required. If you don't want to walk, it's well worth negotiating the narrow Devon lanes to reach this tiny hamlet, just a single row of old cottages lining the foreshore of Start Bay. Less than 100 years ago, Beesands was a busy little fishing village. There are photographs from the 1920s showing fishermen who have drawn their boats laden with lobster, crab and mullet up the beach virtually to their cottage doors. Sadly, the fishing fleet is no longer operating but the mile-long shingle beach is as appealing as ever.

HALLSANDS

11 miles SE of Kingsbridge off the A379

South of Beesands, the only way to follow the coastline is by a well-trodden footpath. It's part of the South West Coast Path and the route takes you through the ruined village of Hallsands which was almost completely demolished by a violent storm in January 1917. Another mile or so further brings you to the lighthouse at **Start Point**, built in 1836, and open to visitors from Monday to Saturday during daylight hours. And if you want to be able to boast that you once stood at the most southerly point in Devon, continue along the Coast Path for about five miles to

Prawle Point, an ancient lookout site where today there is a Coastguard Station.

MALBOROUGH

5 miles S of Kingsbridge on the A381

For anyone travelling this corner of the South Hams, the lofty spire of Malborough's 15th century church is a recurrent landmark. It's a broach spire, rising straight out of the low tower. Inside, the church is wonderfully light, so much so that the splendid arcades built in Beer stone seem to glow.

About half a mile to the east of Malborough, just off the A381, is an outstanding example of a medieval farmhouse. **Yarde** is a Grade I listed manor farm with an Elizabethan bakery and a Queen Anne farmhouse. This is a privately owned working farm but Yarde can be visited on Sunday afternoons from Easter to the end of September, and by groups at any time by arrangement.

SALCOMBE

7 miles S of Kingsbridge, on the A381

Standing at the mouth of the Kingsbridge "estuary", the captivating town of Salcombe enjoys one of the most beautiful natural settings in the country. Sheltered from the prevailing westerly winds by steep hills, it also basks in one of the mildest micro-climates in England. In the terraced gardens rising from the water's edge, it's not unusual to see mimosa, palms, and even orange and lemon trees bearing fruit. The peaceful gardens at **Overbecks**

Museum & Garden (National Trust), overlooking Salcombe Bar, have an almost Mediterranean character. Otto Overbeck, who lived in the charming Edwardian house here between 1918 and 1937, amassed a wide-ranging collection that includes late-19th century photographs of the area, local shipbuilding tools, model boats, toys and much more.

Like other small South Devon ports, Salcombe developed its own special area of trading. Whilst Dartmouth specialised in French and Spanish wine, at Salcombe high-sailed clippers arrived carrying the first fruits of the pineapple harvest from the West Indies, and oranges from the Azores. That traffic has ceased, but pleasure craft throng the harbour and a small fishing fleet still operates from **Batson Creek**, a picturesque location where the fish quay is piled high with lobster creels. The town's seafaring history is interestingly evoked in the **Salcombe Maritime & Local History Museum** in the old Customs House on the quay.

The coastline to the south and west of Salcombe, some of the most magnificent in Britain, is now largely owned by the National Trust. Great slanting slabs of gneiss and schist tower above the sea, making the clifftop walk here both literally and metaphorically breathtaking. At **Bolt Head**, the rock forms a jagged promontory protruding onto the western approaches to the Kingsbridge estuary, and further west, the spectacular cliffs between Bolt Head and **Bolt Tail** are

interrupted by a steep descent at Soar Mill Cove.

HOPE COVE

6 miles SW of Kingsbridge off the A381

There are two Hopes here: Outer Hope, which is more modern and so gets less attention, and Inner Hope which must be one of the most photographed villages in the country. A picturesque huddle of thatched cottages around a tiny cobbled square, Inner Hope once thrived on pilchard fishing but nowadays only a few fishermen still operate from here, bringing in small catches of lobster and crab.

THURLESTONE

5 miles W of Kingsbridge off the A381

One of the most attractive coastal villages, Thurlestone can boast not just one, but two beaches, separated by a headland. Both beaches are recommended, especially the one to the south with its view of the pierced, or "thyrled", stone, the offshore rock

Bolt Head, nr Salcombe

135

from which the settlement gets its name and which was specifically mentioned in a charter of AD846. The village itself stands on a long, flat-topped ridge above the beaches and is an attractive mixture of flower-decked cottages, old farm buildings and long-established shops and inns.

BANTHAM

6 miles W of Kingsbridge off the A379

One mile to the north of Thurlestone (as the crow flies) is another fine sandy beach, at Bantham. This small village has a long history since it was a centre of early tin trading between the ancient Britons and the Gauls. By the 8th century, Anglo-Saxons were well-established here, farming the fertile soil. The sea also provided a major source of income in the form of pilchard fishing. Bantham continued to be a busy little port until the early 1900s with sailing

South Sands Ferry and Sea Tractor, Bigbury on Sea

barges bringing coal and building stone for the surrounding area.

BIGBURY ON SEA

10 miles W of Kingsbridge on the B3392

This popular family resort has a stretch of National Trust coastline and extensive sands. The most interesting attraction here though is **Burgh Island** which is actually only a part-time island. When the tide is out, it is possible to walk across the sandbar linking it to the mainland. At other times, visitors reach the island by a unique **Sea Tractor**, specifically designed for this crossing. It can operate in 7 feet of water, in all but the roughest conditions, and it's well worth timing your visit to enjoy this novel experience.

The whole of the 28-acre island, complete with its 14th century Pilchard Inn, was bought in 1929 by the eccentric millionaire Archibald Nettlefold. He built an extravagant Art Deco hotel which attracted such visitors as Noel Coward, the Duke of Windsor and Mrs Wallis Simpson, and Agatha Christie. The "Queen of Crime" used the island as the setting for two of her novels, *Ten Little Niggers,* (later renamed *And Then There Were None*), and *Evil Under the Sun.* The hotel, which has been described as "a white Art Deco cruise liner beached on dry land" is still in operation, its wonderful 1930s décor meticulously renovated in the 1990s.

AVETON GIFFORD

5 miles NW of Kingsbridge on the A379

Pronounced "Awton Jiffard", this

pleasant small village, little more than one main street, had one of the oldest churches in Devon until it was almost completely destroyed by a German bomb in 1943. The modern replacement is surprisingly satisfying but not in the same class as the buildings designed by the village's most famous son. Robert Macey was born here in 1790, the son of a mason. After learning his father's trade, he also studied as an architect. He then walked all the way to London where he successfully established himself and was responsible for designing many hospitals, factories, churches and theatres, of which the most notable were the Adelphi and the Haymarket.

At the southern end of the village, just before the three-quarter-mile long medieval causeway, a lane on the right is signposted to Bigbury. This very narrow road runs right alongside the River Avon and is very beautiful, but be warned – the river is tidal here and when the tide is in the two fords along the way are impassable.

LODDISWELL

3 miles NW of Kingsbridge off the A379

After the Norman Conquest, Loddiswell became part of the 40,000 acre estate of **Judhel of Totnes**, a man with an apparently insatiable appetite for salmon. Instead of rent, he stipulated that his tenants should provide him with a certain number of the noble fish: Loddiswell's contribution was set at 30 salmon a year.

The benign climate of South Devon has encouraged several viticulturists to plant vineyards in the area. The first vines at **Loddiswell Vineyard** were planted in 1977 and since then its wines have been laden with awards from fellow wine-makers and consumer bodies. Visitors are welcome, Monday to Saturday.

MODBURY

9 miles NW of Kingsbridge on the A379

Modbury's main street climbs steeply up the hillside, its pavement raised above street level and stepped. The many Georgian buildings give this little town an air of quiet elegance and the numerous antique, craft and specialist shops add to its interest. **St George's Church** contains some impressive, if damaged, effigies of the Prideaux and Champernowne families; the White Hart and Assembly Rooms are 18th century, the Exeter Inn even older. Once a coaching inn, this inviting old pub dates back to the 1500s.

Modbury's Fair Week in early May is a jolly affair, though perhaps not as riotous as it was in the 19th century when it lasted for nine days and the town's 10 inns stayed open from morning to night.

In May 2006 this quiet little town sparked off a green campaign that attracted national attention. It was masterminded by Rebecca Hoskins, a young Modbury-born-and-raised wildlife camerawoman who was appalled by the appalling plastic bag pollution she found and filmed in remote parts of the Pacific Ocean, On her return to Devon she found the sea equally infested. She called a meeting of all 43 Modbury shop-owners, showed them her film, and convinced them to stop handing out plastic bags to customers. More than 3 years later, the town is still a plastic-bag-free area and throughout the country major supermarkets have followed the example set by this modest little town.

Accommodation, Food & Drink
and Places of Interest

T he establishments featured in this section includes hotels, inns, guest houses, bed & breakfasts, restaurants, cafes, tea and coffee shops, tourist attractions and places to visit. Each establishment has an entry number which can be used to identify its location at the beginning of the relevant chapter or its position in this section.

In addition full details of all these establishments and many others can be found on the Travel Publishing website - www.travelpublishing.co.uk. This website has a comprehensive database covering the whole of Britain and Ireland.

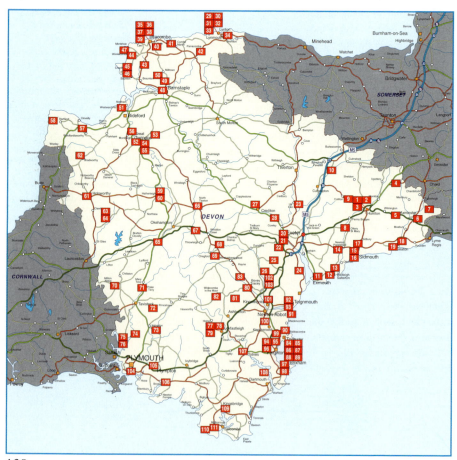

DEVON

2   THE THREE TUNS

133 High Street, Honiton,
Devon EX14 1HR
Tel: 01404 42902
e-mail: ruth_pearce@live.co.uk

The Three Tuns is situated in a central location in Honiton, inviting both visitors and locals alike in to the warm and welcoming atmosphere that has been offering great food and drink for the last 20 years.

Andy and Ruth Pearce are managers of this 17th century coach house , it boasts many traditional features, such as exposed beams, whilst also having a cosy and homely feel. Andy and Ruth have been providing top quality and wonderfully prepared food for many years, always using local produce, ensuring that each dish is as fresh as possible. You wont find any packaged foods here either, just home cooking and an extensive menu, including the well renowned steaks.

Open from 10am-11pm Monday to Saturday and 12pm-6pm on Sundays, food is available from 12-2pm and 6-9pm. There are jacket potatoes with wonderful toppings, such as brie and bacon and prawn marie rose and sandwiches with home cooked beef and cheese and onion for those wishing to have a light snack at lunch time. Breakfasts are also served during the lunch period, the large seeing two pieces of bacon, two eggs, two sausages, hash brown and more on one plate for just £5.95- a breakfast fit for a king. The main menu has a great variety of dishes, to suit all tastes. Starters include homemade soups daily, whitebait with bread and butter and a gorgeous platter of hot 'n' kicking wings with sweet chilli or garlic dip. Main courses have a tremendous amount of homemade dishes, including cottage pie, chicken tikka masala, steak and kidney pie and liver, bacon and onions. There is also an array of meats from the grill, steaks with all the trimmings, gammon, quarter pound burgers and there is even a choice of seafood, with fishcakes, salmon and prawn salad and the ever traditional home beer battered cod.

If you still have room after the main course, there is a splendidly English dessert menu, featuring treacle sponge, apple crumble and stuffed backed apple pudding, which is divine. This can all be washed down with one of the lovely real ales available here. Menu is subject to change according to seasonal produce.

DEVON

1 THE COFFEE HOUSE

46 High Street, Honiton,
Devon EX14 1PG
Tel: 0140444816

Enjoying a prominent position in Honiton's High Street and open all year round, **The Coffee House** is a family run business offering a lot more than just coffee. Friendly owners, Lindsay and Teresa Norris have created a popular venue catering for all tastes. The bright and welcoming interior has seating for 60

while the pretty courtyard tea garden seats an additional 12. Using fresh local produce whenever possible, The Coffee House offers a wide range of breakfasts, snacks, baguettes, sandwiches and homemade lunches as well as cream teas and homemade cakes. This little gem is open from Mon-Sat, 9.00am-4.30pm and is closed on Sundays and bank holidays.

3 ALLHALLOWS MUSEUM

High Street, Honiton, Devon EX14 1PG
Tel: 01404 44966
e-mail: info@honitonmuseum.co.uk
website: www.honitonmuseum.co.uk

The building housing the museum is the oldest in Honiton, dating from 1327. It started life as part of a chapel when people from the 'new town' grew tired of climbing the hill to St. Michael's. They got permission for a chapel in the town centre and called it All Saints or Allhallows. The first gallery is the chancel of the chapel, which was shortened last century to make

room for St. Paul's, just outside. Fifty years ago the chapel was bought by the townspeople and opened as a museum. It has three galleries, Murch, Nicoll and Norman, in which are housed selections of an extensive lace collection as well as local antiquities.

4 THE OLD VICARAGE

Yarcombe, nr Honiton,
Devon EX14 9BD
Tel: 01404 861594
e-mail: jonannstockwell@aol.com
website:
www.theoldvicarageyarcombe.co.uk

Jon and Ann Stockwell have been the owners of **The Old Vicarage** for 10 years now and the warm welcome received when walking through the door is testament to the experience that comes with time in the hospitality trade. The Old Vicarage is set amongst the spectacular scenery of the Yarty valley in East Devon and welcomes all visitors to the area. The red brick built premises were constructed in the 19th century and the landscaped gardens along with the 800 year old church complete the stunning surroundings. The interior does not disappoint either, decorated in a Georgian style; many of the original features remain and create a classy atmosphere to stay in. There are four rooms available in this B & B and they are all spacious, comfortable and one

even has a **four poster bed** for those romantic nights away from home. The tariff includes a full English breakfast and all tastes are catered for. The B & B also boasts a pool table in the games room, ample parking, an elegant dining room, guests lounge and an excellent BBQ area.

141

5 BURROW FARM GARDENS

Dalwood, near Axminster,
Devon EX13 7ET
Tel: 01404 831285
website: www.burrowfarmgardens.co.uk

The beautifully landscaped ten-acre gardens of **Burrow Farm Gardens** were created over the last 40 years by Mary Benger and will appeal to both plantsmen and those seeking a relaxing walk around a tranquil landscape that also offers extensive views. The gardens include a fascinating woodland garden created in an ancient Roman clay pit and the most recent addition – Millennium mill garden. Sweeping lawns lead between island beds of unusual shrubs and herbaceous plants down to the lake whilst the pergola walk features old roses and

herbaceous plants. The terrace and courtyard gardens feature later summer flowering plants. Burrow Farm Gardens has been awarded star status in the Good Gardens Guide.

6 CASTLE INN

Castle Hill, Axminster, Devon EX13 5NN
Tel: 01297 34944

Situated in the ancient market town of Axminster, the **Castle Inn** is a pleasant town centre pub, offering an extensive range of wines, spirits and ales, but most importantly a warm welcome. The main bar/lounge is a comfortable traditional room with a pool table, darts board and state of the art jukebox. Bar food is served

Monday to Friday 12-2pm, on Thursday meals are buy one get one free. An enclosed rear courtyard makes for an ideal smoking area. Dogs are allowed in the public bar on a lead. Come along soon to this friendly pub.

7 THE OLD INN

Hawkchurch, Axminster,
Devon EX13 5XD
Tel: 01297 678309
e-mail: oldinn@hawkchurch.com
website: www.hawkchurch.com

The Old Inn in Hawkchurch certainly lives up to its name since it was first built in the 1540s as a Church House, a place that provided for festivities, the brewing and dispensing of ale, and accommodation for the rector's manor tenants. Strangely, in 1806 that building was

deliberately burned down, along with the parish poorhouse and three or four adjoining cottages. It was then rebuilt and has continued to be an inn ever since. It is now the home of Ricky and Jean Woodham who extend a warm welcome to all to wine and dine in their atmospheric old hostelry.

In their cosy and friendly bar which looks out to the village church, they offer a range of traditional ales from local producers along with a good choice of wholesome and appetising meals including many home-made and freshly prepared dishes. Food is served every lunchtime and evening, except Sunday evening.

The inn also offers 3-star en suite accommodation in 3 attractively furnished and decorated rooms charmingly located in a secure courtyard to the rear of the inn. If you prefer self-catering, a 2-bedroom cottage is available.

8 VOLUNTEER INN

Broad Street, Ottery St Mary,
Devon EX11 1BZ
Tel: 01404 811755
e-mail: bealeworthy1@yahoo.co.uk
website: www.volunteerinnottery.co.uk

Few things are as welcoming as a real fire, and the **Volunteer Inn** feels genuinely warm and homely. The pub was built in approximately 1670, and to the back of the building is a courtyard access under an original arch (part of the coach house), which was a recruiting station for volunteer soldiers for the Napoleonic War, hence its name. Open for food and drinks including real ale, keg beer, lagers, ciders and wines. Food is available daily from 12 noon until 2.30p.m, 6 - 8.30pm Monday-Saturday, and 12 noon until 3p.m on Sundays when a delicious home cooked Sunday lunch is added to the menu.

Bed and Breakfast is also available so you can come and enjoy Ottery and the surrounding areas with a cosy base to explore from. Accommodation consists of a large

family room as well as two smaller rooms complete with shower facilities. A fantastic time to book accommodation here, is on November 5th, Guy Fawkes night, when the town becomes host to the famous Flaming Tar Barrels. For reasons lost in antiquity, local born residents carry flaming tar barrels on their backs through the streets...and the crowd! Its seriously hot stuff and the pub is ideally situated for the night as it sits smack bang in the middle of it all.

9 RIDGEWAY FARM

Awliscombe, Honiton, Devon EX14 3PY
Tel: 01404 841331 Fax: 01404 841119
e-mail: jessica@ridgewayfarm.co.uk
website: www.smoothhound.co.uk/hotels/
ridgewayfarm

Set in an area of outstanding natural beauty with stunning views, **Ridgeway Farm** is a traditional 18th century farmhouse with cosy, comfortable accommodation, decorated to a high standard. The farm is a peaceful retreat situated on the outskirts of Awliscombe, 3 miles from the market town of Honiton and tucked away from the hustle and bustle of everyday life. The road through the village leads to an Iron Age settlement of Hembury Fort where you can enjoy quiet walks. There is much to admire at Ridgeway Farm, not least of which being the genuine and inclusive hospitality which has such a positive impact upon the guest experience.

10 OLD BRIDWELL HOLIDAY COTTAGES

Bridwell Avenue, Uffculme,
Devon EX15 3BU
Tel: 01884 841464
e-mail: Jackie@oldbridwell.co.uk
website: www.oldbridwell.co.uk

Set deep in the glorious Devon countryside and in the quiet hamlet of Old Bridwell, these holiday cottages are the perfect location from which to explore the Devon Heartland. In the past cider production was an integral part of rural life and some of the cottages were originally used for the storage of apples, barrels and straw for the farm brew. Locally made cider can still be purchased nearby today.

In the 1980's the original estate was divided into two parts. Bridwell Park with its parkland, ornamental lakes and resident deer herd was separated from the old farmstead which then became Old Bridwell. It was transformed into idyllic holiday cottages and includes the ancient walled fruit garden which is a wonderful place to relax. **Old Bridwell Holiday Cottages** are easy to find being just five minutes from junction 27 of the M5. The little villages of Exmoor and Dartmoor are a short drive and the dramatic coast of North Devon only an hour away. The lovely South Devon beaches are just a 40 minute drive.

The nearby village of Uffculme, placed upon the banks of the river Culme, provides some picturesque walks and has a rich history. It's Cold Harbour Mill, which has in the past been a paper mill, corn mill, and more recently a woollen mill is still a working mill spinning wool from local alpacas. It has a museum which is a great place to absorb some of this rich history.

To really experience the ambience of a traditional Devonshire village and the timeless countryside a stay in one of the authentic country cottages at Old Bridwell is a must.. There are 10 self-catering cottages in total, all can sleep up to six people, and some can accommodate eight, making them perfect for family holidays. Smaller parties are also welcome at discounted rates. They are individually decorated and furnished, with their own special touches, so a return trip can be a charmingly new experience. They are all fully equipped with everything that you would expect to find at home and are centrally heated for out of season breaks. Some have private rear gardens and all have patios with furniture for relaxing when you are not out exploring the pretty countryside and the many and varied local attractions. Small pets are welcome and the cottages are available all year round.

11 THE STRAND COFFEE HOUSE

**49 The Strand, Exmouth,
Devon EX8 1AL
Tel: 01395 273439**

Just 4 minutes from the beach, in the lovely seaside town of Exmouth is the traditional tearoom **The Strand Coffee House.** Offering delicious homemade cakes, scones and soups, this friendly property is popular with locals, tourists and many coach day-trippers, coming to visit the surrounding areas.

Hosts Sheila and Roger provide a great menu for 30 covers inside and a further 16 outside. There are a great variety of speciality teas, including herbal and fragrant as well as a simple traditional English. The food served is a fantastic price and value and includes soups served with a buttered roll, breakfasts, for all appetites and a large selection of dishes such as omelettes, macaroni cheese and chicken curry. There is also a selection of lighter bites, such as sandwiches and jacket potatoes. The coffees are popular here

and see specialities such as cappuccino, latte and mocha, as well as American, café au lait and a regular filter or decaffeinated coffee.

The Strand Coffee House is located in a wonderful location, just a few minutes from the splendid shopping area, making this business a great one to visit after an afternoon of shopping.

12 TEA AND TITTLE TATTLE

**2 Fore St, Budleigh Salterton,
Devon EX9 6NG
Tel: 01395 443203**

Steaming teapots, homemade cakes and lashings of scones with clotted cream; are just some of the delights from this Devonshire tearoom. Having fast become a Budleigh Salterton staple – **Tea and Tittle Tattle**, as the name suggests, are rather into their hot beverages and merry conversation.

Owners, Denise and Gareth have created a popular destination with locals and a welcome stop off point for many visitors to this unspoilt seaside town. The reasons aren't hard to find - quick friendly service, quality food at affordable prices and a warm, inviting atmosphere. Open for breakfast, lunch and afternoon tea.

Denise makes all of the delicious cakes and desserts as well as the scones which are baked fresh daily. The lunch menu changes daily and there is always a good choice of hearty homemade dishes including pies, roasts, casseroles and salads – all made on the premises using fresh locally sourced produce.

On Sundays, traditional roast lunches with all the trimmings are added to the menu, so popular are these that advanced booking is recommended. Here you can also enjoy a chilled glass of Chardonnay or Merlot to compliment your meal since the tearoom is fully licensed.

13 FANCY THAT

Lower Budleigh, East Budleigh,
Devon EX9 7DL
Tel: 01395 445919

Next to Bicton gardens and close to the sea is the ever so tropical and traditionally Caribbean **Fancy That**. Set in the countryside, in a village famous for being the home of Sir Walter Raleigh, this stone built., historical building oozes charm and character, whilst also offering a fun and friendly atmosphere.

Janice Voce is the host here and she is famous for growing her own traditional fruits- so much so that she featured in the *Western Morning News*. Her passion is food and she provides a

tremendous Caribbean menu with traditions such as jerk chicken, curried mutton, cream of peanut soup, served with jonny cake and rice and peas. As well as a vegetarian aubergine in coconut rundown sauce, which is divine. Fancy That caters for special dietary requirements, such as gluten free, dairy free and for diabetics, meaning that this business is suitable for all. Lighter bites such as sandwiches, breakfasts and cream teas are also available.

The opening times are Tuesday-Sunday from 9.30am- 5pm and in the evenings on a Friday and Saturday from 6.30pm- 9.30pm.

14 SOUTHERN CROSS GUEST HOUSE & TEA ROOMS

Newton Poppleford, nr Sidmouth,
Devon EX10 0DU
Tel: 01395 568439
e-mail: timothy.flaher@btconnect.com
website: www.southerncrossdevon.co.uk

The **Southern Cross Guest House** offers award winning bed and breakfast accommodation in its historic 14th century thatched cottage, constructed of cob, wattle and dorb, oak beams and thatch roof. Situated just a few miles from Sidmouth with World Heritage Coast Status, the Southern Cross Guest

House is ideally located to allow you to enjoy all that this historic town and the surrounding area has to offer.

There are five stylish bedrooms to choose from, most with en-suite facilities, colour TV, well-stocked complimentary beverage refreshment tray, ironing facilities, hair dryer and radio alarm clock. A substantial breakfast is served in the elegant dining room and of course includes a traditional full English breakfast.

The cottage is also home to the celebrated **Southern Cross Tea Rooms** founded in the 1950's by an Irish actress called Eileen McKenna. This dynamic lady created 'The Cream Tea Experience' that has won international fame and become part of the Devonshire Heritage. Savour an intriguing mix of the rustic and the elegant in the charming, low beamed tea room, with its hotch-potch of antique tables, or in the lounge, where a fire once burned on the floor, giving warmth to both man and beast.

15 THE LONGHOUSE BED & BREAKFAST

Salcombe Hill Road, Sidmouth,
Devon EX10 0NY
Tel: 01395 577973
e-mail: pvcia@aol.com
website: www.holidaysinsidmouth.co.uk

The Longhouse B&B, formerly a part of the Norman Lockyer Observatory, has been lovingly restored into a beautiful home. Lynne and Pete Vincent have since 2003 updated the house to include the benefits of modern living and this has been reflected in its second five star rating and silver award by Visit Britain.

Surrounded by woodland, the Longhouse sits just below the top of Salcombe hill, at six hundred feet above sea level, with views across Sid Bay and Sidmouth town. Only a five-minute stroll from the Jurassic Coast path makes it an ideal place for ardent walkers. Just under a mile from the town centre and sea front puts it in easy touch with the town's facilities. Though the acre of landscaped gardens provides a peaceful haven to relax in.

Both double rooms are on ground level with easy access, have recently been fully refurbished and are gas centrally heated. Each has en suite shower, towels and linen supplied, TV/DVD and full tea/coffee making facilities. A range of films are available.

Breakfast is cooked in the Aga, using fresh local produce, and served daily from 8 a.m. to 9.30 a.m. During the summer months you may like to take the option of enjoying breakfast in one of many seating areas around the garden. The gardens combine both formal and woodland in just over an acre of ground and are constantly a work in progress. For those enthusiasts all advice will be gratefully received.

It would be difficult to mention the Longhouse without giving a moments thought to its interesting history. Built in 1912 by Sir Norman Lockyer as a part of the Hill Top Observatory, it served as office, laboratory and library. When astrophysics was at it's most popular in the late 1930's it employed ten full time scientists and won international acclaim. Since it's decline in the mid 1970's the Norman Lockyer Observatory has been restored and with a growing enthusiastic membership is open to the public throughout the year.

A warm welcome is guaranteed, please phone and speak to Lynne or Pete Vincent for further booking information, tariff and availability.

16 NORMAN LOCKYER OBSERVATORY

Sidmouth, Devon   EX10 0YQ
Tel: 01395 512096
website: www.normanlockyer.org

There are few public access observatories in Britain; the **Norman Lockyer Observatory** has a planetarium and large telescopes, including those used to discover helium and establish the sciences of astrophysics. Lockyer's achievements include the establishment of meteorology, astro-archaeology, the science journal, Nature, the Science Museum and government departments for Science and Education. The radio station commemorates the contribution of Sir Ambrose Fleming, a local hero, to the invention of the radio valve. Programme of public events available on the website above.

HIDDEN PLACES GUIDES

Explore Britain and Ireland with *Hidden Places* guides - a fascinating series of national and local travel guides.

Packed with easy to read information on hundreds of places of interest as well as places to stay, eat and drink.

Available from both high street and internet booksellers

For more information on the full range of *Hidden Places* guides and other titles published by Travel Publishing visit our website on

www.travelpublishing.co.uk
or ask for our leaflet by phoning
01752 697280   or emailing
info@travelpublishing.co.uk

findSOMEWHERE.CO.UK

For people who want to explore Britain and Ireland

Places to Stay

Our easy-to use website contains details and locations of places to stay, places to eat and drink, specialist shops and places of interest throughout England, Wales, Scotland and Ireland.

Places to Stay:	**Places to Eat and Drink:**	**Places of Interest:**	**Specialist Shops:**	**Gardens:**
Hotels, guest accommodation, bed & breakfast, inns, self-catering accommodation	Restaurants, pubs, inns, cafes, tea rooms	Historic buildings, gardens, art galleries, museums, nature parks, wildlife parks, indoor and outdoor activities	Fashion shops, art and craft shops, gift shops, food and drink shops, antique shops, jewellery shops	Garden centres and retail nurseries

17 ROSE COTTAGE

Greenhead, Sidbury, Sidmouth,
Devon EX10 0RH
Tel: 01395 597357
e-mail: roz.kendal@btinternet.com
website: www.rosecottagesidbury.co.uk

Boasting a Visit Britain Quality in Tourism rating of four stars, **Rose Cottage** is a delightful 17th century former estate house office that is now a comfortable family-run guest house. It is located in the picturesque village of Sidbury, just two miles from the Regency coastal town of Sidmouth with its award-winning gardens and clean safe beaches. The East Devon Way passes through the village and the surrounding countryside is an Area of Outstanding Beauty. Rose Cottage provides an ideal base from which to explore the Jurassic Coast (a World Heritage Site), and the neighbouring towns and villages of East Devon.

Rose Cottage has recently been refurbished and is attractively decorated with lots of original artwork and several charming dolls houses. Outside, there is around an acre of gardens and an orchard from which there are enchanting views of the East Devon countryside.

Owner Roslyn Kendall takes pride in offering her guests a delicious Full English Breakfast and Buffet which will set you up for the day. Roslyn also offers a four course dinner at which you will experience first class home cooking that makes use of the very best local produce such as Lyme Bay crab and local beef. Hearty Sunday lunches are also available and Roslyn is happy to cater for vegetarians and other special diets.

The accommodation at Rose Cottage comprises 6 attractively furnished and decorated rooms, all with en suite facilities and each equipped with a television, hair dryer and facilities for making hot drinks.

Rose Cottage has teamed up with 'Out To Play Golf' to offer guests the opportunity to play a selection of golf courses in Britain on a discounted Green Fee basis. Guests can enjoy Discounted Green Fees at participating golf courses with 'Out To Play Golf' discounted Green Fee vouchers! The vouchers entitle golfers to Green Fee savings ranging from 10% discount up to multi-player offers of 2 Green Fees for the price of 1!

Rose Cottage is open all year round; credit cards are accepted, but please note that the premises are unsuitable for children under 5 years of age.

18 THE HARBOUR INN

Church Street, Axmouth, Seaton,
Devon EX12 4AF
Tel: 01297 20371
e-mail: theharbourinn@live.co.uk
website: www.harbourinnaxmouth.co.uk

The Harbour Inn is a quintessential traditional English village pub set on the River Axe estuary, a famous and important bird migratory conservation area. The picturesque building is surrounded by hanging baskets, flower boxes and wonderful shrubbery, giving the property an intimate and inviting atmosphere to all who visit.. Typically from 12th century origins the exterior oozes charm and is eye-

catching from the thatched roof. The interior is old and traditional, with wooden floors, beams throughout and a fantastic 10 feet inglenook fireplace, perfect for colder evenings, intimate gatherings and the ancient custom of burning The Ashen Faggott every Christmas Eve.

Mark and Jan Baldaro have been running the premises since 2008, bringing their experience from pubs in Somerset and Cornwall, ably assisted by loyal and long-serving staff.

There is plenty of local activity here, including darts, boules and even a twin skittle alley, as well as occasional music and events, enjoyed by many tourists, campers and those in caravans and walkers, visiting the surrounding area. There are intentionally no juke boxes, piped music, games/ pool tables or fruit machines.

Whilst definitely a pub, not a gastro restaurant, dining is a main focus here, with 3 dining areas seating 18-30 covers in each, as well as a delightful patio/courtyard seating 40 and a luscious beer garden, seating up to another 75 people. There is also a (fully laid) 100 seat function room available to hire.

The main menu and specials boards change daily with everything sourced locally and made on the premises, including the wonderfully tempting desserts. There is always a good choice of locally caught fish and vegetarian dishes. The bar menu is a mixture of local and traditional favorites with the emphasis on quality and value.

Open 11am-3pm and 6pm-11pm everyday (Sundays 12-3pm and 6pm-10.30pm), with food served daily from 12-2pm and 6.30-9pm, The Harbour Inn is a place that caters for all. Suitable for disabled, children, with a small garden play area outside the Inn also welcomes well-behaved dogs.

150

19 BEAUMONT

Castle Hill, Seaton, Devon EX12 2QW
Tel: 01297 20832
e-mail: tony@lymebay.demon.co.uk
website: www.smoothhound.co.uk/hotels/
beaumont.html

Beaumont is a delightful Victorian guest house, which enjoys an unrivalled location in the charming, seaside town of Seaton. The bustling town is situated at the heart of the Jurassic Coast and bordered by a large area of outstanding natural beauty and a site of special scientific interest, which is popular among visitors. The tastefully decorated, child-friendly, guest house boasts fully en-suite bedrooms, which are all spacious and airy with many facilities, including a colour TV and clock radios. The first floor rooms have spectacular views overlooking Lyme Bay and the cliffs of Beer. Keen walkers can enjoy rural rambles and town walks and the more energetic can take on the 400 mile South Coast Walk. There are many attractions and activities in the vicinity with zoos, theme parks and private gardens to enjoy, as well as Seaton Bay.

Beaumont is close to Dorchester, Taunton and Exeter, allowing visitors to get a taste of more than one place. Tony and Jane Hill, who run the guest house, have a lot of local knowledge and will happily spend time advising guests on specialized restaurants and pubs in the area.

The guest house, close to the long and winding River Axe, does allow for small dogs to stay, but this has to be pre-arranged. There are National Trust estates to enjoy in the area as well as Seaton's own historical tramway. Close by is the fishing village of Beer and slightly further away are the great moorlands of Exmoor and Dartmoor to explore.

findSOMEWHERE.CO.uk

For people who want to explore Britain and Ireland

Places to Eat and Drink

Our easy-to use website contains details and locations of places to stay, places to eat and drink, specialist shops and places of interest throughout England, Wales, Scotland and Ireland.

Places to Stay:	**Places to Eat and Drink:**	**Places of Interest:**	**Specialist Shops:**	**Gardens:**
Hotels, guest accommodation, bed & breakfast, inns, self-catering accommodation	Restaurants, pubs, inns, cafes, tea rooms	Historic buildings, gardens, art galleries, museums, nature parks, wildlife parks, indoor and outdoor activities	Fashion shops, art and craft shops, gift shops, food and drink shops, antique shops, jewellery shops	Garden centres and retail nurseries

Montgomery House, 144 Fore Street,
Exeter EX4 3AN
Tel: 01392 678965

Fore Street, just off Exeter's High Street, is well known for its independent traders and quirky shops. It's here you'll find **Let's Do,** a distinctive and individual café occupying one of the few ancient buildings in Fore Street to have survived the World War II bombings.

Owner Ben Parry's extensive menu offers customers an appealing choice of dishes based on fresh, locally sourced ingredients. Start the day with one of the 20+ varieties of breakfast, ranging from the "full works" to a simple but tasty bowl of porridge with honey or brown sugar. Throughout the rest of the day, the choice includes home-made burgers, omelettes made with free range eggs, jacket potatoes, salads, hot and cold sandwiches and melts, and for tea-time some delicious cakes, muffins and cookies. The regular menu is supplemented by daily specials.

The hot drinks include Fairtrade and decaffeinated coffee, as well as several varieties of fresh leaf tea. If you prefer a cold drink, the choice ranges from fresh smoothies to iced tea.

Let's Do is open from 8am to 5pm, Monday to Friday; from 9am to 5pm on Saturday; and from 10am to 3pm on Sunday.

21 EXETER'S UNDERGROUND PASSAGES

Romangate Passage, Off High Street,
Exeter, Devon EX4 3PZ
Tel: 01392 665887
website: www.exeter.gov.uk

Dating from 14th century, the medieval passages under Exeter High Street are a unique ancient monument: no similar system of passages can be explored by the public elsewhere in Britain. They were built to house the pipes that brought fresh water to the city. Their purpose was simple: to bring clean drinking water from natural springs in fields lying outside the walled city, through lead pipes into the heart of the city. The pipes sometimes sprang leaks and repairs could only be carried out by digging them up as we do today. To avoid this disruption the passages were vaulted and it is down some of these vaulted passageways that visitors are guided.

HIDDEN PLACES GUIDES

Explore Britain and Ireland with *Hidden Places* guides - a fascinating series of national and local travel guides.

Packed with easy to read information on hundreds of places of interest as well as places to stay, eat and drink.

Available from both high street and internet booksellers

For more information on the full range of *Hidden Places* guides and other titles published by Travel Publishing visit our website on

www.travelpublishing.co.uk
or ask for our leaflet by phoning
01752 697280 or emailing
info@travelpublishing.co.uk

22 POACHERS INN

55 High Street, Ide, Devon EX2 9RW
Tel: 01392 273847
e-mail: tony@poachersinn.co.uk
website: www.poachersinn.co.uk

The **Poachers Inn** is a delightful village inn, situated on the outskirts of the popular Dartmoor city of Exeter. The inn has an air of the traditional about it, offering great food, well-kept local ales and a comfortable bed for the night if required. The landlord, Tony Steadman, has a keen interest in real ales and boasts an impressive knowledge about all things mead! The bar always has Branscombe Branoc and there will be four others available, mainly from Devon, Cornwall, Dorset and Somerset.

The premises themselves date back to the 16th century and the original slate roof is accentuated by the white washed walls and wrought iron details. The interior is exceptional; the main bar is a magnificent wooden example, adorned with real ale hand pumps and coasters of beers gone by! The bar area is an eclectic mix of comfortable chairs, wooden stools and old iron tables, all located near the open fireplace. Pictures and mirrors in charming frames adorn the walls, ensuring there is always something to pique your interest. The restaurant area is located just off the main bar and can be as social or relaxed as you like, there are tables in little cubby holes for a more relaxed evening, for the more social gatherings, the main dining room accommodates everybody. For the long summer evenings, there is an alfresco option, the well kept garden is enormous and boasts a spectacular view over Devon hills. The popular BBQ is available for private parties or even for hire, should you want to cook for yourself.

The menu is extensive and is created using the finest of locally sourced produced, even the bread is baked in house. Typifying the menu starters are deep fried crispy whitebait with tartare sauce, new season asparagus topped with a poached egg and celery and Cornish blue cheese soup. The mains are equally sumptuous; slow roasted pork belly with sage mash, seafood and fennel risotto and a fresh ostrich steak with crushed new potatoes are just some of the delicious dishes on offer. Lunch is served between 12 pm and 2.30 pm and dinner between 6 pm and 9.30 pm all year round and full sample menus are available on the Poachers Inn website. The restaurant is very popular so reservations are recommended to avoid disappointment.

The inn also provides accommodation; three well-appointed and comfortable rooms are available at reasonable prices all year round. The breakfast, supplied by Tony, has to be one of the best in England!

23 THE THREE TUNS

Exeter Road, Silverton, Devon EX5 4HX
Tel: 1392 860352
e-mail: the3tunsinn@aol.com
website: www.thethreetunsinn.com

Silverton is a pleasant large village which in medieval times was an important borough with its own weekly market and fair. In 1819 it was by-passed by what is now the A396 so it has been spared the worst of 21st century traffic. It's an attractive place with many cob and thatch buildings, including the delightful **Three Tuns** pub which dates back to the 1500s.

It's owned and run by the Pink family – Michael and his wife, who is the chef, their daughter and son-in-law. The low-beamed bar has an open fire and a choice of 4 permanent brews plus one guest ale. A major attraction at the Three Tuns is the excellent food on offer. The blackboard menu always includes good old English dishes such as Lamb Shank or grilled plaice fillet, along with more exotic offerings like the Mexican Chicken Sizzler. For vegetarians, there are options such as Vegetable Crumble or Leaf Spinach and 3 Cheese Lasagne. Everything, including the wonderful desserts, is freshly prepared to order.

If you are planning to stay in this scenic corner of the county, the Three Tuns has 4 attractively furnished and decorated rooms, all with en suite facilities. The inn accepts all major credit cards and there's a peaceful beer garden and ample off road parking.

*A visit to The Three Tuns will be
one you wish to repeat more than once.*

24 CHI RESTAURANT, BAR AND B&B

Fore Street, Kenton, Devon EX6 8LD
Tel: 01626 890213
e-mail: enquiries@chi-restaurant.co.uk
website: www.chi-restaurant.co.uk

If you would like to experience the authentic taste of the orient, make your way to Stephen and Sui Choy's outstanding **Chi Restaurant and Bar** in Kenton, just south of Exeter. The restaurant occupies a substantial former country pub which has been dazzlingly converted into a stylish restaurant with an understated oriental theme. Diners approach the restaurant by way of a peaceful garden with lily ponds and a fountain. Inside, the eye is immediately caught by the open kitchen which, as well as the popular favourites of Chinese cuisine, also provides the dishes you want but can never find in the South West - a delicious combination of classic and modern Chinese cuisine in a delightful contemporary setting.

Stephen is the Chef and has more than twenty years experience in preparing Oriental dishes using the finest fresh ingredients from scallops to local oysters. Where possible, he sources fresh local ingredients such as wild sea bass for his popular dish of Thai style sea bass. Stephen refuses to use colouring or that staple of some Chinese restaurants, MSG. Without compromising on quality, he does not need the use of flavour enhancers. Each dish is beautifully presented and accompanied by exquisite flowers and small animals expertly carved from different fruits - look out for the swan carved from apples.

Stephen specialises in fish dishes based on the 'catch of the day' - his lemon sole in Thai chilli sauce is particularly spectacular.

The restaurant's beautifully landscaped enclosed garden is lit in the evenings and creates an unforgettable atmosphere. It also provides the perfect location for special events such as parties, weddings or even business events.

Chi Restaurant also offers B&B accommodation in 5 comfortable en-suite bedrooms all with colour TV, tea/coffee making facilities with complimentary biscuits and mineral water, hair dryer, in-room safe, telephone, alarm clock\radio and free broadband internet access. A photo copying and fax service is available at a small charge. At breakfast, guests are offered the choice of a full English breakfast, or if you prefer something different, a Chinese breakfast of freshly steamed dim sum and Jasmine tea.

The restaurant is located just 6 miles south of Exeter and 5 miles from Dawlish on the edge of the Powderham Estate. Powderham Castle, the historic home of the Earl of Devon, built more than 600 years ago is just a few minutes walk away.

155

25 HALDON BELVEDERE (LAWRENCE CASTLE)

Higher Ashton, Exeter EX6 7QY
Tel: 01392 833668
e-mail: enquiries@haldonbelvedere.co.uk
website: www.haldonbelvedere.co.uk

Haldon Belvedere, also known as **Lawrence Castle** is situated in a secluded woodland spot on Haldon Hill, some six miles south of the cathedral city of Exeter. From its high vantage point, breathtaking views of the Exe Valley and the beautiful Devon countryside can be seen. Haldon Belvedere was built in 1788 by Sir Robert Palk in memory of his friend, Major-General Stringer Lawrence, credited to be the father of the Indian army. The building itself is triangular in shape, with turrets at each corner. One turret houses the spiral staircase which leads to the upper rooms and the roof terrace. The other turrets contain ante rooms at each level.

The ground floor room has been dedicated to Stringer Lawrence where one can see the original memorial tablets recording Lawrence's exploits, there is also a stone statue of the General which dominates the room from the centre. On the first floor is a miniature ballroom, where Sir Palk would have entertained special guests, King George III was once a visitor here. Features of this room include large Gothic windows, delicate plasterwork and the original mahogany flooring. In one of the ante rooms there is a fireplace depicting Lawrence's coat of arms; each of the rooms in this turret has its own fireplace which was the only form of heating until the restoration of the building in 1995. The chimneys are invisible from below; they come out of the crenellations at the top of the turret. The top floor is a luxury apartment which is rented for holidays and special occasion short breaks and has been featured in the BBC holidays programme.

The apartment has been tastefully converted and is accessed by the spiral stone staircase with cantilevered steps, wrought iron balustrade and mahogany handrail. Leading from the main living area, which sleeps 2, there is a separate bathroom and fitted kitchen built into the circular turret rooms. The 360 degree views at this level are just stunning. Because of the spiral staircase, the property is not suited to the very young, the elderly or the infirm.

The miniature ballroom on the first floor is often used for civil ceremonies which may be taking place during your stay, however, any evening functions will be not be taken without your approval.

The building also opens to the public each Sunday and most bank holiday afternoons between February and October.

26 THE VANILLA POD AT THE CRIDFORD INN

Trusham, Teign Valley, Newton Abbot,
Devon TQ13 0NR
Tel: 01626 853694
e-mail: reservations@vanillapod-
cridfordinn.com
website: www.vanillapod-cridfordinn.com

Nestled in the idyllic village of Trusham in the Teign Valley, **The Vanilla Pod at the Cridford Inn** is the perfect place to come and indulge in some beautifully crafted food. The main site dates back to 1086, and was probably one of the small holdings mentioned in the *Domesday Book*. The age of the inn is evident in the medieval window frame seen in the current bar area; probably the oldest example of such in the country.

Before the husband and wife team Ian and Tracey realised their dream of running a bar/restaurant in the country, they ran the widely renowned and acclaimed Vanilla Pod Restaurant in Torquay since September 2003. Ian is also the Head Chef with an absolute passion for fine food; he has won many accolades as well as collecting his top award for deserts at the Hilton London Metropole. Tracey runs the management side of the business, ensuring that excellent, friendly service (the last ingredient needed to make a night at the Vanilla Pod unforgettable) is always at the highest standard.

When you come to the Vanilla Pod, it really must be for the excellent food which is already synonymous with quality in the area. Dishes such as pan-fried sirloin steak on a potato Rosti with carrot puree, wild summer mushrooms, and roasted globe artichoke, or seared fillet of seabass with wilted baby spinach, slow roasted cherry tomatoes and dauphinois potatoes, are served from their monthly renewed menu. Just be sure to save enough room for one of Ian's award winning desserts! His signature vanilla pod chocolate cup with hand crafted Tuille biscuit cup and saucer (complete with teaspoon) filled with a dark chocolate mousse, topped with vanilla cream is not to be missed, and neither are his hand-made chocolates. All the dishes can be accompanied with wine if you so wish, and you can consult the knowledgeable staff for their recommendation. In addition there is an extensive bar menu that changes seasonally and daily changing specials boards. Their opening times are; Monday - Friday open 11-3pm, 6-11pm, (food served 12-2.30pm, 6.30-9.30pm) Saturday open 11am-11pm (food served 11am-2.30pm, 6.30pm-9.30pm) Sunday 12-10.30pm (food served 12-3pm, 6.30-9.00pm)

There are four cosy and elegantly decorated suites available at the Cridford Inn, all of which have en-suite bathrooms.

They also cater for wedding functions of up to 40 people and can provide flowers, cars and cakes for the big day. They are within 2 miles distance from Haldon Belvedere castle.

28 THE CROWN & SCEPTRE

Newton St Cyres, nr Exeter,
Devon EX5 5DA
Tel: 01372 851278
e-mail:
cathy@thecrownandsceptre.eclipse.co.uk

Located about half way between Exeter and Cretiton, in the village of Newton St Cyres lies the ever so popular **Crown & Sceptre.** Now one of the social hubs of the village, the public house was built in 1962 on the site of a pub, which was devastated by a fire. Although a fairly new building, you would never guess as the building has all the finest features of an olde worlde village hostelry. This can be found from the warmth and genuine welcome that you will experience whilst visiting, as well as the relaxed atmosphere, heightened by the real log fires, well-kept ales and good, honest home cooking.

Owners and spectacular hosts Richard and Cathy Wightman have been here for the past 5 years and although their first venture into the business of this trade, they have made a well-respected client base, with many locals and repeat visitors.

The inn is open seven days a week, lunchtime and evening Monday to Friday and all day on Saturdays and Sundays. There is something for everyone at the Crown & Sceptre. Coffees are available throughout the day, with fair-trade favourites such as espresso and café latte. Two permanent real ales and a guest ale are on tap also, to quench the thirst of those exploring the nearby countryside and the food available will satisfy even the heartiest of hungers.

The menu really does cater for all tastes and even special dietary requirements can be catered for. For those with a smaller appetite, there is a large array of salads, with chicken and bacon, greek salad, with feta cheese and a delicious red onion confit and melting goats cheese. Sandwiches and ploughmans are also popular at lunchtimes. Steaks and other pub favourites are served throughout the day, with dishes such as fresh cod coated in homemade beer batter, hand linked sausages, homemade fresh chicken kiev, homemade lasagne, and a splendid homemade pie of the day, which features on the specials board. All meals can be enjoyed anywhere throughout the bars, restaurant or outside by the tumbling Shutten brook, which runs through the plush garden. There is also a child's play area, making this a fabulous business for all the family.

159

29 THE NORTH CLIFF HOTEL

North Walk, Lynton,
North Devon EX35 6HJ
Tel: 01598 752357
e-mail: holidays@northcliffhotel.co.uk
website: www.northcliffhotel.co.uk

In a glorious setting high on the wooded hillside above Lynmouth and a 200 metre walk to Lynton, is just one of the attractions of **The North Cliff Hotel**. The owners, sisters Sue and Kate have quickly made their mark at the hotel, where major improvements include a new reception, boot/drying room (ideal for walkers), bar and restaurant. The bar is an excellent place to relax and meet new friends over a drink, and in the restaurant, well-named The View, Kate has raised the cooking to new heights. Her 3-course menu offers plenty of choices to suit all tastes. The hotel has a lovely breakfast room with a collection of teapots on display and an outside area enjoying amazing views.

The spacious individually styled en suite bedrooms can accommodate family gatherings or walking parties as there are 7 doubles, 2 twins, 1 single and 4 family rooms (can be used as twins or doubles). All the bedrooms at the North Cliff command beautiful views over Lynmouth Bay, Countisbury Hill, Watermeet Valley and the Welsh coastline.

Attached to the North Cliff is a self-contained flat which consists of a bedroom sleeping 4 (double and bunk beds), a large lounge/dining room with a double settee bed, kitchen, shower room and toilet. There is a patio, which has the stunning views over Lynmouth Bay.

Local activities include walking, riding, tennis and putting, and the North Cliff is ideally situated for exploring the coastline and Exmoor National Park. The road in front of the hotel forms part of The South West Coastal Path and the remarkable Valley of the Rocks is a 2-mile walk. The famous water powered Cliff Railway linking Lynton and Lynmouth passes within a few feet of the hotel and is accessed by the garden.

The North Cliff has its own private parking, and welcomes well behaved dogs.

30 LEE HOUSE

Lee Road, Lynton, Devon EX35 6BP
Tel: 01598 752364
e-mail: info@leehouselynton.co.uk
website: www.leehouselynton.co.uk

You can be sure of a very warm and friendly welcome at **Lee House** from your hosts, Ken and Caroline Blakey. Lee House is a delightful Victorian Residence set in the heart of Lynton village, making it an ideal destination for holidays of any duration, whether for an extended stay, a short break or a special occasion. Lee House enjoys 4 star rating from Visit Britain and is fully licensed.

All guest rooms are en-suite, comfortable, well furnished and fully equipped with tea and coffee making facilities, television, clock radio, hair dryer and quality complimentary toiletries. Guests can choose from a range of rooms including the popular balcony rooms overlooking Lynton and the hills beyond and a four-poster room. All rooms are tastefully and individually decorated in keeping with the style of Lee House.

In the morning, generous home cooked breakfasts are served in the tranquil dining room with choices to satisfy both traditional and vegetarian tastes, while vegan and other special diets can be fully catered for. At the end of the day, guests can enjoy the views from the comfort of the South facing lounge and garden terrace while relaxing with a drink from the bar.

A short walk from Lee House will take you to the dramatic landscape of the Valley of Rocks, or the marvellous Victorian cliff railway that links Lynton with its twin village of Lynmouth. There are also many interesting art & craft shops, tea rooms, inns and restaurants close by in the two villages. For those wishing to venture further afield, the superb location of Lee House makes it an ideal base for exploring the North Devon coast and Exmoor National Park, allowing you to experience the breathtaking natural beauty and relaxing pace of life.

Lee House is situated in the walking capital of Exmoor, just minutes from the South West Coast Path and close to the Tarka Trail and Two Moors Way. Boot trays and drying facilities are available for your convenience.

Private parking is provided for all rooms at the rear of the house, allowing guests to make the most of the local walking routes. Cycling, horse riding, golfing and fishing activities are also found nearby. Ken and Caroline are always happy to fill your flask with a hot drink or provide packed lunches with advance notice. They look forward to meeting new and returning guests.

31 LYNTON COTTAGE HOTEL

Lynton Cottage Hotel
North Walk, Lynton, Devon EX35 6ED
Tel: 01598 752342
e-mail: enquiries@lynton-cottage.co.uk
website: www.lynton-cottage.co.uk

The cliff-top location of **Lynton Cottage** commands some of the finest sea views in England with panoramic views of Lynmouth bay, Countisbury, Watersmeet and on a clear day, Wales. Heather & David try to offer the ultimate escape with peace and tranquillity in a relaxed and informal hideaway within beautifully manicured gardens. Being one of the finest three star hotels in North Devon, and also an AA two rosette restaurant, they pride themselves on an international reputation for cuisine and comfort.

So let the stress of today's hectic lifestyle drift away in the comfort of the Lynton Cottage Hotel.

33 SINAI HOUSE

Lynway, Lynton, North Devon EX35 6AY
Tel: 01598 753227
e-mail: enquiries@sinaihouse.co.uk
website: www.sinaihouse.co.uk

Carmel and Colin Wilkins offer a warm to visitors to their beautifully appointed former vicarage set on a steep hillside above Lynton. **Sinai House** has eight guest bedrooms – 5 doubles, a twin and 2 singles – all with en suite bath or shower, television and tea/coffee trays with proper teapots and a supply of biscuits. The lounge is well-stocked with reading material, and the house has a charming little bar decked with golfing memorabilia – Colin can arrange golf at the Ilfracombe course.

In the dining room, a superb breakfast gets the day off to a perfect start, while towards the evening the flag-stoned patio is a delightful spot for a pre-dinner drink. This area is great walking country but Sinai House (which is open from mid-February to early November), is popular not just with walkers but with visitors who come from all over the world to enjoy the delights of coast and countryside, and the particular brand of hospitality provided by Carmel and Colin.

32 SEAWOOD HOTEL

North Walk, Lynton,
North Devon EX35 6HJ
Tel: 01598 752272
e-mail: admin@seawoodhotel.co.uk
website: www.seawoodhotel.co.uk

Enjoying peace and tranquillity yet remaining close to the heart of Lynton, is the fabulous **Seawood Hotel**, a magnificent grade 2 listed Victorian House boasting spectacular sea views. This stunning hotel is family owned and run, and offers an unpretentious service helping guests to relax, unwind and feel a little pampered. The location itself gives guests the opportunity of exploring Exmoor, boarding the unique Cliff railway (at the end of the garden), visiting the many attractions in the surrounding area or just simply relaxing in the hotel gardens. The seaside town of Lynton is in an area known locally as 'Little Switzerland' which appears almost prehistoric in places such as the valley of the rocks where the poet Shelley used to promenade to, passing the entrance of this hotel.

The hotel has a traditional feel with classic styling and has an atmosphere of comfort and elegance throughout. All the rooms enjoy stunning seaviews of the bay around Lynmouth and the coast of Wales. Guests can watch the sun setting and the lights of the Welsh coastline twinkling, making the perfect backdrop for a relaxing break. The twelve en-suite bedrooms, vary in size from four poster, to double, twin and single bedded and all have digital flat-screen televisions with DVD players and IPod dock, connection to freeview with 40 channels, Wi-Fi internet access, hairdryer, tea and coffee making facilities, clock radio, dressing gowns and a selection of toiletries.

The varied choice of breakfasts is vast with local organic produce being used whenever possible. The restaurant is open to non residents for dinner between 7pm-8pm so pre-booking is advised. The food served here is of exceptional quality and the six-course dinner menu includes culinary delights such as sirloin steak - cooked the way you like it served with a peppercorn sauce; stuffed Chicken Breast served with a red pepper coulis; and lamb shank slowly cooked and served with a rich gravy. The mouth watering desserts are changed daily and the dinner starts with a surprise from the chef to begin the meal. Specialist diets are catered for and there is an extensive choice on the quality wine list.

The owners take great pride in their service and at every stage provide the extra care, personal attention and friendly atmosphere that so often completes the perfect break. All guests can be assured of a warm and friendly welcome along with first class customer service. Well behaved dogs are also accepted.

34 RIVER LYN VIEW

26 Watermeet Road, Lynmouth,
Devon EX35 6EP
Tel: 01598 753501
e-mail: riverlynview@aol.com
website: www.riverlynview.com

River Lyn View is a great Bed & Breakfast situated in the coastal town of Lynmouth, North Devon, and with the B & B just a short stroll from the picturesque harbour; it is a prime position within the town. The 18th century building has clearly been looked after; there are many hanging baskets, providing bursts of colour and the quality continues inside. With traditional high ceilings, exposed beams and a light and airy décor, the River Lyn View provides an ideal place from which to explore the surrounding countryside and coastline. Lynmouth itself is an outstandingly pretty little town at the mouth of the Lyn valley where the rivers of the East and West Lyn meet in the harbour.

The husband and wife owners have created spacious and welcoming accommodation, there are four en suite rooms available

and all of them are well appointed, comfortable and quiet. The cost of the rooms includes a breakfast and there is quite a choice; various fruit, cereals, porridge or the classic full English breakfast are available to provide the ideal start to your day.

35 THE STEAK HOUSE

Searock Apartments, Wilder Road,
Ilfracombe, Devon EX34 9AR
Tel: 01271 879394
e-mail: simonkino@yahoo.co.uk

The **Steak House** is a very popular, family run restaurant set in the Victorian town of Ilfracombe, North Devon. Owned and run by Simon, Andy and Lorraine Kino, the Steak House provides diners with the best of locally sourced meat and seafood at very reasonable prices.

Experience is certainly not lacking within the owners; Simon has been a chef for 10 years and Andy and Lorraine have been in the catering industry for 25 years. The wealth of knowledge that comes from working in the hospitality industry shines through when entering the Steak House, the exterior is clean and fresh with well kept, colourful window boxes and the interior is no different. Large windows span the wall providing plenty of light, all of the tables are immaculately laid out, complete with linen tablecloths and sparkling cutlery.

The village of Ilfracombe has been declared a conservation area to preserve the Victorian look and the building is adorned with Victorian features. The location of the restaurant makes it an ideal spot to break and have a bite to eat following a hard days exploring! With Ilfracombe being known as the doorway to Exmoor there are some amazing local walks which take in the rugged North Devon countryside and coastline.

The main draw has to be the extensive menu, including the superior quality Exmoor beef, hung for a minimum of 28 days, enhancing the tenderness, succulence and traditional flavour. The meat used is approved by the English Beef and Lamb Executive (EBLEX) and is fully traceable back to the farm it originated from. The high quality Exmoor beef can be accompanied with a range of delicious home made sauces; such as pepper, garlic, diane and blue cheese. Other highlights on the menu include the Exmoor pork, duck and chicken, all sourced from farms practicing the "five freedoms" as set by the Animal Welfare Council ensuring a quality standard of life for the animals.

You can also choose from the blackboard daily specials; sumptuous dishes based around fresh locally caught fish. If there is any room left after the huge main course, the Steak House has a daily sweet board as well as the regular creamy Devon ice cream selection or a West Country cheese board.

The restaurant boasts space for 50 covers but fills up very quickly, so reservations are recommended to avoid disappointment. The Steak House is open 7 days a week from 7pm between May and October and Thursday, Friday and Saturday from 7pm during the winter.

36 WENTWORTH HOUSE HOTEL

2 Belmont Road, Ilfracombe,
Devon EX34 8DR
Tel: 01271 863048
e-mail: wentworthhouse@tiscali.co.uk
website: www.hotelilfracombe.co.uk

Providing some of the top hotel accommodation in Ilfracombe and North Devon with first class facilities is the **Wentworth House Hotel.** An excellent example of the fine architecture of a bygone era, this beautiful Victorian house was built as a Gentleman's Residence in 1857. It has since been lovingly restored and furnished, still retaining its former elegance. With an abundance of character and charm, it is open all year round offering the perfect place for family summer holidays, romantic getaways, business trips and shorter breaks. The location is superb with the high street, promenade and harbour just minutes away. As well as being awarded a 5* Food and Hygiene certificate by Devon District Council, in 2008 Wentworth House was also awarded B&B of the year by *Insight Magazine*; it's no wonder many guests return year after year to sample the fine hospitality on offer.

Guests can choose to unwind with a drink in the comfortably furnished, spacious Residents lounge which overlooks the gorgeous gardens or simply relax in peace with a good book. Whatever the choice, the attentive hosts do their utmost to ensure guests have a comfortable stay, even sleeping periodically in the bedrooms themselves to check the beds are 'cumfy not lumpy' of prime importance here. The eight elegantly furnished, en-suite rooms all have excellent views of either the sea or the surrounding countryside and are equipped with top class facilities including free view televisions, electric shaver points and full central heating. The bathrooms are stocked with complimentary toiletries and hair dryers and irons are available if required.

The hearty full English breakfast is served in the delightful dining room where guests are also welcome to dine in the evening if they wish. Wentworth House takes great pride in providing good old fashioned cuisine, serving generous portions and fresh homemade desserts. All cuisine is freshly prepared on the premises using locally sourced produce. Vegetarian meals and any special dietary requirements can be catered for on request. Ilfracombe is a resort for all seasons and North Devon offers its visitors stunning coastal scenery, rural tranquillity, the breathtaking Exmoor National Park as well as the finest surfing beaches. All in all, Wentworth House Hotel offers the perfect place to stay to enjoy a relaxing break in beautiful surroundings while having an abundance of interesting places to visit all within easy reach.

37 THE CAIRN HOUSE

43 St Brannocks Road, Ilfracombe,
Devon EX34 8EH
Tel: 07802 592136
e-mail: info@cairnhousehotel.co.uk
website: www.cairnhousehotel.co.uk

Cairn House Hotel is a warm, family run business located in the beautiful seaside town of Ilfracombe in North Devon. The Adorian family welcome those of all ages, families, singletons or couples, locals to the area or visitors from afar. They are committed to making your stay relaxing, enjoyable and memorable; wanting to make sure your stay will be one you want to repeat again and again.

The Cairn House has nine bedrooms all of which are en suite, centrally heated and tastefully decorated. Each room also has its own tea and coffee and hot chocolate making facilities along with colour T.V ensuring that your stay will be as comfortable and hassle free as possible. There is a range of single, twin, double and family rooms, four poster beds also available. Many of the rooms have opportunity of waking up to stunning sea views across the Bristol Channel to the south of Wales.

The house itself has a charming period feel to many parts of it as it has retained many of its original features, one of which is a beautifully carved wooden staircase. Cairn House boasts a fully licensed bar stocking a good variety of wines, spirits, beers and soft drinks. The bar is adjacent to a comfortable residents' lounge which is the perfect spot to relax of an evening with friends, old or new. The house is also set in its own well kept grounds which are truly glorious in the summer months when in bloom.

Each morning a hearty full English breakfast is served to give you a good start to the day, although your hosts endeavour to cater for any dietary requirements, providing an alternative cooked menu and a selection of fresh fruit, fruit juices, cereals, yoghurts, with plenty of tea and coffee. Once filled up and ready to go you are just a 10 minute walk from the town centre which is very close to many local attractions such as the promenade and harbour. The sea is just a 12 minute walk away and Woolacombe Bay with its sandy beach is only a few minutes drive away. Cairn House has a Private Car Park and is conveniently located right opposite the hotel is the beautifully landscaped gardens of Bicclescombe Park complete with children's play area and tennis courts, making Cairn House a relaxed family getaway.

WATCH OUT FOR:

EQUITEENIE WORLD, West Penhill Farm, Fremington, North Devon EX31 2NG
Tel enquiries: 07802 592136   website: coming soon.

Situated near the Tarka Trail, **Equiteenie World** (opening soon) is a new stud farm for the smallest horses in the world. There are onsite parking facilities and the stud farm is within easy access to many towns and activities. Bicycles are also available for hire.

38 SHERBORNE LODGE

Torrs Park, Ilfracombe, Devon EX34 8AY
Tel: 01271 862297
e-mail: visit@sherborne-lodge.co.uk
website: www.sherborne-lodge.co.uk

North Devon is renowned for its beautiful countryside, rugged coast and quaint villages; with so much to explore a place to stay is essential and **Sherborne Lodge**, in Ilfracombe is one of the best. Sherborne Lodge is in a great location in Ilfracombe; right at the start of Torrs Park, one of the most popular areas of Ilfracombe, yards from the famous Torrs walk, close to the promenade and Ilfracombe Bay and only a five minute walk from the town centre.

There are 10 rooms available, including three family suites. The rooms are all en-suite with the exception of one which has it's own private bathroom. All the rooms are very comfortable, well appointed and contain all the modern amenities. The 200 year old property houses facilities for a range of activities; a freezer for bait/catch from fishermen, cycle storage and two gun safes for clay pigeon shooters.

There are also plenty of things to keep you occupied inside; pool table, darts board, piano, board games, internet access and a large TV in the bar area. There is a hearty English breakfast in the mornings and a full bar menu for the evening.

40 CHAMBERCOMBE MANOR

nr Ilfracombe, Devon EX34 9RJ
Tel: 01271 862624
website: www.chambercombemanor.org.uk

Although the manor here was mentioned in the *Domesday Book*, the present **Chambercombe Manor** was not built until the 12th century and it still retains much of its medieval charm and character today. When, exactly, it fell from being a manor house to a farmhouse is unknown but fortunately such features as its plaster frieze and barrel ceiling in the bedrooms can still be seen. Displaying period furniture from Elizabethan times up to the Victorian era, this is a delightful house that allows visitors to soak up the atmosphere of what was also a family home. Along with the Great Hall, there is the private chapel of the Champernon family, the manor's first owners, an old kitchen and the Coat of Arms bedroom that was once occupied by Lady Jane Grey and it is the Grey coat of arms, who were descendants of the Champernons, that is depicted above the fireplace.

Meanwhile, outside there is a paved courtyard, with ornamental ponds, a delightful garden of lawns, shrubbery and herbaceous borders, and a water garden beyond which lie the extensive grounds that take in the peaceful, secluded wooded valley in which the manor house is situated.

168

39 THE ILFRACOMBE CARLTON HOTEL

Runnacleave Rd, Ilfracombe,
North Devon EX34 8AR
Tel: 01271 862446   Fax: 01271 865379
e-mail: enquiries@ilfracombecarlton.co.uk
website: www.ilfracombecarlton.co.uk

At the heart of the exciting resort of Ilfracombe, in North Devon, **The Ilfracombe Carlton Hotel** is an ideal destination for every holiday. Built in 1850, this attractive building was converted in the late 19th century to a guest house, and then to a hotel where it

has been catering for paying guests ever since. The communal rooms still retain original cornicing and picture rails.

This family-run, fully licensed 2 star hotel is a short level walk from all the attractions Ilfracombe has to offer, the Landmark theatre and a ten minute stroll from the harbour. The abundance of local activities makes the Ilfracombe Carton a great base for an invigorating holiday; for example golf, sailing, scuba diving, sea fishing, horse riding, quad biking, and clay and pheasant shooting. If you have a passion for shooting, the Carlton can cater your needs with a police approved secure gun room, and they can even organise all inclusive shooting breaks for you on request. If you want a slower paced break, the fresh air, tranquillity and gentle pace of life can make for the relaxing holiday you are looking for. There are also many walks around the stunning coast and countryside, both in Ilfracombe and surrounding areas.

There are a range of light, tastefully decorated suites available, from single, double, twin and family rooms, to Superior double or twin rooms which come with super king-size beds. All rooms come with en-suite (shower or bath, with WC), colour TV and the price can be with bed & breakfast or dinner, bed & breakfast (there is a reduced rate available for bookings over four nights). There is on-site parking for up to 15 cars, and a lift which serves all floors.

There is a lovely spacious dining room and restaurant, which can also cater for parties, wedding receptions and large groups. The large bar with sprung dance floor, offers entertainment on most evenings, so you can dance the night away in style. The menu is a lovely array of fresh home-made British dishes; for example roast chicken breast with caramelized red onions and parsnip crisps, or fillet of plaice with a lemon and parsley butter. Where possible local produce is used and there are options for vegetarian diets. Breakfast is served 7:30am until 9am (an hour later on Saturdays, Sundays and Bank holidays) and dinner is served 6:30pm until 8pm.

169

41 THE ROYAL MARINE

Seaside, Combe Martin,
North Devon EX34 0AW
Tel: 01271 882470 Fax: 01271 889198
e-mail: theroyalmarine@btconnect.com
website: www.theroyalmarine.co.uk

Located in the stunning village of Combe Martin, **The Royal Marine** is an impressive free house with amazing seaside views. The village has an interesting history, with sites such as a well preserved strip field system, and the remains of eighteenth century silver mines to visit. Also it has the longest village high street in the country, so you can come and enjoy many small, individual shops of every type. The market town of Barnstable is within 10 minutes away and also short drives away are Lynton and Lynmouth with

the breathtaking Valley Of The Rocks and the famous Cliff Railway. Combe Martin is a great place to come if you like to be active on your holidays, as there is plenty to do! There are extensive walks to explore, which really is the best way to take in this beautiful part of Devon. Or you can go swimming, golfing, surfing, fishing... the list is endless.

The Royal Marine is a perfect place to come and rest during your stay in this lovely sea-side village. They have six rooms, all with en-suite and most with views of the beach, Hangman cliffs or both. The views are especially impressive at night when the bay and cliffs are floodlit. The tastefully decorated suites all include colour television, tea and coffee making facilities, hairdryer and radio alarm clock. Also included in the price is a breakfast served in the restaurant, with tea or coffee, juices, cereals, toast, or a full English breakfast. A self contained apartment is available for those staying at The Royal Marine as a group, it sleeps 6 with one double room with 4-poster bed and en-suite shower room, one twin room with en-suite, a lounge with two sofa beds, a flat screen television, dining area and sea views, and a fitted kitchen. The Royal Marine is open all year round, and the accommodation tariff is constant through the year. There is a parking area for all residents.

The restaurant, which is open for lunch and dinner, serves a delightful array of locally sourced seasonal dishes which are sure to satisfy. There is also a children's menu, or choice of having a reduced version of some of the adult dishes for adventurous young taste buds. There is also a very popular and established carvery, specials such as pure Devon fillet of beef which are changed regularly and a lovely selection of homemade desserts.

Parracombe, Barnstaple,
Devon EX31 4PE
Tel: 01598 763239
website:
www.foxandgoose.parracombe.co.uk

As **The Fox & Goose** is the only hostelry in the Exmoor village of Parracombe, the villagers can consider themselves lucky that it is a very good one in every way. It was built in traditional style in 1894 and still retains its log fires in winter. A piano is always kept fully tuned and the walls are adorned with animal heads and an abundance of memorabilia. Outside, there's a peaceful riverside patio area beside the Hedden and flower-filled raised beds.

Mine hosts, Nikki and Paul, who arrived here in early 2005 have more than 15 years experience in the hospitality business. During their tenure they have established the Fox & Goose as a top quality eating place with an extensive menu based on locally sourced ingredients wherever possible. The bill of fare changes regularly but a typical menu might include amongst the starters Taw Torridge Mussels, a Greek salad and a smooth home-made chicken liver pâté. Locally caught fish takes pride of place amongst the main courses and might include a Lobster Thermidor with lobster caught in the waters around Lundy Island; a large bowl of traditional bouillabaisse; wild sea bass fillet or cod with tiger prawns. Meat dishes could offer a choice of beef and venison steaks; an Exmoor Venison Casserole; and a traditional Steak & Kidney Pie. For vegetarians, typical options include a Leek & Stilton 'Open' Pie; Mushroom Stroganoff, and Fresh Egg Pasta.

For dessert, the offerings might include a Velvet Chocolate Mousse; Rhubarb Fool or, for a minimum of two people, a Foxy Fondue – dark chocolate melted with Cointreau and orange essence and served with mixed fruits and marshmallows for dipping. If you prefer a savoury conclusion to your meal, the pub's cheese board offers a selection that includes Hawkridge Farmhouse vintage Cheddar; Cropwell Bishop Stilton and Cornish yarg wrapped in nettles.

To accompany your meal there's a good selection of wines available as well as two real ales Cotleigh and Exmoor. From the spring of 2010, the Fox & Goose will be offering accommodation in the form of Bed & Breakfast, four en suite rooms will be available.

Food is served every day of the week from noon until 2pm, and from 6pm to 9pm. (7pm to 9pm on Sundays). The bar is open daily from noon until 2.30pm and from 6pm to 11pm (7pm to 10.30pm on Sundays).all major credit cards are accepted; dogs on leads welcome.

West Down, nr Braunton,
North Devon EX34 8NU
Tel: 01271 863757
e-mail: enquiries@foxhuntersinn.co.uk
website: www.foxhuntersinn.co.uk

A 300 year old hostelry of exceptional charm and character, the **Foxhunters Inn** provides an atmosphere of genuine warmth and hospitality. Cosy inglenooks, roaring log fires, original stonework and softly lit bars all add to the appeal. Another major attraction here is the quality of the cuisine on offer. The varied menu includes locally supplied steaks, fish, and a good selection of vegetarian options. The Sunday carvery is very popular, offering a selection of succulent meats, a mix of delicious vegetable dishes and again, a vegetarian option for those wanting a carvery without meat.

Mine hosts, Pauline and Mick Webb, also pride themselves on the inn's family-friendly environment. It has its own special family area with a licensed café-bar. The Fishing Fox is located by the large car parking area so the children can access the play area containing a Wendy House and a stationary train ride, plus the beer garden where adults can enjoy the summer weather whilst eating and drinking. The beer garden is dog-friendly too – a dog bin is provided and dogs must be kept on a lead at all times. The Fishing Fox has its own fish and chip restaurant, opens everyday and closes late in the evening, depending on demand. This facility is only open in the summer season.

The inn also offers comfortable accommodation. There are eight bedrooms in total, all with en suite facilities including wc, wash basin, bath and shower. The rooms available include 4 poster double rooms, double rooms, and there is also a shared family room with bunk beds for the children. The rooms are all non-smoking and equipped with TV and hospitality tray. The bed and breakfast is open all year round. There is also the added attraction of a free bottle of house wine if the Hidden Places guide is mentioned at the time of booking!

The Foxhunters Inn is a popular meeting place for those taking part in local country sports in the area. There are many renowned shoots in the area for both pheasant and partridge. Walked up shooting, walked up driven shooting and clay pigeon shooting are all popular within the area – there are two clay pigeon shoots and a game shooting centre within a 4-mile radius of the inn. By arrangement, the Foxhunters Inn can prepare breakfasts and evening meals to fit in with your days shooting schedule.

44 THE ROCKS HOTEL

Beach Road, Woolacombe,
Devon EX34 7BT
Tel: 01271 870361
e-mail: enquiries@therockshotel.co.uk
website: www.therockshotel.co.uk

Located in the heart of Woolacombe, **The Rocks Hotel** used to be known as the Caertref Hotel. But when Wendy and Martin Lambert purchased the hotel in January 2008, they re-named it and spent 12 months totally refurbishing and modernising the premises ready for the 2009 season.

The hotel is situated only 300 yards from the beach and other attractions within easy reach include the North Devon coastal path, the Tarka Trail and some excellent surfing beaches.

All 9 bedrooms have en suite bathrooms, and all are equipped with a flat screen TV/DVD player , Wi-Fi internet,

hairdryer and tea/coffee making facilities. The bedroom are a mix of family(sleeps 5), King, double,twin and single. The hotel also has a self-catering 2-bedroom apartment to let with its own courtyard and parking, details of which can be found on the hotel's website.

The Rocks Hotel has a surfboard stone, outside shower, and decked patio area, for relaxing in the sun. Also free parking for our guests.

All credit cards accepted apart from American Express and Diners cards.

45 MOORSANDS

34 Moor Lane, Croyde Bay,
Devon EX33 1NP
Tel: 01271 890781
website:
www.croyde-bay.com/moorsands.htm

Formerly a small Victorian hotel, **Moorsands** has more recently been a private house. Having been restored to its past glory, it is now a family home and a well established bed and breakfast and is capably run by Paul and Faith Davis. The property was built in 1880 and is very well kept and the exterior is warm and inviting, hanging baskets adorn the walls and complement the relaxed feel of the place. Inside there are four rooms available, all of which are en-suite, there are twin, double and family rooms and they all have great views over Croyde Bay or the rugged North Devon countryside.

The B & B is very keen to be green and tries to minimize its impact on the environment. Paul and Faith will gladly

collect you from the station or coach stop should guests want to arrive using public transport.

The breakfast available is varied, prepared by Faith and there is a choice for everybody, including vegetarians. The food is mainly sourced from local suppliers and there is much organic produce. Croyde Bay is famous for its surfing, the beach said to be the best surfing beach in Devon, as such, the guesthouse will gladly provide room to store surfboards and wetsuits.

46 CROYDE HOLIDAY BUNGALOWS

Stock Farm, Brayford, Barnstaple,
Devon EX32 7QQ
Tel: 01598 710498
www.croydeholidaybungalows.co.uk

Situated in the beautiful North Devon coastal village of Croyde, **Croyde Holiday Bungalows** offer a peaceful and quiet beach holiday experience. Both bungalows are carpeted throughout, fully furnished and thoroughly cleaned by the owner between guests.

The bungalows have spacious lawns to relax on and are within easy reach of the dunes and the golden sandy beach of Croyde, well known for the quality of its beach. Also within easy walking distance is the picturesque village with its shops, churches, restaurants, inns and south west coast path.. Only 2 miles away is Saunton Sands which hosts an 18 hole golf course.

'Gilonica' is a modern residential bungalow situated in a quiet cul-de-sac close to the beach, recently refurbished to a high standard it boasts one double bedroom and one twin room. There is an extra

bed if required which means that Gilonica can sleep 5. The other bungalow is called 'Seashells' and has three bedrooms capable of sleeping six people. Seashells has the added

bonus of its own private entrance onto the sand dunes. Both bungalows supply bedding, and the kitchens are very well stocked with appliances. Well behaved dogs accepted.

47 LUNDY HOUSE HOTEL

Chapel Hill, Mortehoe, Woolacombe,
North Devon EX34 7DZ
Tel: 01271 870372
e-mail: info@lundyhousehotel.co.uk
website: www.lundyhousehotel.co.uk

Enjoying a fabulous location, **Lundy House Hotel** is set directly on the rugged North Cornwall coastline between the village of Mortehoe and Woolacombe, facing south and looking directly across to Lundy Island. The Hotel's terraced garden leads directly onto the North Devon Coastal path giving access to Combesgate and Grunta beaches. The hotel has been in the safe hands of Victoria and Tim Cole for over 13 years and appeals to a wide range of Clientele having nine en-suite bedrooms, all enjoying fabulous views, of which four are family rooms. All rooms have excellent facilities and there is free Wi-Fi connection throughout the hotel.

Traditional home cooking is a priority here using fresh local produce in the superb cuisine. The Lundy House Big Breakfast has earned quite a reputation and includes locally award-winning sausages as well as organic porridge served

with or without Devon clotted cream.

The Hotel is non-smoking, welcomes pets and offers a friendly, personal service to all its valued guests. The hotel's stunning location enjoying spectacular sunsets makes this undoubtedly the best location in the bay. Saunton Golf club is close by and the hotel offers clubs and a trolley for hire. Other leisure pursuits nearby include horseriding, surfing, fishing and Clay pigeon shooting.

48 MARSHALS

Boutport Street, Barnstaple,
North Devon EX31 1SX
Tel: 01271 376633
website: www.marshalspub.co.uk

Located in the heart of Barnstaple, adjacent to the Queen's Theatre and close to the famous glass-roofed Victorian Pannier Market, **Marshals** is a popular town centre pub where your welcoming hosts are Debbie and Bill

Furnifer. Behind the cheerful yellow-painted façade, the pub has an inviting old world look, complete with oak beams. It's a good spot for enjoying a glass of well-kept cask ale for which this hostelry is well-known - it's also on the Real Ale Trail.

Marshals also has a reputation for serving good, home-made food at lunchtimes. All the old favourites feature on the menu - cottage pie, chicken curry and sausage & mash made with local sausages. Other options include a tasty fish bake, a home-made lasagna and a dish called Boozy Cow - braised steak, shallots and carrots, slow cooked in rich ale gravy. Also available is a good range of light snacks such as jacket potatoes, ploughman's and sandwiches. Coffee is available all day and breakfast is served from 10.30am to 2pm, Monday to Saturday.

Another attraction here is the live music sessions which are held on Sundays at 3.30pm.

49 RING O' BELLS

Prixford, Barnstaple, Devon EX31 4DX
Tel: 01271 343836
e-mail: info@ringobellsprixford.com
website: www.ringobellsprixford.com

Serving mouth-watering dishes, created from the best local produce, **The Ring O'Bells** is a traditional village pub located in the charming village of Prixford, near Barnstaple. Martin and Janet Squire, who bought the pub at the end of 2007 have a wealth of experience in the hospitality industry and have won several awards, including Best Gourmet Restaurant in Devon and Best pub food 2001 for previous establishments they have owned.

The solid oak tables add to the character of the pub, which has an extensive choice of wines, spirits and beers for guests to indulge in. Visitors can enjoy excellent, real ales and freshly cooked food in the bar or restaurant area. The U-shaped bar area can seat 50 people and the restaurant, which is in two sections, can jointly seat 40 people on its luxurious leather chairs. The owners are extremely passionate about the business and this is evident in the quality of the food and service that is extremely popular among locals and visitors.

The pub, which is just 2.5 miles away from the busy town of Barnstaple, has its own skittle alley that can be booked for parties as well as a games room.

Parking is not a problem, with a spacious rear car-park that can hold up to 40 cars.

175

50 MARWOOD HILL GARDENS

Marwood, nr Barnstable,
North Devon EX31 4EB
Tel: 01271 342528
e-mail: info@marwoodhillgarden.co.uk
website: www.marwoodhillgarden.co.uk

Marwood Hill Gardens is one of North Devon's best hidden assets. Situated just four miles north of Barnstable and just nine miles from Ilfracombe signposted on the A3123 is 20 acres of simply glorious gardens, lakes and a garden tea room.

The gardens themselves are a true labour of love and were started in the 1950s by Dr Jimmy Smart who was a ship's doctor for six years in the war. He was awarded an MBE after swimming from raft to raft treating survivors when HMS Hermes sunk. After the war Dr Smart settled in Marwood as a GP and began to resurrect the beauty hidden by years of neglect. It took many years to restore some sort of order including the purchase of new land, the damning of the stream to create the two of the garden's three lakes and the building of a spectacular greenhouse which holds a fantastic collection of camellias.

Dr Smart sadly died in 2003 but Marwood Gardens today stand a tribute to his life's work. Throughout the year Marwood becomes a canvas for nature's colours - welcoming the daffodil yellows and snowdrops whites of spring, the drift of colour blooms of Primulas, Wisterias and Roses in the summer months and the burnt oranges and surprising bursts of Cyclamen that only autumn can bring.

Marwood also sells a wide range of plants throughout the year many of which are raised from seed or cuttings from the unusual variety growing within its walls. They grow a variety of Magnolias, shrubs and trees including Eucalyptus and silver Birch. There is also a large collection of herbaceous plants which aren't available in garden centres, including a selection of oriental grasses. The gardens are particularly famous for their Camellia and Astilbe collection which are the largest in the country and world respectively.

The gardens also provide an idyllic spot to enjoy the stunning views in the outside eating area and tea room which offers a home cooked and locally sourced menu of light snacks and lunches, cakes, hot and cold drinks and of course good old Devonshire cream teas and ice cream.

Marwood is a true testament both to hard work and nature – these gardens contain some rare carefully tended plants alongside nature's own influence in a relaxed and natural beauty you'll be hard pushed to find elsewhere. Open daily from 10am-5:30pm in spring and summer, and 10:30am-4pm in autumn and winter.

51 | THE VILLAGE INN

Youngaton Road, Westward Ho!
Devon EX39 1HU
Tel: 01237 477331
e-mail: info@villageinndevon.co.uk
website: www.villageinndevon.co.uk

The Village Inn has had a long and varied history. It started life as Youngaton Farm in around 1750 and is reported to be the oldest building in Westward Ho! In 1870 it was described as "a small farm with a dining or picnic shed", and a few years later as "a lodging house". The census of 1881 showed the farm occupied by Theophilus M Kelsall, his wife, 6 daughters, 2 sons, his sister-in-law, nurse and 3 servants. In 1904 the whole site was offered for sale and at that time comprised 8 bedrooms, 1 bathroom,

drawing room, dining room, morning room, kitchen, scullery, larder and 2 WCs. The property also had stabling for 3 horses, a harness room, coach house, two poultry houses, a gymnasium, workshop and 2 fives courts. It remained a private dwelling until World War II when it was used as a private school for children evacuated from the London area. After the war, it became a small hotel trading under the name of The Grenville Arms Hotel at a time when Westward Ho! was in its heyday as a family holiday resort. Julie and Stuart Hudson, together with their daughter Clare, arrived on the scene in December 1999 and carried out a programme of refurbishment to restore the fine old building to its former glory. They changed the name to The Village Inn in 2000.

Today, the inn is famed for its outstanding food, based on local produce wherever possible. The quality meat and poultry are supplied by Barton Farm at Woolfardisworthy (Woolsery). Fresh vegetables come from Littles of Bideford, and the fresh fish from S&P Fish in Barnstaple. Meals can be enjoyed either in the elegant restaurant, the airy conservatory or, weather permitting, in the colourful patio garden.

The Village Inn also offers really comfortable accommodation in beautiful, spacious en suite family, double and twin bedrooms, most with sea views. All rooms have central heating and are equipped with generous hospitality trays, a remote controlled colour TV with Teletext, and an alarm clock/radio. Guests can enjoy a hearty full English breakfast, served in the intimate and cosy restaurant.

Fore Street, Torrington,
Devon EX38 8HQ
Tel: 01805 622220
e-mail: globehotel.torrington@yahoo.co.uk
website: www.theglobetorrington.co.uk

The Globe Hotel has been a hotel since 1800, in the welcoming town of Torrington, in an area of unspoilt natural beauty above the river Torridge. Recently it has been taken over by new owners, who have quickly been making a name for themselves locally for their amazing *à la carte* menu. The hotel attracts an eclectic mixture of people; from walkers and cyclists who come for the surrounding trails and picturesque walks to actors and artists from the Plough arts centre conveniently positioned next door, which gives it a lovely lively atmosphere.

There is a range of tastefully decorated suites available; with single, twin, double and family rooms, all newly decorated with an elegant style. There are also double rooms with dramatic wooden four-poster beds, one of the beautifully unique touches which make The Globe Hotel so special. All of the rooms come with stylish en-suite bathrooms and digital television with Freeview. Tariff for rooms include breakfast, and there is reserved parking for guests. The hotel is pet friendly, so you needn't leave the last member of the family behind.

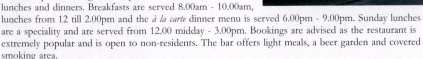

The sumptuous surroundings of the hotel's restaurant are surpassed only by the quality of the food. Award-winning chef Jamie Goodman serves mouth-wateringly delicious food, such as West Country lamb shank, with crushed baby potatoes & seasonal vegetables, and traditional home made apple pie. All of the food is cooked using local produce wherever possible, vegetarian options are available for lunches and dinners. Breakfasts are served 8.00am - 10.00am, lunches from 12 till 2.00pm and the *à la carte* dinner menu is served 6.00pm - 9.00pm. Sunday lunches are a speciality and are served from 12.00 midday - 3.00pm. Bookings are advised as the restaurant is extremely popular and is open to non-residents. The bar offers light meals, a beer garden and covered smoking area.

There is much to see during your stay at the Globe Hotel, with the coast being close by and Bideford within striking distance. Also local attractions include the Dartington crystal factory, Rosemoor RHS garden centre, pannier market and the Torrington 1646, a re-enactment centre at the time of the Civil War (a tradition very proudly upheld in Torrington, with a yearly torch-lit procession held through the town). Also there is the Tarka trail, a network of paths, cycle ways and a former railway route which covers 180 miles stretching to both Exmoor and Dartmoor, and the Common, an enjoyable 20 mile network of footpaths covering 365 acres of common land.

53 THE CORNER HOUSE

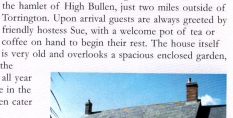

High Bullen, Torrington,
North Devon EX38 7JA
Tel: 01805 623430
e-mail: brithome@supanet.com
website: www.brithome.supanet.com

The Corner House is a delightful B&B situated in the hamlet of High Bullen, just two miles outside of Torrington. Upon arrival guests are always greeted by friendly hostess Sue, with a welcome pot of tea or coffee on hand to begin their rest. The house itself is very old and overlooks a spacious enclosed garden, perfect for relaxation, while children can play in the adjoining paddock. This charming house is open all year round, has full central heating as well as a log fire in the winter, welcomes children of all ages and will even cater for pets.

The well furnished accommodation consists of three en-suite rooms (two double and one twin). All rooms have Televisions, tea and coffee making facilities and hairdryers.

Breakfast is traditional style with a large and varied menu, catering for all tastes. There are several good eating places in the area, however if guests wish, they can arrange a good, home cooked evening meal in The Corner House.

There are many local attractions worth visiting within easy reach including the RHS Rosemoor Gardens, The Dartington Crystal Centre and The Tarka Trail.

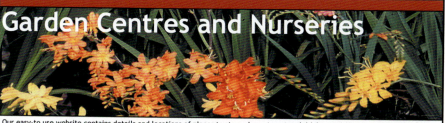

54 RHS GARDEN ROSEMOOR

Rosemoor, Great Torrington,
Devon EX38 8PH
Tel: 01805 624067 Fax: 01805 624717
e-mail: rosemooradmin@rhs.org.uk
website: www.rhs.org.uk/rosemoor

The Royal Horticultural Society Garden **Rosemoor** is acclaimed by gardeners throughout the world, but visitors do not have to be keen gardeners to appreciate the beauty and diversity of Rosemoor. Whatever the season, the garden is a unique and enchanting place that people return to time and time again. Situated on the west-facing slopes of the beautiful Torridge

Valley, Rosemoor is undeniably one of the jewels in the West Country crown. Generously donated to the Society by Lady Anne Palmer in 1988, Rosemoor is now established as a garden of national importance, famous for its variety and planting.

To Lady Anne's collection of rare and interesting plants a wide range of varied features has been added. They include a formal garden, where the object is to display an enormous selection of plants and planting schemes. Then there is a series of individual gardens such as the renowned Rose Gardens, Foliage Gardens, the Cottage, Square and Spiral Gardens, and the Winter Garden which provides some stunning effects in the colder months. Other attractions include a lake, a bamboo and fern planted rock gully, an arboretum, three Model Gardens, and a marvellous Fruit and Vegetable Garden.

Also on site is a Plant Centre and Shop which stocks a wealth of colourful, rare and beautiful plants. Each plant comes with a 2-year guarantee. The Shop stocks a delightful selection of beautiful gifts, local produce and drinks including Rosemoor's own apple juice produced from fruit in its own garden.

Round off your visit by sampling the fare on offer in the licensed Restaurant with its garden views, or in the Wisteria Tea Room. Visitors can use the restaurant, plant centre and shop all year round without having to pay a garden entry fee.

55 APARTMENTS AT ROSEMOOR

RHS Garden Rosemoor, Great Torrington,
Devon EX38 8PH
Tel: 01805 624067 Fax: 01805 624717

Apartments at Rosemoor offer quality self-catering accommodation in a delightful setting.

Rosemoor House was built around the 1780s and was donated to the Royal Horticultural Society in 1988 along with the exquisite Rosemoor Garden. The 3 apartments are in the northern and western wings of the house. 'Magnolia', on the ground floor, can sleep 2 guests; 'Camellia' on the first floor also sleeps 2; while 'Azalea', also on the first floor, can accommodate up to 4 people. All enjoy lovely garden views.

56 THE CYDER PRESSE

Weare Giffard, nr Torrington,
Devon EX39 4QR
Tel: 01237 425517
e-mail: info@cyderpresse.co.uk
website: www.cyderpresse.co.uk

The village of Weare Giffard, located off the A386 three miles south of Bideford, has claims to be the longest riverside village in England, straggling for almost two miles along the banks of the River Torridge. It was here that scenes for the film *Tarka the Otter* were shot. The village is rich in old world charm and one of its most delightful buildings is **The Cyder Presse**. Dating from the late 1700s and once at the heart of a working farm, the inn announces itself with a huge painting of a cider press on its white painted exterior. Inside, the atmospheric bar sports masses of black beams and an impressive stone

fireplace with a wood-burning stove. Malcolm and Judy Passmore took over here in the spring of 2007, together with Rusty, their friendly King Charles spaniel. This was their first venture into the hospitality business but they have taken to it like ducks to water. Their chef has created an interesting and varied menu, based wherever possible on local produce, that includes mussels espanola, rosemary roast lamb shank, and a vegetarian chilli. Children have their own menu which offers healthier alternatives to deep fried food. In good weather, meals can be enjoyed at tables in the pleasant beer garden at the side and rear of the inn. Food is served every lunchtime and evening.

The Cyder Presse has always been well-known for its real ales and local ciders. The resident brews are Tribute and Exmoor ales, supplemented by guest ales. This lively pub also provides the "headquarters" of the local skittles and cricket teams, and also hosts a regular Quiz Night.

If you are planning to stay in this lovely part of the county, The Cyder Presse offers comfortable bed & breakfast accommodation in 2 attractively furnished and decorated en suite rooms.

The inn has ample parking and all major credit cards are accepted.

57 THE MILKY WAY ADVENTURE PARK

Clovelly, Bideford, Devon EX39 5RY
Tel: 01237 431255
e-mail: info@themilkyway.co.uk
website: www.themilkyway.co.uk

For kids and families wanting a fantastic, fun-filled day out, **The Milky Way Adventure Park** is a definite must. With five major rides and exciting, live shows The Milky Way has attractions to suit all ages, whatever the weather.

The adventure park in North Devon has it all, including the tallest, fastest and longest roller coaster in Devon, which is sure to satisfy any thrill-seeking visitors. New to the park this year is Professor Nebula's galaxy show time and kids in space quest, which add to other live shows on offer. For those

with younger children the Fantasy Farm and Toddler Town offer an astonishing 6573 square feet of fun for the under 5's with puzzles, soft play, ball pools, mini ride on tractors, sand pits and much more. They will have the perfect opportunity to learn and play and will love taking a ride on Humphrey the caterpillar around the Big Apple track, which is an extremely popular ride at the site. The Big Apple attraction was built in 2008 to make sure smaller children didn't feel left out, because of the bigger roller coasters.

The whole family will be begging to come back again and again when they discover North Devon's biggest indoor adventure play area, which will be just as much fun for the adults.

When the whole family has exhausted themselves they can rest and watch the amazing live shows the park has to offer, which feature Merlin from Britain's Got Talent as well as fantastic displays from the North Devon Bird of Prey Centre. They are performed indoors and outdoors, ensuring visitors don't miss out if it is raining.

The park has its own train, which visitors can ride as many times as they like to take in the surrounding scenery. The wheel-chair friendly Torridge Rose provides a relaxing trip around the site, allowing passengers to experience spectacular views of the North Devon Coast and Dartmoor.

Two cafés on the site provide the perfect resting spot, while visitors decide what to do next. A pet's corner, archery, golf, maze, museum and laser shooting are just some of the many more things to do at the park. The all weather attraction is extremely popular among locals and visitors and one of the many good things about the park is that all of the rides are included in the entrance fee.

58 THE CHURCH OF ST. NECTAN

Stoke, nr Hartland, Devon EX39 6DU
Tel: 01479 810000
e-mail: pinebankchallets@btopenworld.com
website: www.pinebankchalets.co.uk

St. Nectan, the patron saint of this church and parish, was one of many Celtic hermits and missionaries associated with early Christian sites in South-West Britain, South Wales and Ireland in the fifth and sixth centuries. The most important feature of the interior is the fifteenth century oak screen, one of the longest and finest in Devon, and unrestored except for some attention to the paintwork and varnish around 1850. It is over 14 metres long and some 3 metres high, with tracery of high quality.

Above the north porch, and entered by a door in the north aisle, is a room traditionally called Pope's Chamber, in which some local antiquities are stored, most notably parts of an early pulpit purchased in 1609 for 30 shillings and recarved in 1629, apparently on the occasion of the death of James I (the pulpit in the church dates from 1848). The room contained a fireplace and may have been used by a priest or sexton, and to store the parish armour in Elizabethan and Stuart times.

The church as we have it is in the Perpendicular style of the fourteenth century, subject to restoration, particularly the windows, in 1848. Although situated some 3 kilometres from the village of Hartland, the centre of the manor, the church is one of the largest in this part of Devon, Hartland parish being in the top ten percent of Devon parishes by population till the 17th century.

59 THE BRIDGE INN

Bridge Street, Hatherleigh, Devon EX20 3JA
Tel: 01837 810085
e-mail: contact@thebridgeinnhatherleigh.net
website: www.thebridgeinnhatherleigh.co.uk

Set in a beautiful riverside location just after entering Hatherleigh, **The Bridge Inn** reopened in 2008 following a major refurbishment by their owners Pauline and Steven. Having been in the trade for more than 10 years, Pauline and Steven have a well deserved great reputation for hospitality and the warm and friendly atmosphere certainly confirms that. There are two bars; the games bar has darts, pool and large screen TV, whilst the lounge bar offers a more serene environment with background music and local banter at the bar.

Outside there is a riverside patio area overlooking the River Lew, a tributary of the river Torridge, which is renowned for its fishing. There is also a large function room available for private hire. The food is all home made using the

best of local produce and the menu is extensive, featuring all the pub favourites with a few exotic dishes thrown in. There are 5 well appointed en-suite rooms available, comprising 3 double rooms, 1 twin and 1 single with a hearty English breakfast included as well.

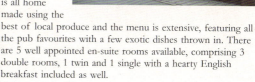

2 Higher Street, Hatherleigh,
Devon EX20 3JD
Tel: 01837 811278
e-mail: relax@thomasrobertshouse.com
website: www.thomasrobertshouse.com

Thomas Roberts House is an elegant and comfortable Georgian House with a sense of history. It is situated just off the centre of Hatherleigh - a lovely little market town in the heart of Devon's Ruby Country just to the north of Dartmoor - and offers three well-appointed en-suite bedrooms, all with king-size beds (alternatively, one super-king-size bed can be converted to twin beds). The town is ideally located for exploring Devon and Cornwall, with Dartmoor, the coast, the Eden Project and the major cities of Exeter and Plymouth all within an easy drive.

Fully centrally heated with off-road parking, a genuinely warm welcome is guaranteed by the owners, Angela and Stephen Caddy, who go out of their way to ensure that your stay is as relaxing and enjoyable as possible. The area is blessed

with a number of good pubs and restaurants renowned for their good food, some of which are within easy walking distance.

After a comfortable night's sleep, wake to a hearty English breakfast (consisting of local produce), which is normally served between 8.00 a.m. and 9.30 a.m.

The owners regret that debit and credit cards cannot be accepted currently and that payment is by cheque or cash only.

61 THE OLD MARKET INN

Chapel Street, Holsworthy,
Devon EX22 6AY
Tel: 01407 253941
e-mail: info@oldmarketinn.co.uk
website: www.oldmarketinn.co.uk

Located in the ancient market town of Holsworthy, **The Old Market Inn** is a handsome old hostelry which dates back to the 1700s and still has some original features. A free house, the inn is owned and run by the Sycamore family who arrived here in September 2006. They have carried out extensive refurbishment to the highest standard and such is the quality of their ales, food and accommodation, the inn was in last 5 finalists in the 'Devon Pub of the Year' award in 2009.

The heart of the Old Market Inn is its bar with its fine choice of beers, and real ales. When Lee Sycamore took over the Old Market Inn, there was not a real ale in sight and Lee was assured by the former landlord that "You can't sell real here, you'll never sell it". This did not deter Lee from having two hand-pulls installed before the inn re-opened. Within a month, a third hand pull was installed, with the fourth coming two months after that. Then, in August 2007, The Old Market Inn was awarded the 'Cask Marque' for outstanding real ales. As the advertising says *'For pubs which serve the perfect pint'*. Five months after being awarded the 'Cask Marque' the inn was recommended by 'North Devon Camra' and now appears in the *CAMRA Good Beer Guide*. The bar also stocks a fine selection of wines, available either by the glass or by the bottle, as well as a delicious range of malt whiskeys and fine brandy. Cocktails are the specialty of the house, with a choice of around 30 varieties.

Good food is another top priority here. The restaurant offers an extensive menu with dishes based on locally sourced ingredients and prepared by 2 exceptional chefs. Every Sunday throughout the year there's a Carvery starting at 12 noon and continuing until 4pm.

The accommodation at the inn comprises three recently refurbished en-suite letting rooms. All the rooms are equipped to the highest standards with all the luxuries of home. These include central heating, free digital wide screen, flat screen TV, tea and coffee making facilities, as well as a spacious shower room. The Old Market Inn also offers guests the use of free internet access through WiFi connection.

Bradworthy, Holsworthy,
Devon EX22 7SQ
Tel: 01409 241964
e-mail: mail@lewbarn.co.uk
website: www.lewbarn.co.uk

Located in the village of Bradworthy, near Holsworthy, **Lew Barn B&B** occupies an imaginatively converted barn standing in large diverse gardens with a fish stocked lake and bordered by two streams. Guests are welcome to enjoy these lovely grounds, have a barbeque or just sit and watch the fish in the lake. You could even try your hand at catching a few but make sure your rod licence is up to date. Then, later on as the day begins to draw in, you could amble up the road to Bradworthy village, a short 5 minute walk. Call in at the local 14th century inn and sample their fine ales and delicious food. If you time it just right you might be walking back beneath one of the magnificent sunsets for which the area is famous. And your hosts, Carole Veness and Pete Vick will even provide you with a torch and umbrella for the walk!

Lew Barn itself, with its vaulted ceilings and old beams, was built of stone in 1860 and converted in 1986. It now offers comfortable accommodation with a choice of single, double and family rooms. All rooms have en suite facilities and are equipped with digital TV and hospitality tray. Also available is Kingfisher Cottage, which has been recently converted and decorated. This self-catering cottage has everything needed for a very comfortable stay, sleeping up to 4 people plus cot. The pine kitchen is well equipped and has a fitted oven and hob, washing machine, fridge, microwave oven and kettle.

At breakfast time, B&B guests will find a good choice that includes a full English, Continental or vegetarian options.

Lew Barn is a dog friendly guest house - Carole and Pete have their own Newfoundland dogs and plan to provide dog kennel facilities during the course of 2009. Guests will then be able to enjoy a day out without their pet if they wish, at owners' risk.

Lew Barn is just two miles from the North Devon/Cornwall border and is perfectly situated for exploring both counties. It is close to the seaside town of Clovelly, the surfing beaches of Bude, Westward Ho and Hartland Point, the shopping towns of Bideford and Barnstaple, and the National Parks of Exmoor and Dartmoor. It is also close to the Tarka Trail and the South West cycle route (no.3).

63 BRADDON COTTAGES & FOREST

Braddon Cottages, Ashwater, Beaworthy,
Devon EX21 5EP
Tel: 01409 211350
e-mail: holidays@braddoncottages.co.uk
website: www.braddoncottages.co.uk

Braddon Cottages was once farmed before being lovingly converted into holiday cottages by current owners George and Ann, comprising four barn conversions and two purpose built houses, there is certainly no shortage of accommodation space. All of the cottages are solidly built stone or masonry buildings with slated roofs surrounded by gardens and lawns landscaped in local stone with fine views over Braddon lake and Dartmoor national park. The secluded nature of the cottages, they are situated at the end of a long drive, guarantees peace and quiet in this lovely rural setting.

The four barn conversions are called Haybarn, Stables, Granary and the Bullocks House. Haybarn, which sleeps 6 is a Napoleonic corn barn facing south with spectacular views of Braddon lake and Dartmoor. The Stables boasts a magnificent conservatory dining area and sleeps up to 10 people. Granary has a very large and unique lounge with an interesting ceiling and landing with massive exposed beams, capable of sleeping up to 9 people, Granary also hosts a large private patio and garden area. The Bullocks House sleeps up to 9 people and has a wonderful large stone fireplace with a wood burning stove. The two purpose built houses are equally spectacular and have the added bonus of being able to be split into two apartments each, so each house sleeps up to 15 people or two apartments capable of sleeping up to 7 or 8. There is a well established fishing lake with large carp, mirror carp, Bream, Tench and Rudd amongst others.

Braddon Cottages can now offer unique low carbon holidays by installing central heating and domestic hot water systems that are served by underground heat mains from a hi-tech Austrian woodchip boiler concealed in a shed in the North Ride area of Braddon. The woodchips are harvested locally.

There are pleasant walks through 150 acres of parkland and woodland, 3 miles of newly created stone pathways that meander through the woodlands, along the streams and around the lake where you can see plenty of wildlife.

Facilities include an all-weather tennis court, games field, children's indoor and outdoor play areas and a full sized snooker table. In the grounds is a large lake with two islands, a jetty, a rowing boat and free fishing for guests. Well behaved dogs are welcome at Braddon.

187

64   EAST LAKE FARM

East Chilla, Beaworthy, Devon EX21 5EP
Tel: 01409 221323
e-mail: eastlakeholidays@bt.com
website: www.eastlakeholidays.co.uk

East lake Holiday Cottages are situated between the rugged glory of Dartmoor National Park and the beautiful North Devon coastline, near the towns of Bude, Widemouth and Sandymouth. Just minutes from the A30, access to East Lake is ideal, rural enough for peace and quiet, yet close enough to the big cities of Bristol, Exeter and Plymouth so that it is not cut off. A key feature of East Lake is that it is also a working farm that holds over 200 head of

cattle and 400 ewes, the farm owners Elizabeth and Dennis encourage guests to help out at feeding time! The cattle is principally made up of Charolais, Belgian Blue and Limousin and through there certification supply Tesco with beef among others. 99% of the sheep are taken by Waitrose, 6-700 lambs are produced a year from the flock of 400 Suffolk Cross Mules ewes and they welcome a helping hand during lambing season! Another benefit of the 150 acres of land on which the farm stands is the game shooting, the farm rears Pheasant and Partridge which are reared from day old chicks to adulthood in purpose designed areas, as only around 40% of the reared stock is shot during shooting season, plenty escape to the wild.

There are three beautifully converted barns to choose from; Lake View Cottage has three bedrooms and sleeps six people over two floors and offers panoramic views over cultivated farmland towards the lake, Spring Lake Cottage has four bedrooms and sleeps eight people with a large private lawn and a cosy wood burning stove in the lounge for those cold wintry nights and finally Ship Lake Cottage has two large en-suite bedrooms and sleeps four people. All of the cottages are fully equipped with modern appliances including TV's and DVD players and are furnished to a high standard

The farm boasts its own 1 acre fishing lake packed full of Brown and Rainbow Trout and coarse fish such as Orfe, Rudd, Roach and Common Carp, overlooked by all of the cottages and just a quarter mile away, fishing in the lake is a great way to spend a morning.

65 PREWLEY MOOR ARMS

Sourton Down, nr Oakhampton,
Devon EX20 4HT
Tel: 01837 861349
e-mail: sue-alecmatth@hotmail.com

This country side public house is situated on
the edge of Dartmoor National Park, right next
to a cycle trail, the **Prewley Moor Arms** is well
positioned to provide that well deserved pint at
the end of a day's sightseeing. Rebuilt in 1995,
the Prewley Moor Arms has a traditional slate
roof, well kept
hanging
baskets and an
outdoor
playground for
children. The
pub serves real
ales and great
home cooked
food sourced
from local producers as well as providing B & B
accommodation in five en suite rooms. The
Prewley Moor Arms is open daily for food and
drink and has disabled access.

HIDDEN PLACES GUIDES

Explore Britain and Ireland with
Hidden Places guides - a fascinating
series of national and local travel
guides.

Packed with easy to read information
on hundreds of places of interest as
well as places to stay, eat and drink.

Available from both high street and
internet booksellers

For more information on the full range
of *Hidden Places* guides and other
titles published by Travel Publishing
visit our website on

www.travelpublishing.co.uk
or ask for our leaflet by phoning
01752 697280 or emailing
info@travelpublishing.co.uk

66 COPPER KEY INN

Fore Street, North Tawton,
Devon EX20 2ED
Tel: 01837 82357
e-mail: martin@inspectbuild.com

The Copper Key Inn sits in the ancient village of
North Tawton, surrounded by gorgeous mid-Devon
countryside close to the spectacular ruggedness of the
Dartmoor National Park. The 16th century inn boasts
a thatched roof, beautifully kept hanging baskets and a
large garden outside, inside the rustic nature continues;
classic slate and wooden floors, an open fire, old exposed
wooden beams and an unspoilt ancient main bar. Martin
and Bernice are a local couple who have been running the
Copper Key Inn for three years, keen to play their part
they support both the local rugby and football teams and
the local industry; coming from farming backgrounds,
Martin and Bernice make sure that all of the food is made

with the finest
of Devon
produce. The
Copper Key
Inn is a real
local pub, there

is a warm communal atmosphere and the pub caters for all
ages with a continually changing selection of home made
Devon fayre which includes some great local ales. The food is
well worth the visit and to make it even more tempting,
Martin has said that anyone presenting this guide at the bar
will receive a 10% discount off their meal.

189

67 THE SEVEN STARS

South Tawton, Okehampton,
Devon EX20 2LW
Tel: 01837 840292
e-mail: info@sevenstarsdartmoor.com
website: www.sevenstarsdartmoor.com

Virginia Creepers adorn the side of this classic stone building and accompanies the well kept hanging baskets that provide beautiful bursts of colour. It is clear that **The Seven Stars** has been cared for and the interior does not disappoint either; polished wooden floors,

exposed stone pillars, an open fire place and old wooden beams create a warm and welcoming atmosphere only found in the best of traditional English pubs. A nice touch are the old photos of the pub and the village throughout the years. The location could hardly be bettered as well; standing opposite the historical Tudor church house, set among the thatched cottages of South Tawton and on the edge of the rugged Dartmoor National Park, the Seven Stars is certainly a special place to eat.

The menu is littered with English dining classics, home made on the premises using locally sourced ingredients; highlights include

battered fish and handcut chips, Devon steak and Otter ale pie and the local ham with free range eggs and chips. Where better to enjoy the food than in the spacious beer garden along with a glass of your favourite wine on a glorious summer's evening. Food is served between 12pm – 2.30pm & 6pm – 9pm, children are very welcome and dogs can be catered for as well!

68 CASTLE DROGO

Drewsteignton, near Exeter EX6 6PB
Tel: 01647 433306
e-mail: castledrogo@nationaltrust.org.uk

Castle Drogo (National Trust) is spectacularly sited on a rocky outcrop with commanding views out over Dartmoor and the Teign gorge. It was built for Sir Julius

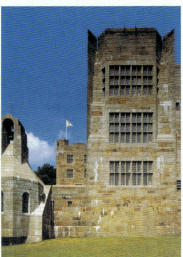

Drewe, a self made millionaire, on land once owned by his Norman ancestor, Drogo de Teigne. Surrounding this 20th century dream country home, lies an equally impressive garden – the highest in the Trust.

The square shape of the castle and the large rotund croquet lawn exemplifies the simple ethos of the architect, Lutyens, of "circles and squares". From spring bulbs in the formal garden, the rhododendron garden, the stunning herbaceous borders, the rose garden and the winter garden there is colour and interest here all year round.

69 CYPRIAN'S COT

47 New Street, Chagford,
Devon TQ13 8BB
Tel: 01647 432256

Shelagh Weeden makes her Bed & Breakfast guests feel really welcome at **Cyprian's Cot**, an early 16th century Grade II listed building of great charm and character. The whole place has an inviting , home-from-home feel, and the bedrooms, prettily furnished with country cottons, combine old features with the amenity of a private bathroom (with the double room) or an en-suite shower room (in the twin). Guests can relax and plan their days or watch television in the lounge, where on cooler evenings a log fire is lit in the large inglenook fireplace.

An original oak screen separates the lounge from the oak panelled dining room, where guests start the day with a breakfast choice that makes good use of local free range produce. The cottage is conveniently located close to the centre of Chagford, but the countryside is also close by – the garden leads straight onto fields, and the views over the Moor are particularly stunning in the setting sun.

Chagford has its own attractions, including interesting shops and highly rated pubs. It's a popular centre for country lovers and walkers are most welcome at Cyprian's Cot; there are local maps available. Pets can be accommodated by arrangement.

70 EDGECUMBE ARMS

The Village, Milton Abbot, Tavistock,
Devon PL19 0PB
Tel: 01822 870603

Situated in Milton Abbot, halfway between Tavistock & Launceston on the B3362. Tony & Glynis Wilson a local couple took over the **Edgcumbe Arms** in March 2009. This small village pub is once again the buzzing centre of village life, much to the delight of the locals. Due to the couple's hard work & Glynis' homemade specials, which offers good taste & value for money, it has the locals & visitors returning time & time again.

HIDDEN PLACES GUIDES

Explore Britain and Ireland with *Hidden Places* guides - a fascinating series of national and local travel guides.

Packed with easy to read information on hundreds of places of interest as well as places to stay, eat and drink.

Available from both high street and internet booksellers

For more information on the full range of *Hidden Places* guides and other titles published by Travel Publishing visit our website on

www.travelpublishing.co.uk
or ask for our leaflet by phoning
01752 697280 or emailing
info@travelpublishing.co.uk

191

Peter Tavy, Nr. Tavistock,
Devon PL19 9NN
Tel: 01822 810348
website: www.petertavyinn.com

On the edge of Dartmoor lies the ever so popular **Peter Tavy Inn.** Surrounded by wonderful woodland, this charming 15th century pub is set in what feels like a remote village, however it is easily accessible, just a mile off the A386, close to Tavistock.

There are 3 special features, which this public house is renowned for- hospitality at the forefront, cuisine and real ales. The Owners Chris and Jo Wordingham have been running this establishment for the past 4 years and they most definitely have something to show for it. The exterior of the building is quaint and traditional, surrounded by shrubbery, giving the building an intimate feel. Throughout the interior you will find ancient timber beams, travelling the length of the property as well as warming log fires, perfect on winter days. On warm days, the garden is a tremendous setting to enjoy a meal or drink and take in the wonderful views of the Dartmoor countryside.

Well-kept real ales are a key focus here and they are wonderful, changing depending on the time of year. 3 ales are available during the winter and a massive 5 ales are served during the summer months. Regulars include jail ale and the other ales available are all brewed in the West Country, keeping in with the pub's roots.

The cuisine here is varied and there are wonderful ingredients used, to create some spectacular tasting dishes. During the lunch service, 12-2pm there is wonderful steak and stilton pie, smoked chicken, bacon and cashew nut salad, minted lamb and orange casserole and a twist on gammon steak, served with apricot and mango sauce. As well as the traditional dishes of roast beef and Yorkshire puddings and ham, egg and chips. Throughout the evening service, 6.30-9pm, there are wonderful meals of lamb shank, Mexican fajita, and salmon fillet with pancetta and pork tenderloin in a mango and chilli sauce. There is also a great selection of fish, steaks and vegetarian options available.

The Peter Tavy Inn is the perfect business for families and children are very much welcomed. The scenic location and quietness of the surrounding village, makes this public house a peaceful and enjoyable getaway, allowing you to enjoy a wonderful meal within the Dartmoor national park.

72 SAMPFORD MANOR

Sampford Spiney, Yelverton,
Devon PL20 6LH
Tel: 01822 853442
e-mail:
manor@sampford-spiney.fsnet.co.uk
website: www.sampford-spiney.fsnet.co.uk

Sampford Manor is a fine example of a Devonshire manor farm house, with a rich history predating the *Domesday Book* (interestingly it once became part of Sir Francis Drake, the famous Westcountry seafarer's, estate. He is thought to have won it for £500 as part of a wager). It is situated on

the edge of the wilds of Dartmoor, just three miles from the market town of Tavistock. The present occupiers have carried out extensive renovations since 1987, to restore the manor to its full beauty and character. It is now an enchanting small holding and bed & breakfast, open all year round (apart from Christmas), the granite foliage-covered exterior, slate floors and beamed ceilings brimming with authentic quality. Much admired at Sampford Manor is their award winning herd of alpaca, and there are free range chickens and ducks.

The accommodation is cosy and in keeping with the atmosphere of the rest of the grounds; double and twin rooms are available with bed and breakfast. Dinner or packed lunches for walkers or bicyclists can be arranged on prior notice. The food is all cooked from local produce, and the eggs used are from their own hens. The manor is well placed for walking, bicycling, riding and other outdoor activities. With stabling and grazing available for horses and dogs welcomed.

The Village Green, Meavy, Dartmoor,
nr Yelverton, Devon PL20 6PJ
Tel: 01822 852944
e-mail: info@royaloakinn.org.uk
website: www.royaloakinn.org.uk

Set in the picturesque village of Meavy, within the Dartmoor National Park and just a few minutes from Yelverton, lies the **Royal Oak Inn.** Owned by the parish council, this free house has been leased to Julie and Stephen Earp and they have been here for the last two years. It is clear that the couple have a wealth of experience in the licence trade, and this definitely makes the Royal Oak a place to visit.

Dating back to the 15th Century, the building oozes charm and history. It was originally a place for pilgrims to stop on their travels and was owned by the church. The property is very eye-catching, surrounded by hanging baskets and potted plants, and it sits right on the village green. The interior is warm and inviting, with the traditional inglenook fireplace and exposed beams. The beams in the lounge bar are from a Spanish galleon that was sunk in the Armada, and there is evidence that Sir Francis Drake visited the Royal Oak. The original slate flooring is still in situ. Both Julie and Stephen believe one of the strengths of the pub is its many original features. Not

much has changed in centuries and you get a real sense of history here.

The Royal Oak is open for every session. It is open all day Saturday and Sunday all year round, and during the summer months it is open all day, every day. The food and drink available at the inn is top notch. There are four real ales to enjoy. Jail ale and Dartmoor IPA are regulars, with a national and Cornish guest ale. Moreover there are two real scrumpy draught ciders to mull over. They are obviously committed to providing fine quality cask ales here.

Food is served seven days a week, from 12-2.30pm and 6-9pm. Due to the popularity of the food here it is definitely best to book at all times, to avoid any disappointment. Stephen is the main chef and he produces a wonderful homemade steak and ale pie, and a fine blue steak. All the beef and lamb used is slowly reared on Dartmoor for a fuller flavour. He also serves mussels mariniére when in season, and a delicious mushroom and goats cheese tartlet. Friday night is fish and chip night in the bar, with the fish being freshly battered to order in the Royal Oaks' own beer batter. The pub has the Taste of the West accreditation for the use of so many local foods and ales.

This real old-fashioned village inn is fantastic for families and couples, and there is plenty of entertainment. There is a quiz night from 9.30pm on Thursdays, which is popular with locals and many visitors. Euchre is played weekly, the Morris men regularly meet here and dance, and there are often impromptu music sets and sing-alongs. There is a games box, and there is also the ultimate curry night once a month – all you can eat for one price. The website provides regular updates on what's on.

Milton Combe, Yelverton,
Devon PL20 6HP
Tel: 01822 853313
e-mail: chris.lisney@hotmail.com
website: www.whodhavethoughtitdevon.co.uk

The **Who'd Have Thought It Inn** in Milton Combe is fast establishing itself as one of West Devons destination eateries thanks to the professional and welcoming stewardship of young proprietors Chris and Ruth.

The ingredients used in Chris's kitchen are sourced from local suppliers, including fresh fish from the Devon coast and rivers, seasonal game from nearby Maristow Estate and traditionally raised beef, lamb and poultry. Vegetables, fruit and herbs used, are likely to have been grown in the village gardens or purchased that day from Tavistocks award winning Farmers Market, offering a refreshing choice of truly seasonal fayre. Vegetarian dishes are created by Chris with the same genuine appreciation of good food and fine flavour that everything on his menu is given and many choices from the à la carte and 'Specials' menu are available as portions for the smaller appetite.

In addition, the Deli-Board offers a Tapas style alternative to starters and dishes to share, including anti-pasta, charcuterie, cheeses and fish, and is available until 10pm.

Originating as a licensed premises in 1540, the lovely stone and slate clad building exudes historical charm with original beams and copper work, stone flagged floors and roaring log fires. As a freehouse, The Who'd Have Thought It Inn has a fine selection of real ales, lagers, ciders and an extensive wine list. Freshly ground Lavazza coffees and warming hot chocolate are always available.

The Inn now features newly appointed en-suite bed and breakfast accommodation. Each room has been lovingly styled to enhance the 16th century features which are in abundance throughout this fine old building. With vaulted ceilings, solid oak floors and original stonework, the rooms have been luxuriously furnished and only the finest cotton linens and non-allergenic bedding has been used to complete the perfect retreat.

With a wide selection of places to explore in the surrounding area as well as nearby Tavistock and Plymouth, you won't be short of amusement. From the glorious Buckland Abbey, once home to Sir Francis Drake and now owned by the National Trust, to the craggy backdrop of moorland and tors that makes up Dartmoor National Park, you really will find something for everyone.

75 THE OLDE PLOUGH INN

Fore Street, Bere Ferrers, Yelverton,
Devon PL20 7JL
Tel: 01822 840358
e-mail: info@oldeploughinn.co.uk
website: www.oldeploughinn.co.uk

Sarah and Ted have 15 years experience in the pub trade, running pubs in the West Country and Dorset and moved to **The Olde Plough Inn** in February 2008 and the pub has gone from strength to strength. The 16th century building has all the traditional features: stone walls, slate flooring and a large fireplace to create the warm and welcoming atmosphere during the cold winter months. The pub and grounds are in immaculate condition and the garden is a great place to sit on a summer's eve and enjoy a pint of well kept local ale. With stunning views of the river Tavy, the garden is the best place to partake in some al fresco dining.

The menu is full of traditional favourites, freshly prepared using the best of local produce with daily specials comprised of in season meat supplied from nearby Tavistock and Plymouth. Sunday nights are a popular time to visit the Plough, live music weekly which varies from Traditional Irish Folk music to Jazz, truly something for everyone. The Plough is open daily for food and the growing popularity of the pub means that it is advisable to make reservations for eating.

77 SOUTH DEVON RAILWAY

The Railway Station, Buckfastleigh,
Devon TQ11 0DZ
Tel: 0845 345 1420
e-mail: info@southdevonrailway.co.uk
website: www.southdevonrailway.org

One of the most delightful ways of exploring the Dart river valley is by taking a journey on the nostalgic **South Devon Railway.** It was originally built in 1872 as the Buckfastleigh, Totnes and South Devon Railway and became part of the Great Western Railway four years later. The line provided much needed support to the local agricultural and woollen industries and continued to serve the local economy during two world wars. Declining traffic led to the line being closed to passengers in November 1958 and to freight traffic in 1962.

However, local enthusiasts managed to re-open the line in 1969 and the most scenic stretch, from Totnes to Buckfastleigh, survives today as the South Devon Railway. It follows the lovely Dart river valley for some 6 miles and the majority of the services are operated by steam engines.

There are regular daily services from mid-March to late October, with special services on other days. At Buckfastleigh Station, you will find a railway museum, railway workshops, cafés serving hot and cold meals, a model railway and the Expressway model railway, gift and book shop.

76 TAMAR BELLE

Bere Ferrers Station, near Yelverton,
Devon PL20 7LT
Tel: 07813 360066
e-mail: stationmaster@tamarbelle.co.uk
website: www.tamarbelle.co.uk

The Tamar Belle is a real treat for those with a passion for trains, or with a sense of adventure for whom normal hotels just don't cut it. Uniquely converted 1930's Gresley teak carriages make up the accommodation and with the restaurant, revive all of the glamour and elegance of the station in an earlier era. Part of the 1890's Victorian Bere Ferrers station, the Tamar Belle heritage centre, is a perfect way to explore the history of this beautiful waterside village, between the rivers Tavy and Tamar.

The visitor centre carriage is a wealth of information and photos of the station and the history of the area. There are also many working railway artefacts around the site including a yard crane, operational turntable and pump trolley (which provides a great way to work off any excess calories from their fine cuisine!) Or why not try your hand at signalling in an authentic ex LSWR signalling box equipped with unique inter-active computer train control simulator?

The accommodation is just delightful; uniquely converted sleeper cars, with original carriage partitions, restored wood trim, seats and luggage racks. Though the novelty of these suites has not been in sacrifice of comfort; both of the carriages have been fitted with double or twin beds, en-suite bathrooms, and tea and coffee making facilities. Interconnecting units to accommodate families can be arranged, as can a day lounge for that extra bit of luxury. All the carriages have been fully fitted with heating and insulation for all year round occupancy. The price for stay is very reasonable, at £30 per person per night for the first night, and reduced prices for subsequent nights with the seventh night complimentary if staying for six or more. There are also appropriate reductions for children and teenagers. The legendary "platelayers" breakfast can be added to your stay for only an additional £5.

To complete any visit to the Tamar Belle heritage centre you must stop off at the restaurant and kitchen car, where you can get breakfast and evening meals served by liveried stewards in a leisurely style reminiscent of the old Pullman Car Company. The menus are changed daily, so there is always a great selection of seasonal food available, made with fresh local produce. Special diets or vegetarian alternatives can be accommodated by prior arrangement. There is a reduction in price on the four course evening meal for people staying overnight.

78 THE WHITE HART

2 Plymouth Rd, Buckfastleigh,
Devon TQ11 0DA
Tel: 01364 642337
e-mail: her_ladyship49@hotmail.com

The White Hart is a 17th century pub full of tradition and character; Devon stone walls, slate roof and a large welcoming wood burning stove inside. Taken over by Dawn in January 2008, the White Hart now provides great ales, fresh quality food and live entertainment. The ales are all well kept and include the local favourite Jail Ale.

The food is all homemade using the best of local produce, popular dishes include the Jail ale & steak pie, lamb hot pot, vegetarian lentil loaf and sticky toffee pudding. Twice a month the White Hart plays host to live music from bands, this live entertainment is very popular and everybody is welcome; including dogs.

The location of the pub means that it is an ideal end point for a walk and with the world famous Dartmoor Tors close by, walkers make up a large part of the clientele.

The White Hart is open all year round and is open for food every day, including Christmas and Easter, so there is no reason not to visit for that special occasion.

79 DARTMOOR OTTERS & BUCKFAST BUTTERFLIES

Buckfastleigh, Devon TQ11 0DZ
Tel: 01364 642916
e-mail: contact@ottersandbutterflies.co.uk
website: www.ottersandbutterflies.co.uk

The tropical landscaped gardens at **Dartmoor Otters & Buckfast Butterflies** are home to a wide variety of exotic butterflies from around the world that live, breed and fly freely here along with small birds and other tropical creatures such as terrapins and leaf cutting ants.

Meanwhile, in specially designed outside landscape, three species of otter, including the native British otter, can be seen both on land and in the water.

The otters, some of whom have been rescued and some that have been bred here, are fed three times a day and both they and the butterflies provide plenty of opportunity for budding wildlife photographers to hone their skills.

80 THE EDGEMOOR

Haytor Rd, Bovey Tracey, Devon TQ13 9LE
Tel: 01626 832466
e-mail: reservations@edgemoor.co.uk
website: www.edgemoor.co.uk

The romantic architectural style of **The Edgemoor** hotel and restaurant will impress any guest; the 1870's school is surrounded by beautifully kept gardens and mature trees. This peaceful setting creates a feeling of being miles from anywhere, but is actually easily accessible from the A38 Exeter to Plymouth Devon Expressway. Close to the historic town of Bovey Tracey, The Edgemoor is located right on the Eastern boundary of Dartmoor National Park, providing a great base from which to explore the beauty of Devon. The exterior is a myriad of fauna, growing up the stone walls of the premises and creating a warm welcome. Inside the opulence continues, huge windows let light flood into the large rooms, all decorated with comfort and relaxation in mind.

The bar, which used to be the schools' gym, hosts a lovely stone fireplace which has a roaring log fire through the winter months and the country cottage style helps guests feel right at home. The lounge boasts a high ceiling and picture windows, framing the lovely gardens and creating a light and airy atmosphere whilst guests enjoy afternoon tea, or just some peace and quiet. The candlelit restaurant offers magnificent food, wonderful service and a truly excellent wine choice. The Edgemoor menu is extensive and the kitchens pride themselves on only using the very best of local produce in a manner that helps sustain local businesses. The beef, for example, is from Dartmoor farms, not only is this reared locally, but supporting Dartmoor farmers also helps to sustain the Dartmoor environment, without the grazing of the cattle, Dartmoor would deteriorate into an overgrown wilderness. Whilst the menu is huge, the kitchen brigade are happy to prepare tailor made dishes for any dietary requirements.

The hotel has 16 beautiful en suite rooms, 5 of which have their own terrace, perfect for enjoying a cool summer evening. Whether you choose to have a four poster, half tester or other, every possible convenience will be made available, all the rooms are stocked with telephones, hair dryers, colour televisions, trouser press and an ample tray of refreshments. The 5 rooms which boast their own terrace have all been individually named; Baskerville, Merrivale, Wilhays, Wistmans and Honeybags, providing that little bit of individuality missing from mainstream motels. The hotel is open all year round and offers special deals in the off season, as well as full disabled access, there are also two downstairs rooms.

81 BAGTOR HOUSE

Ilsington, Dartmoor, Devon TQ13 9RT
Tel: 01364 661538
e-mail: sawreysue@hotmail.com
website: www.bagtormanor.co.uk

Set in the staggeringly rugged beauty of the Dartmoor National Park is a bed and breakfast offering two sumptuously decorated bedrooms; a master double room, wood panelled with its own private bathroom that looks out over **Bagtor**

House's five acres of picturesque gardens where dragonflies dance over the trout ponds in the summer months and in the spring bluebells carpet the woodlands. There is also a spacious family room with a large double bed and two comfy single beds for the kids complete with its own private bathroom at the top of the house

Bagtor provides a comfortable base for adults and children alike to truly envelope the wilderness of the moor. The manor itself is a grade II listed building and makes an appearance in the ancient doomsday book, with original oak beams, flagstone floors and inglenook fireplaces, outdoor seating area and grass tennis court. Any stay here gives the atmosphere of the 15th century that much of the house owes its architecture to, but with all the modern comforts with a stellar breakfast served each day from 8-9am in front of a roaring fire with fresh organic eggs from the manor's own ducks, chicken and geese, local bacon and sausage, homemade bread and museli. Guests find themselves just 30mins from the seaside, within easy reach of many National Trust properties and moorland activities.

83 PRIMROSE TEAROOMS

Lustleigh, Dartmoor, Devon TQ13 9TJ
Tel: 01647 277365
e-mail:
primrose.tearoom@btconnect.com

Lustleigh is a picturesque village, set amongst the Dartmoor countryside and home to several thatched cottages, one of which is Primrose Cottage, where the **Primrose Tearooms** can be found. Ewa and Claudette Collier, the owners, have recently refurbished the tearooms to a high standard, bringing them stylishly into the 21st century. The cottage boasts well kept hanging baskets and a spectacular view over a lovely terraced garden to the rear of the premises.

The tearooms specialise in cakes, Devon cream teas with locally sourced clotted cream and soups, which are all home made on site daily. Also available are sandwiches and panini with a variety of fillings made to order and served with a fresh salad and crisps. Even more impressively, there is a range of traditional teas,

traditional leaf teas, black leaf teas, herbal teas and green leaf teas;

there truly is a tea for everybody! As well as the tea selection, there are various coffees; expresso, lattes, etc and soft drinks.

The tearooms are open daily between 10.30 am and 5 pm except Sundays when they open at 11.30 am. They are closed Wednesdays and Thursdays. The premises have wheelchair access; no disabled toilets.

Widecombe in the Moor,
nr Newton Abbot, Devon TQ13 7TA
Tel: 01364 621257

Set in the picturesque village of Widecombe in the Moor amongst the rugged beauty of Dartmoor's national park, the **Café on the Green** will provide a warm and friendly welcome to all. The kind welcome ensured by the local, enthusiastic staff under husband and wife team, Fiona and Robert Wallace, embrace visitors from all over the country. Just 100 yards from the famous 'Cathedral of the Moor', this fine eatery has a great location in the heart of Dartmoor with views over the village green and the church. Built in the 1920's to accommodate the growing popularity of the Charabanc Tours, the café has been providing delicious cream teas for tourists for nearly 90 years. The large spacious garden can entertain 120 people and in the summer it really is a nice place to spend time, especially when the wild Dartmoor ponies visit! Inside the atmosphere doesn't change; light and airy, the décor is accentuated by the original Lloyd Loom furniture and the wood-burning stove.

The menu is extensive and caters for groups large or small, Café on the Green uses the best of local produce to create sumptuous offerings, including famous Devon cream teas with Devonshire tea. Other examples include fresh salads, soups and

Photos by Tracey-Elliot - Reep

home made cakes. The gorgeous ice cream and clotted cream comes from nearby Langage Farm. Also stockists of the world renowned Tracey Elliot- Reep Collection, local dartmoor photographer and author.

The Café on the Green is open all year round from 9 am to 5 pm, 7 days a week, except during the summer months when they are open slightly later. Fiona and Robert welcome children and well-behaved dogs. There are full disabled facilities, wheelchair access and designated parking bays.

84 THE WESTBANK

54 Bampfylde Rd, Torquay, Devon TQ2 5AY
Tel: 01803 295271
e-mail: westbnk@hotmail.com
website: www.thewestbank.co.uk

A family-run Victorian guest house in Torquay, just a few minutes walk from the stunning seafront and beaches, **The Westbank** is the ideal destination for business or pleasure. This 4 star silver awarded Guest Accommodation boasts a range of elegantly decorated suites, a perfect base from which you can explore the many places of interest Torquay and the surrounding areas, and is also near the conference centre for business visits.

The rooms start at the lower priced full en-suite accommodation, which includes a full English breakfast and the option of having a 4 course traditional evening meal made from fresh and locally source produce. There

are also the large Luxury rooms, which have en-suite and a lounge area or the Four-poster rooms, which have the en-suite and lounge area as well as an elegant four-poster bed; the height of luxury! All rooms include Wi-Fi, hairdryer, hostess tray and all the amenities you need to make your stay as easy and relaxing as possible. There is a minimum of two nights on all room bookings.

The hotel itself has a beautiful cosy lounge area, where you will be greeted with a complimentary tray of teas and biscuits.

85 KINGSHOLM

539 Babbacombe Road
Torquay, Devon TQ1 1HQ
01803 297794
e-mail: enquiries@kingsholmhotel.co.uk
website: www.kingsholmhotel.co.uk

You would struggle to find better accommodation than the Kingsholm. The combination of location, AA 4-star guest accommodation, excellent value, and the individual service offered by Debbie and Alison is unique in Torquay. The high level of repeat guests is proof of quality.

Kingsholm is an Edwardian house with wonderful bay windows overlooking Torwood Gardens. It is a few minute's walk to the bustling harbour with its fine restaurants and theatre, or just ten minutes to the isolation and splendid views of the South West Coast Path. The 9 en-suite bedrooms show the attention to detail in decoration, facilities and cleanliness essential to win 4-stars, yet the relaxed atmosphere gives the easy feeling of visiting an elegant and spacious home. Parking is provided and you can relax from the moment your bags are carried to your room.

In addition to B&B, you may choose to enjoy Debbie's award winning 3-course dinners which feature home-cooking and home-grown produce. There is a modern bar and the lounge is well-stocked with local information. Of course you can book on-line but why not get a feel for where you will stay by telephoning and speaking to Debbie or Alison in person. (Double en-suite £56-70).

86 BARCLAY COURT

29 Castle Road, Torquay,
Devon TQ1 3BB
Tel: 01803 292791
e-mail: enquiries@barclaycourthotel.co.uk
website: www.barclaycourthotel.co.uk

Ever since the Victorian times, Torquay has been one of the UK's top holiday destinations and back then, anyone who was anyone had a villa in this popular area. Built in 1872, **Barclay Court** hotel retains many of the original features of a classic Victorian house; the high ceilings and large rooms for example. The exterior of the hotel is very well kept and creates a very good first impression on approach. The terraced garden offers several places to sit a while and enjoy the clement weather and the pleasant fish pond is soothing after a hard day's sightseeing.

Inside the décor is subtle and creates a feeling of warmth and comfort, the dining room conservatory is south facing and so light and airy and provides the perfect atmosphere in which to enjoy a fabulous full English breakfast. The ten en suite rooms are all very well appointed, with tea and coffee making facilities, hair dryers and an LCD television with free view. The ten rooms are all various sizes, singles, doubles, family suites and even a four poster with a Jacuzzi for that special occasion. The rooms also give very good views over the town of Torquay, the hotel being right at the heart of the action.

Colin and Maz are the convivial owners of this great hotel and have succeeded in creating a warm and welcoming atmosphere in which to relax and enjoy this 'home from home'. The hotel even has a games room, with amusement provided for all ages in case of gloomy weather. Set in the heart of Torquay, the Barclay Court Hotel provides an excellent base from which to explore and enjoy the local area. 'Leave your car in the car park' boasts the excellent website, within 15 minutes walking distance are the beaches, the harbour and the town centre. Also within easy travelling distance are the local popular tourist attractions; Agatha Christie's Mile, Torre Abbey, Cockington Village, Kents Caverns, The Living Coast and Torquay Museum. Torquay makes up one of the towns of Torbay, an area of South Devon which enjoys 22 miles of coast featuring 20 beaches, so whether it is fishing, sunbathing or swimming, there is a beach for everyone.

535 Babbacombe Rd, Torquay,
Devon TQ1 1HQ
Tel: 01803 292900
e-mail: ravenswoodtq@aol.com
website: www.ravenswoodhotel.co.uk

Simon and Saiko are your gracious hosts at the **Ravenswood** B & B, situated in the heart of Torquay and which offers great value for money. The location of this superb hotel is the main draw, just 400 metres from Torquay harbour and town with shops, restaurants and nightlife, as well as just 800 metres from the beach. The hotel also has the added bonus of being just a kilometre away from the station and popular tourist attractions; Kents Cavern and Torre Abbey.

This Edwardian town house was built in 1906, is currently Grade 2 listed and has retained many of its original features, such as sash windows, white render, tiled roof and the terraced gardens. Set above the road, many of the rooms offer great views of Torwood Gardens Park, a perfect place to wander and relax after a hard day's sightseeing. The interior is just as appealing, littered with Edwardian features and decorated in a warm and comfortable manner; the rooms pretty much guarantee a peaceful and restful night's sleep. There are nine rooms and they are all supplied with wash basin, shower and toilet as well all of the basic amenities; tea and coffee making facilities etc. Six of the rooms are doubles, and the other three are single with one of the doubles and one of the singles having a connecting door to create a family suite. The hotel is remarkably well stocked with extras, there is free to use Wi-Fi internet access available all over the hotel, free parking and free view TV's in all of the rooms.

Breakfast is served in the bright and airy dining room with lovely views over Torwood Gardens Park, the menu is large and caters for anyone. There is a continental buffet of juice, cereals, fruit and breads. For the slightly hungrier there is the option of a Full English breakfast consisting of bacon, sausage, sauté potato, mushroom, fried egg and beans. Less filling hot breakfasts come in the form of eggs on toast, beans on toast, mushrooms on toast, bacon sarnies or boiled eggs. Breakfast is served as standard between 8.30 am and 10 am, but earlier breakfasts are available on request. The whole hotel is non-smoking and all major credit cards are accepted.

88 RICHWOOD SPA GUEST ACCOMMODATION

20 Newton Road, Torquay,
Devon TQ2 5BZ
Tel: 01803 293729 Fax: 01803 213632
e-mail:
enq@richwood-hotel-torquay.co.uk
website:
www.richwood-hotel-torquay.co.uk

Nigel and Maxine Fisher own and run this great hotel in the heart of Torquay, itself a main attraction on the English Riviera. Torquay is one of Britain's premier resorts, and is part of Torbay, an area of South Devon made up of Torquay, Brixham and Paignton. Famous for being the place to be seen on holiday by the Victorian's, the architecture of these three towns is mainly Victorian in construction and the **Richwood Spa Guest Accommodation** benefits from the style of building. Large windows and high ceilinged rooms create a light and airy feeling inside the hotel which adds to the warm and friendly welcome offered by Nigel and Maxine. The décor inside is contemporary and modern with wooden flooring and bright colours.

There are seventeen rooms available, in a variety of shapes and sizes and all with en suite facilities. All of the rooms are comfortably furnished and the hotel is fully centrally heated. The rooms are provided with clock/radios, colour TV's and tea & coffee making facilities. The main draw to this excellent hotel though is the amount of things to do; the hotel boasts two bars, the Tavern bar, with the appearance of a small country inn and the second bar is adjacent to the dining room for that pre dinner aperitif. There is a games room which features a pool table and a darts board, as well as a variety of activities for the rare occasion of inclement weather. The main draw however, is the fine 30ft x 15ft heated swimming pool, maintained at around 26°

Celsius throughout the season. Built on the south side, the pool and its adjoining gardens become a sun trap and so a magnet for sun worshippers! In the evening, the area is floodlit for guests to sit a while and contemplate their time in Torquay.

From May to September, weekly entertainment provides the guests with a chance to enjoy themselves and get footloose and fancy free with music and dancing. Out of season a number of short breaks are organised, with a candlelit dinner and dance a very popular choice. The kitchen is stocked with excellent chefs who carefully prepare a four course evening meal for guests who choose to eat in. Special dietary requirements can be catered for with prior arrangement.

89   AVENUE PARK GUEST HOUSE

3 Avenue Road, Torquay,
Devon TQ2 5LA
Tel: 01803 293902
e-mail: avenueparktq@googlemail.com
website: www.avenuepark.co.uk

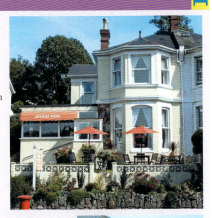

Ever since the Victorian times, Torquay in South Devon has been "The" place to go. The English Riviera has long been known for its recuperative qualities and **Avenue Park Guest House** embodies these qualities perfectly.

Owned and run by Keith and Sandra, the emphasis is on making your stay as **comfortable** and **enjoyable** as possible in a **friendly** and **relaxed** atmosphere, where excellent service and good food awaits you. Please contact us for more information and our tariff.

This Victorian villa, with delightful open views and sunny guest garden and dining room offers the chance to relax. The décor has been individually designed for each room, rather than one style for all. Comfortable beds and little extras as well as Free WiFi and Freeview TV/DVD ensure a comfortable stay.

Eight en-suite rooms - superior, double, twin and family - with two on the ground floor for those who have trouble getting around. The two superior rooms have new en-suites and offer the chance to relax in more space with king sized beds, soft seating and views over the garden and park.

The family rooms can cater for groups of up to 5 people and are perfect for families looking for an idyllic holiday or a place to stay for that special occasion. Double and twin rooms can offer single occupancy.

Ideally located the Avenue Park offers views over parkland and remarkably short level walks to the sea front, the train station and Princess Theatre. Torquay is part of Torbay, which is made up of Torquay, Paignton and Brixham. This cluster of towns means there is a lot to see and do, and the Avenue Park is the perfect base from which to explore this great part of South Devon including nearby Dartmoor.

The Avenue Park is also just a two minute walk from the Riviera Centre with its conference facilities, heated swimming and wave pool, gym, health facilities, bar & restaurant.

Breakfast is served in the light and airy dining room, and the full English breakfast is freshly cooked. Fresh fruit, yoghurt, cereals & toast etc offer a good choice, along with vegetarian or other dietary options. Evening meals can be catered for with prior arrangement.

DEVON

90 BABBACOMBE MODEL VILLAGE

Hampton Avenue, Babbacombe, Torquay,
Devon TQI 3LA
Tel: 01803 315315 Fax: 01803 315173
e-mail: mail@model-village.co.uk
website: www.babbacombemodelvillage.co.uk

Why not experience the ever changing miniature world of **Babbacombe Model Village**. Take time out from the hustle and bustle of every day life and feel on top of the world as you see it re-created in miniature. Thousands of miniature buildings, people and vehicles set in 4 acres capture the essence of England's past, present and future. It's not just the humour, nor the animation – it has a life of its own.

Towering above a medieval village, Merrivale Castle is a miniature tourist attraction full of visitors enjoying a day out re-living medieval England. The whole scene comes to life with superb animated effects featuring all the bawdy, comic events of old England. Dramatically illuminated at night, part of this feature is the Dastardly Dungeon, where characters are stretched to their limit, and hysterical scenes at the

Celebrity Banquet- see who's been invited to the feast. After its popularity in 2005, the fabulous Silvers Circus has returned to town – a unique opportunity to see this amazing animated model of a three-ringed circus with over 120 animated effects and moving figures.

Open all year, and summer evenings until late - times vary so phone or check website for details.

91 POTTERS MOORING HOUSE

30 The Green, Shaldon,
Devon TQ14 0DN
Tel: 01626 873225
e-mail: info@pottersmooring.co.uk
website: www.pottersmooring.co.uk

Potters Mooring was formerly a sea captains residence and dates from 1625 when Shaldon was a small fishing community. Today, Potters Mooring has been lovingly refurbished to the highest standards whilst retaining its quiet charm and historic appeal. Potters Mooring occupies a great position in the small village of Shaldon, overlooking the picturesque village green, surrounded by elegant houses and cottages, and only minutes from the mouth of the river Teign and the nearby beaches.

Bob and Linda have created a friendly and warm atmosphere in this quaint hotel, which is steeped in history and offers an educational experience for any and all visitors. If you book early you could choose a river view room, overlooking the river Teign towards Teignmouth or a room overlooking the

tranquil bowling green so enjoyed by locals and visitors to the UK alike.

Alternatively there are one or two bedroomed

cottages for families and groups of friends. All five rooms and cottages are en suite and are decorated and furnished to a high specification in order to create a home from home. There is an extensive breakfast menu and for the truly hungry there is the famous captain potters full English breakfast, not for the faint hearted!

207

92 LYNTON HOUSE

7 Powderham Terrace, 'Seafront',
Teignmouth, Devon TQ14 8BL
Tel: 01626 774349
e-mail: stay@lyntonhouseteignmouth.com
website:
www.lyntonhouseteignmouth.com

Lynton House boasts a truly unique location, yards from the popular beach and promenade sea front of Teignmouth. Ably run by the husband and wife team Chris and Lorraine Lunn, Lynton House has a warm and welcoming atmosphere and service that has guests returning time and time again. The striking building has an interesting history, being part of Powderham Terrace, an impressive example of Victorian architecture which was erected in the 1860's by the Courtenay family, Earls of Devon. The interior is equally welcoming, clean, well kept and cosy, a good example is the lounge bar; tastefully decorated and with comfortable furnishings, this is the ideal place to sit and relax. The large picture windows look out over the sea front and promenade and there is endless scope for just watching the world drift past.

Lynton House has 12 en suite rooms available, almost all of which have stunning views of the sea or the river from which Teignmouth gets its name. All the rooms have comfortable beds, colour television, tea & coffee making facilities to create the feeling of a home away from home. The hotel has a spacious dining room, situated on the ground floor of the three floors and offers a quiet and luxurious place to enjoy breakfast and dinner. The hearty breakfasts and the four course dinners are created using only the finest of locally sourced produce. A typical four course dinner consists of a home made soup; West Country crab cakes with a parsley sauce, home made bread and butter pudding with custard and a selection of cheese and biscuits.

As mentioned earlier, Lynton House overlooks the well kept promenade of Teignmouth, which boasts, amongst other things, a new state of the art children's play area, an adventure golf course and the grand old Victorian Pier. Opposite the pier is a large grassed area, ideal for a game of football or cricket. Chris and Lorraine have installed a stair lift to the first landing for guests with mobility problems. Unfortunately there is no parking available at the hotel but there are parking bays along the sea front and a large car park a few minutes walk away.

DEVON

93 OYSTERCATCHER CAFÉ

12 Northumberland Place, Teignmouth,
Devon TQ14 8DD
Tel: 01626 774652
website: www.oystercatcherscafe.co.uk

Off the beaten track and by the back beach of Teignmouth, you will find the **Oystercatchers Café**, just 50 yards from the river side and a 5 minute walk to the promenade; this quaint little café provides food and drink all year round, seven days a week. Inside, the large wall to wall window lets the light flood in and the airy atmosphere inside helps promote the nautically themed décor. There are paintings and pictures all around the premises depicting scenes by the ocean and comfy sofas from which to study them.

The café serves extremely good home cooked meals; the menu is extensive and caters for every taste. There is a large range of breakfasts, and not just cooked; muesli, croissants and smoothies are available for those who prefer a lighter breakfasts. For lunch you can choose from jacket

potatoes, baguettes, sandwiches and omelettes with a variety of fillings. For people with a larger appetite, there is a selection of more hearty meals, including home made chilli, bangers and mash and beer battered fish and chips.

Open daily from 8 am, the Oystercatchers café is a must for visitors to Teignmouth.

94 BRISTOL HOUSE

16 Garfield Road, Paignton,
Devon TQ4 6AU
Tel: 01803 558282
e-mail: info@bristolhousehotel.com
website: www.bristolhousehotel.com

Located just off the Esplanade and only 100 yards from the seafront, the **Bristol House** is a family run guesthouse offering value for money accommodation. The guesthouse is close to both the shopping centre and parks, and just a 3-minute walk from the train and bus stations. All of the 8 rooms are comfortable, full centrally heated and are equipped with colour TV and hospitality tray. There's a choice of family en suite and double en suite rooms, and there are toilets and shower units on each floor. Guests have the use of a comfortable TV lounge and at breakfast time there's a good choice that include a Full English and one for children. Evening meals are available on request as are packed lunches for your day trips.

Owners Nancy and Leon de Jong hail from the Netherlands so multiple languages are spoken. Open all year round, the guesthouse offers early and late season reductions; children under 4 years stay free and there's a 50% reduction for children aged 4 to 12 years. In addition to Paignton's many attractions, the guesthouse is also within easy reach of Paignton Zoo, Kents Cavern, Babbacombe Model Village and the Becky Falls Woodland Park.

209

95 THE CLIFTON AT PAIGNTON

9-10 Kernou Road, Paignton,
Devon TQ4 6BA
Tel: 01803 556545
e-mail:
enquiries@cliftonhotelpaignton.co.uk
website: www.cliftonhotelpaignton.co.uk

The Clifton at Paignton is a late Victorian terraced establishment, offering warm and comfortable accommodation, excellent service and wonderful breakfast and optional dinner. Situated in a central location, within a five minute walk is the seaside, harbour, pier and the cinema. Also close by are the popular tourist attractions: Oldham Mansion, the Steam Railway and the Palace Theatre.

The Clifton boasts fourteen excellently appointed rooms, with all having en suite or a private bathroom. The décor in all of the rooms is superb and really brings home the view that this hotel is high quality. Some of the rooms even have sea views, which shows just how close to the action The Clifton really is.

The Clifton at Paignton currently holds the Welcome Host award and a big part of that is the excellent food produced by head chef and owner Steve. Breakfast consists of a continental buffet and a choice of cooked English breakfasts. Optional is the evening meals, the menu is based on an international home cooked dishes, examples include pasta with a mushroom and garlic sauce and breast of turkey steak with a wine cream and tarragon sauce. Steve is proud of the fact that they can cater for most dietary requirements and welcomes requests.

96 THE BLACK TULIP

56 Victoria Street, Paignton,
Devon TQ4 5DS
Tel: 01803 552987

The Black Tulip café and eatery is a small but classy family run business nestled in the bustling centre of the seaside village of Paignton. Owners of the Black Tulip Susan and Annette believe that the customer always comes first and guarantee satisfaction.

Their tastefully decorated café is raised over a split level with elegant wooden flooring and modern leather seats for every guest. They serve a wide variety of breakfasts, sandwiches, salads, jacket potatoes, omelettes and toasties, also with a comprehensive main menu and children's menu and the option of choosing from the daily specials board which serves a variety of the best seasonal produce. Local favourites from the main menu are the homemade pie of the day, or bubble and squeak breakfast served with crispy bacon and a free range egg.

There is also a tempting range of deliciously home baked cakes and scones to accompany the selection of coffees and teas or for those fancying themselves an afternoon tipple – the Black tulip is also licensed.

It is open 9am-9pm Aug-Sept and 9am-4pm Sept-Jul and only a 5 minute walk to the beach and pier and just one minute from the station so the perfect spot to stop for lunch on a sunny Devonshire afternoon.

Berry Head Rd, Brixham,
Devon TQ5 9AF
Tel: 01803 856738
website: www.thebreakwater.co.uk

The Breakwater is a family run coffee shop & bistro in stunning surroundings overlooking the coastal Devon town of Torbay. The brightly decorated exterior gives a beach, summery feel and the interior carries on the seaside feel; hardwood floors and pine furniture promote an easygoing atmosphere. The bank of windows all along the side of the restaurant allows views over towards Torbay for the diners and gives a wonderful light and airy feel to the premises. The warm and friendly welcome received when walking through the doors encourages the informal ambiance and The Breakwater proprietor Lee Tyrrell is keen to keep this going.

The Breakwater has a lunch and snack menu which is served from 12 pm to 5.30 pm every day and offers several options; sandwiches with a variety of fillings, including fresh Brixham crab, supplied by local suppliers Browse Brothers. Other snacks include jacket potatoes, pasta dishes, 'Breakwater Salads', and lunch specialities which features delicious dishes such as king prawns with a house salad and crusty bread, moules mariniére mussels and fresh Brixham fish and chips. There is also a sumptuous selection of cakes and 'naughties'; for example, carrot cake, chocolate fudge cake, toasted tea cakes with butter and jam and Devon cream tea for one 'said to be the best in Devon'.

The extensive evening menu is served between 5.30 pm and 9.30 pm and features a variety of classics cooked to perfection to order. Popular dishes include the home made fish pie made with a mix of seasonal fish in a cream sauce topped with mashed potato and a sprinkle of cheese, belly pork with an apple and cider sauce, line caught mackerel served with red pepper butter, new potatoes and a house salad and the 'Breakwater' paella for 2 which is crammed full of seasonal fish. For the extra hungry, the starter menu is delicious, deep fried whitebait and seafood chowder being highlights. The tempting choice of desserts ensures that you will go away with a very well fed stomach!

The restaurant also boasts a selection of paintings and sculptures on show from the Brixham shoal of artists, which offer the guest some culture to accompany their food. The informal nature of this excellent eatery means that you are welcome for just a coffee and a snack as you are for a full meal. Children and dogs are both welcomed and catered for.

35 Fore Street, Brixham,
Devon TQ5 8AA
Tel: 01803 853546

Located in the picturesque fishing village of Brixham, just minutes from the harbour, it is no wonder that **The Lemon Tree Café and Bakery** has plenty of people visiting and revisiting it. Well-liked among locals and tourists all of the food served on the premises is cooked fresh to order, adding to the quality of the place. The delightful café is set in the ideal location for visitors wanting to take in the breathtaking charm of Brixham, a colourful and lively fishing port at the southern end of Torbay.

Among the tasteful specialties on offer are Devonshire cream teas, which go down well with visitors. Whether it is a breakfast, lunch, main meal or light bite you are after the popular café, situated in the heart of the village, provides the ideal place to go. Located in a place undergoing a programme of regeneration it is the perfect spot for locals and visitors to fall in love with the area. The current owner has been running the café, situated in the bustling village centre, for around a year. He knows what customers want having been in the trade for 17 years and this is evident in the number of customers he attracts back time and time again.

Inside, the café has been tastefully refurbished since he took charge of the premises, creating a light, bright and vibrant feel to the place. Spread over two floors, there is seating for 100 people.

The outdoor secret patio garden is a hidden gem and provides the ideal location for customers to sit and relax, while enjoying the tea, coffee and delights on offer. There is a wide and varied choice of food to choose from on the menu as well as several appealing daily specials. Going that extra mile, the owner is happy to cater for customers' needs and even takes phone orders for people who might like to enjoy a packed lunch or to order meals and light bites to takeaway.

The Lemon Tree Café and Bakery provides the ideal resting place from exploring the streets and alleys or after a busy day sightseeing.

The hilly town has a lot of history that visitors can explore, with the nearby statue of William of Orange just a taster of its diverse history.

The Lemon Tree Café and Bakery is open 8am-3pm Mon-Sat during November-April with longer hours in the summer months, opening from 8am-6pm five days a week from April-October. Saturdays they are open 8am - 4pm and Sundays 10am -4pm.

99 LANSCOMBE HOUSE

Cockington Village,
South Devon TQ2 6XA
Tel: 01803 606938
e-mail: stay@lanscombehouse.co.uk
website: www.lanscombehouse.co.uk

Cockington Country Park is located in South Devon just a short stroll to the sea. The stunning countryside is world renowned and Cockington Village is famous in its own right for the lovely thatched cottages and houses in it. It is among such beauty that **Lanscombe House** stands and it certainly does not disappoint!

The house itself was built in the mid 1800's and the tasteful décor has managed to retain original features that add charm and character to this wonderful hotel.

The refurbishment includes eight individual en suite bedrooms all with showers or baths, a light and airy breakfast room, an elegant guest lounge with seasonal log fires, a cosy bar and peaceful walled gardens.

In the evenings, dinner can be enjoyed at the village's famous

thatched tavern; the Drum Inn, designed by Sir Edward Luytens. A little further afield, South Devon has a vast range of great restaurants, sea front bistros and even Michelin Star establishments.

The 450 acres of Cockington Country Park and its preserved thatched village are hidden away from the hustle and bustle of Torquay, however, it is just a 30 minute level walk or a few minutes by car, the local village even has a shuttle bus service.

100 THE BUTCHERS ARMS

Slade Lane, Abbotskerswell,
Devon TQ12 5PE
Tel: 01626 360731

The Butchers Arms is the essence of South Devon; a beautiful stone built former smithy (Circa 1500), close to the market towns of Newton Abbot and Totnes, and the Dartmoor National Park. Large enough to cater for corporate events and private parties (can seat up to 50 people for a buffet), and yet intimate enough for a lovely meal with all the family. Children are welcome, with an enclosed outdoor playing area, and dogs are also welcome on leads.

The restaurant and bar areas are beautifully cosy and rustic, with beamed ceilings, wooden floors and traditional furniture. The warmth and aroma of their two open wood burning fireplaces will be just the thing you need in the colder months, and a large south-facing beer garden is perfect in the summer. Their menu, including a sumptuous range of char-grilled quality meats, and an extensive wine menu to compliment your meal, is as popular locally as it is with visitors (for this reason it is always best to book your table in advance). Where possible ingredients, such as eggs laid by their own hens, are locally sourced. Food is served Mon-Fri 12-2:30pm and 6-9pm (12noon-9pm on weekends).

There is also a renowned music quiz held weekly on Friday nights, and a traditional meat-draw.

101 THE SANDYGATE INN

Lower Sandygate, Kingsteignton,
Devon TQ12 3PU
Tel: 01626 354679
e-mail: jonlemme@yahoo.com

Jon and Sandra took over **The Sandygate Inn** in October 2008 and together with hard work and over 20 years experience in the hospitality trade, it is now a spectacular place to eat. Originally a 16th century staging inn, as well as a warm and welcoming bar and restaurant, it is also home to Roy, the friendly ghost! Outside, the white washed walls are adorned with old wheels and coaching paraphernalia and inside the old heritage is still visible. Old beams support the ancient walls and a large fireplace crackles during the cold winter months.

The Sandygate Inn is proud to produce solely home cooked food, 'just like your mum used to cook it!' and the

menu is littered with old pub classics such as beer battered fish and chips and steak & ale pie. For those who aren't quite hungry enough for the huge main portions, then there is a light bite section, featuring a host of fillings in a choice of bread; panini, ciabatta, baguette and white or brown bloomer. Food is served between 12 pm and 2 pm, and between 6 pm and 9 pm seven days a week.

214

102 THE ROCK CLIMBING AND CAVING CENTRE

Chudleigh, Devon TQ13 OEE
Tel: 01626 852717
e-mail: trc@globalnet.co.uk
website: www.rockcentre.co.uk

If it is a unique experience or challenging adventure you are after **The Rock Climbing and Caving Centre** offers the ideal activities for any adrenalin junkie. Located in Chudleigh, which falls in South Devon's area of outstanding natural beauty, the centre has something for everyone. Swinging through the trees, children do not need to be supervised by an adult for tree topping and will have an amazing experience that is suitable for all ages. It provides the ideal outing for schools, hen parties and corporate events as tree topping requires no previous experience.

Trained guides will be on hand to make sure visitors are fully equipped with safety kit and will supervise ground level training before taking people on an adventure to remember. If tree topping isn't enough to fill your thrill seeking appetite there is always the opportunity to extend your stay and enjoy other various activities on offer, including rock climbing, caving and abseiling.

Set in beautiful surroundings the site has been utilized imaginatively to create the perfect environment to offer a wide range of activities. The limestone cliffs, caves and trees are set in ten acres of grounds and provide a good learning resource without spoiling the surrounding environment. The centre offers a wide variety of climbs and abseils and allows groups to abseil from cliffs, bridges, viaducts, buildings, dams and trees and with the staff's expertise visitors can also learn ice climbing techniques on the breathtaking sandstone cliffs of Devon. Sea-traversing is another sport the centre encourages people to have a go at. The centre's caving staff are extremely experienced and knowledgeable about all caving areas of Britain. Their passion for caving often puts first time cavers at ease, allowing them to get the full enjoyment out of exploring caves.

On-site there are also undercover facilities, including a wall, which provides a popular practicing or warming up facility that can be used on wet days or dark evenings. The main wall offers nine vertical routes, three overhanging and three slab routes plus a featured wall. These are all intended for top roping and have ropes in place. This facility is available for use by members of the public who have appropriate experience/qualification and instructed sessions are also available. A wide selection of climbing shoes and chalk bags are available for hire. A mobile climbing wall can be hired by schools, youth groups and for parties or fun.

215

103 THE HIGHWAYMAN'S HAUNT

Exeter Road, Chudleigh,
Devon TQ13 0DE
Tel: 01626 853250
website: www.thehighwaymanshaunt.com

The attractive thatched-roofed building of **The Highwaymans Haunt** is seeped in history. Built during the reign of King Edward I (1239-1307), it provided quarters for the Cromwellian cavalry during the English Civil War, and (the origin of its name) is reputed to have been the hideout of local highwayman Jack Witherington when it was a farm house. With this in mind it is hard not to fall in love with this picturesque Inn, which has a lovely rustic atmosphere with low beamed ceilings, oak screens, open stone fire places and a brilliant example of an original bread oven.

Neil Elliott and David Bowden, with their wives Julie and Sylvie, took over the Highwaymans Haunt in November 2005, and have since built a name for themselves for their friendly service and amazing menu. They have an excellent a la carte menu, which includes scrumptious dishes like "Drunken mutton"; succulent roasted leg of lamb served with a rich redcurrant, rosemary and maderia sauce, and "Emily's salmon fillet" smothered in a rich lobster and prawn sauce. Also there is a daily changed specials board, where you are always assured the best in fresh seasonal dishes, vegetarian and children's options, and a range of lighter snacks. On a sunday lunchtime they have a freshly prepared sunday carvery with a good selection of seasonal vegetables. Having built fantastic relationships with local farmers, they are able to offer fresh local produce to use throughout all of the food served.

The real ales and extensive wine list on offer are perfect accompaniment to this delicious food, and are lovely to enjoy on the patio area with its stunning views of the surrounding fields and hills. Lunch is served 11:30 – 2pm Mon-Fri (and from 12 noon on Sundays), dinner is served 7-9:30pm Sun-Fri and 6:30-9:30pm Saturdays. There is a large car park and dog friendly areas.

From the lush countryside and tranquillity surrounding the Highwaymans Haunt it would be easy to assume it is in a remote location, but at only quarter of a mile from the A38 duel carriageway, and with close proximity to the towns of sea-side Plymouth and historic Exeter, it is far from remote. There is also the nearby Ugbrook house and gardens to see; if your senses are not overloaded already from the lush gardens at the Highwaymans Haunt!

216

104 THEATRE ROYAL PLYMOUTH

Royal Parade, UK. PL1 2TR
Tel: 01752 668282
e-mail: info@theatreroyal.com
website: www.theatreroyal.com

The building itself has a glass-fronted exterior which creates a light, spacious and relaxing environment for its patrons, both able and disabled. Split over three levels, the theatre offers two bars and catering facilities which include a coffee shop, cafe and restaurant.

Situated in the heart of Plymouth City Centre, the **Theatre Royal Plymouth** is one of the most recognisable and attractive buildings in the area. Having now been open for 25 years, the Theatre Royal boasts a host of facilites, including a 1300 seated auditorium and a 200 seated studio theatre.

Between the two stages the theatre caters for all tastes, regularly showing dramas, musicals, dance, operas and new, creative pieces of theatre - providing audiences with the best in touring shows and new home-grown productions.

105 PLYM VALLEY RAILWAY

Marsh Mills Station, Coypool Road,
Plympton, Devon PL7 4NW
Tel: 01752 330881
website: www.plymrail.co.uk

The object of the **Plym Valley Railway** is to relay and restore a short section of the former Great Western Railway branch line from Plymouth to Launceston via Tavistock and, in particular, the section that runs from Marsh Mills, Plympton to the local beauty spot of Plym Bridge, a distance of around a mile and a quarter. A series of heritage steam and diesel locomotives

from the 1950s and 1960s operate the services that run on Sundays and there is also a buffet and souvenir shop at Marsh Mills.

HIDDEN PLACES GUIDES

Explore Britain and Ireland with *Hidden Places* guides - a fascinating series of national and local travel guides.

Packed with easy to read information on hundreds of places of interest as well as places to stay, eat and drink.

Available from both high street and internet booksellers

For more information on the full range of *Hidden Places* guides and other titles published by Travel Publishing visit our website on

www.travelpublishing.co.uk or ask for our leaflet by phoning **01752 697280** or emailing **info@travelpublishing.co.uk**

217

106 KITLEY HOUSE

Kitley Estate, Yealmpton, Plymouth,
Devon PL8 2NW
Tel: 01752 881555 Fax: 01752 881667
e-mail: sales@kitleyhousehotel.com
website: www.kitleyhousehotel.com

The spectacular country mansion of the **Kitley House Hotel** has been the family home of the Polloxfens and the Bastards since the time of Elizabeth l. The original Tudor house is believed to have been constructed by a Thomas Polloxfen during the reign of the first of the Tudor kings; Henry VII (1457 – 1509). The house stands in beautiful parkland setting on a promontory of land facing the estuary of the river Yealm. Kitley stands on the bank of a westerly branching creek fed at its head by the Silverlake stream. At one time the lake was well stocked with brown trout, rainbow trout and many other fish. The lake and nearby estuary is an ornithologists paradise.

The mansion, like so many country houses, has changed in appearance a number of times. The foundations are 16th century and experts judge that from the thickness of the interior walls that the original Tudor house was H-shaped, the present staircase hall taking up the centre. The building was thoroughly remodelled in 1820 and took 5 years, the house was not thought to be especially imaginative or fanciful afterwards, but is set apart by the freshwater lake in front, separated from the creek by a purpose built dam.

Nowadays however, Kitley House is one of the most popular destinations for those short breaks and holidays, laying on many events that attract guests from all over the world. One very popular event, now in its tenth year, is the Murder Mystery Dinner, where the Candlelight Theatre Company of Torbay comes to the house. The format for the evening is very simple, starting with a cocktail reception at 7 pm when the actors assume their roles! Other events include musical concerts and plays.

Kitley House is an oasis of quiet luxury, providing the highest standards in comfort, cuisine and personal service. A sweeping staircase leads up to 19 spacious bedrooms and suites. Each has panoramic views over the estate and is richly appointed with furnishings designed to reflect the traditional elegance of the house while incorporating all modern facilities. The rooms vary from the base club rooms up to the four poster state rooms, opulent luxury for those special occasions.

Kitley House is the perfect venue, be it for that important business conference, a big birthday celebration in the stunning restaurant or even weddings, civil ceremonies take place all the time.

218

107 THE BAY HORSE INN

8 Cistern Street, Totnes, Devon TQ9 5SP
Tel: 01803 862088
e-mail: thebayhorse@btinternet.com
website: www.bayhorsetotnes.com

Set at the top of medieval Cistern Street, **The Bay Horse Inn** is a traditional slate fronted house long converted into an excellent inn. The frontage is complimented by window boxes, providing splashes of colour and creating the impression that this pub is well cared for. That impression is only intensified inside, the bar area boasts a flag stone floor, an inglenook fireplace and plenty of snug sofas. The location of this establishment is great, close to the shops and the castle, church and museum are all within short walking distance.

This CAMRA award-winning pub offers an excellent range of local real ales and ciders, along with a quality selection of lagers and wines to suit all tastes. A great surprise is a huge rear outdoor area, comprising a partly covered patio courtyard leading through to a lovely walled garden (pictured). A light bar menu is offered comprising the best of local produce, also supported by seasonal weekend fare such as BBQs in summer and more hearty options in the cooler months. The inn also host regular Sunday night live music, along with some folk nights during the week.

On the first floor there are two bedrooms for hire; one double with an en suite and one luxury double en suite overlooking the garden. The rooms have recently been renovated to a high standard and there are plans afoot to create a twin room. The Bay Horse Inn is ideally situated to enjoy the delights of South Devon and is within easy access to Torbay, the South Hams.

109 ASHLEIGH HOUSE

Ashleigh Rd, Kingsbridge,
Devon TQ7 IHB
Tel: 01548 852893
e-mail: reception@ashleigh-house.co.uk
website: www.ashleigh-house.co.uk

The medieval market town of Kingsbridge boasts many lovely old buildings and one of the finest is the Victorian guesthouse; **Ashleigh House**. Situated within easy walking distance of the picturesque estuary and the many fine pubs and restaurants of Kingsbridge, Ashleigh House is the ideal place from which to explore South Devon.

First impressions when approaching the large Victorian house are very good. The property is well maintained with an attractive exterior. Inside the standard remains just as high, typically for large Victorian houses, the rooms are all very spacious and many retain several original features.

There are eight rooms available in total and all have en-suite facilities as well as the basic amenities expected of a high level B&B. The eight rooms are comprised of 5 double rooms, 1 twin room, 1 triple room with

one double bed and one single and one family room, which with its bunk beds, can sleep 5.

Facilities include a large breakfast room which overlooks the mature gardens and the entrance conservatory provides an informal area for guests to relax..

219

Dittisham, nr Dartmouth,
Devon TQ6 0ES
Tel: 01803 722235
e-mail: redliondittisham@hotmail.co.uk
website: www.redliondittisham.co.uk

Set in the heart of one of Devon's prettiest villages, **The Red Lion** is a traditional pub with log fires, real ales and tasty home-cooked food. Dating back to around 1750 when it was a coaching inn, it maintains the best traditions of country hospitality.

A Free House, it has a well stocked bar with a selection of real ales: Palmers Best Bitter from Dorset, Dartmoor IPA from just up the road in Princetown on Dartmoor plus a guest ale generally from the award-winning Newton Abbot Brewery at Teignworthy. The bar also stocks two lagers, John Smiths, cider and Guinness. The wine list is concise and carefully chosen with wines from around the world to please all palates. The Red Lion is owned by a French lady so, naturally, the cuisine on offer is taken very seriously with everything on the menu home-made. During the winter months you can enjoy your beer and food by the log fire, getting away from the wind and rain outside. Then, when the weather picks up, why not enjoy some refreshment on the patio with its outstanding views of the enchanting River Dart.

The Red Lion also offers bed and breakfast in eight lovely en-suite rooms, two of which could be family rooms, and all of which enjoy central heating, tea-making facilities, telephone and TV. Three of the rooms enjoy outstanding views of the River Dart and are furnished to a very high standard with king size beds. The large bathrooms are equipped with baths and power showers. For those who prefer self-catering, a 2 bedroom flat is available.

Dittisham village borders the 11-mile estuary of the River Dart. This area is renowned for sailing and a variety of craft are available for hire locally. It is perfect walking country and is popular with walkers, ramblers and rambling associations. The Red Lion is also well placed for visiting two steam railways, Dartmoor National Park, the National Marine Aquarium in Plymouth, the Eden Project and many other attractions. There are no fewer than 4 golf courses nearby (with a 25% discount for the Red Lion's guests on both green fees and entry to the Fitness Club at the Dartmouth Golf & Country Club), as well as numerous beaches. But for some, the real attractions of Dittisham lie in its peace and tranquillity and in the unspoilt beauty of the surrounding countryside.

110 PORT LIGHT

Bolberry Down, Malborough, Kingsbridge,
Devon TQ7 3DY
Tel: 01548 561384
Mobile: 07970 859992
e-mail: info@portlight.co.uk
website: www.portlight.co.uk

Port Light hotel, restaurant and bar enjoys a unique position, set nearly 450ft above sea level, amidst acres of National Trust Coastal Countryside. It lies between Hope Cove, with its thatched cottages and small but lovely beach, and Salcombe, the famous yachting haven as featured on ITV's lifeboat series. A former Golf Clubhouse and war-time RAF Radar Station, Port Light is owned and run by Hazel and Sean Hassall who extend a genuinely friendly welcome to all their guests.

The bar is bright, spacious and has its own popular menu, with traditional, home-cooked fayre a speciality. The menu ranges from scrumptious salads and hot dishes cooked to order, to jacket potatoes, sandwiches and home-made vegetarian dishes. The lunchtime menu is available from noon until 2pm. The bar is a favourite meeting place where tourists and locals alike can enjoy the relaxed atmosphere and watch the world pass by. In the evening, settle down to enjoy the unsurpassable "Devon Sunsets" over Bigbury Bay or Hope Cove.

From 7pm to 9pm, an evening menu is on offer with locally caught fish as a speciality, along with prime Devon steaks and a Port Light speciality "Kleftico" - a bowlful of lamb shoulder slow cooked in a clay oven together with root vegetables, a hint of garlic and rosemary and onion. All the fish served here is bought from local markets and delivered to Port Light straight from the boats. All the meats are locally reared within South Devon, are fully traceable and prepared in Port Light's own butcher's facilities. To accompany your meal, there's a good choice of wines by the bottle or by the glass.

The restaurant has received recognition for Outstanding Inn Food and Service which proves Port Light's dedication to cooking and chef David Singline's consistent food quality David has been the chef here since 1997. Unlike other eating venues where the chef does appear to change every year, at Port Light David assures customers of a consistently high standard of cuisine whenever you visit.

If you are planning to stay in this lovely part of Devon, Port Light has six superbly appointed en suite rooms, two with shower, and four with bath and shower. All rooms have digital colour television with Freeview, fixed wall heating, beverage facilities and hair dryers.

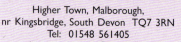

111 THE LODGE HOTEL & SAINTS RESTAURANT

Higher Town, Malborough,
nr Kingsbridge, South Devon TQ7 3RN
Tel: 01548 561405
e-mail: mark.khoury@btinternet.com
website: www.lodge-churchills.co.uk

The Lodge Hotel & Saints Restaurant is open all year round, and has been refurbished to a high standard. For those looking to spoil themselves there is also a luxury suite on the second floor. One double and one twin room are located on the ground floor. All the rooms are en-suite and have TV, DVD player, hair dryer, tea and coffee making facilities. The hotel also has a complimentary DVD library and a broadband wireless connection throughout the hotel for those guests bringing their own laptops. A garden with sun loungers is available for the sole use of the residents and there is ample parking. The Lodge Hotel lies within the quaint village of Marlborough, near Salcombe just a mile from the nearest beach! The village is dominated by a 13th century church, a landmark that can be seen for miles around and it is from this that the Saints Restaurant derives its name.

Following the refurbishment there are 9 en-suite rooms, adjacent to the hotel are two cottages which will sleep up to 6 people each and any well behaved pets.

There is a fresh new look to the restaurant and bar and the new menu created to compliment the changes. Saints Restaurant, with its sensational chef, is the perfect meeting place for guests and locals alike, serving top quality modern cuisine with an emphasis on fresh and seasonal local produce; the very best Devon meat, seafood and organic fruit and vegetables. The menu is changed daily and is well complimented by a wide selection of wines and champagnes. All the meals are cooked a la carte and can be enjoyed inside the unique conservatory, or al fresco style in the private garden. The heated all weather char grill situated in the sheltered garden is open daily throughout the summer months & offers an exciting alternative to the daily menu. Reservations are not essential, but advisable, in order to secure a table in the height of season. The relaxed lounge bar offers a selection of beers, ales & spirits. A varied wine list is also available offering both competitively priced wines and a connoisseur's selection. Sit and enjoy your choice of drink beside the warmth of a cackling fire, or whilst watching your favourite sports event on Sky TV. The friendly staff and vibrant atmosphere ensure the restaurant and bar is a home from home open to hotel guest and non-residents alike.

Tourist Information Centres

BARNSTAPLE

Museum of North Devon, The Square,
Barnstaple, Devon EX32 8LN
e-mail: info@staynorthdevon.co.uk
Tel: 01271 375000

BIDEFORD

Victoria Park, The Quay, Bideford,
Devon EX39 2QQ
e-mail: bidefordtic@visit.org.uk
Tel: 01237 477676

BRAUNTON

The Bakehouse Centre, Caen Street, Braunton,
Devon EX33 1AA
e-mail: info@brauntontic.co.uk
Tel: 01271 816400

BRIXHAM

The Old Market House, The Quay, Brixham,
Devon TQ5 8TB
e-mail: holiday@torbay.gov.uk
Tel: 01803 211211

BUDLEIGH SALTERTON

Fore Street, Budleigh Salterton, Devon EX9 6NG
e-mail: budleigh.tic@btconnect.com
Tel: 01395 445275

COMBE MARTIN

Seacot Cross Street, Combe Martin,
Devon EX34 0DH
e-mail: mail@visitcombemartin.co.uk
Tel: 01271 883319

DARTMOUTH

The Engine House, Mayor's Avenue, Dartmouth,
Devon TQ6 9YY
e-mail: holidays@discoverdartmouth.com
Tel: 01803 834224

DAWLISH

The Lawn, Dawlish, Devon EX7 9PW
e-mail: dawtic@Teignbridge.gov.uk
Tel: 01626 215665

EXETER

Exeter Visitor Information & Tickets, Dix's Field,
Exeter, Devon EX1 1GF
e-mail: evit@exeter.gov.uk
Tel: 01392 265700

EXMOUTH

Alexandra Terrace, Exmouth Devon EX8 1NZ
e-mail: info@exmouthtourism.co.uk
Tel: 01395 222299

HONITON

Lace Walk Car Park, Honiton, Devon EX14 1LT
Email:honitontic@btconnect.com
Tel: 01404 43716

ILFRACOMBE

The Landmark, The Seafront, Ilfracombe,
Devon EX34 9BX
e-mail: info@ilfracombe-tourism.co.uk
Tel: 01271 863001

IVYBRIDGE

Global Travel, 19 Fore Street, Ivybridge,
Devon PL21 9AB
e-mail: bookends.ivybridge@virgin.net
Tel: 01752 897035

KINGSBRIDGE

The Quay, Kingsbridge, Devon TQ7 1HS
e-mail: advice@kingsbridgeinfo.co.uk
Tel: 01548 853195

LYNTON AND LYNMOUTH

Town Hall, Lee Road, Lynton, Devon EX35 6BT
e-mail: info@lyntourism.co.uk
Tel: 0845 660 3232

MODBURY

5 Modbury Court, Modbury, Devon PL21 0QR
e-mail: modburytic@lineone.net
Tel: 01548 830159

NEWTON ABBOT

6 Bridge House, Courtenay Street, Newton Abbot,
Devon TQ12 2QS
e-mail: natic@Teignbridge.gov.uk
Tel: 01626 215667

OKEHAMPTON

Museum Courtyard, 3 West Street, Okehampton,
Devon EX20 1HQ
e-mail: okehamptontic@westdevon.gov.uk
Tel: 01837 53020

OTTERY ST MARY

10a Broad Street, Ottery St Mary,
Devon EX11 1BZ
e-mail: tic.osm@cosmic.org.uk
Tel: 01404 813964

PAIGNTON

The Esplanade, Paignton, Devon TQ4 6ED
e-mail: holiday@torbay.gov.uk
Tel: 01803 211211

PLYMOUTH MAYFLOWER

Plymouth Mayflower Centre, 3-5 The Barbican,
Plymouth, Devon PL1 2LR
e-mail: barbicantic@plymouth.gov.uk
Tel: 01752 306330

SALCOMBE

Market Street, Salcombe, Devon TQ8 8DE
e-mail: info@salcombeinformation.co.uk
Tel: 01548 843927

SEATON

The Underfleet, Seaton, Devon EX12 2TB
e-mail: info@seatontic.freeserve.co.uk
Tel: 01297 21660

SIDMOUTH

Ham Lane, Sidmouth, Devon EX10 8XR
e-mail: sidmouthtic@eclipse.co.uk
Tel: 01395 516441

SOUTH MOLTON

1 East Street, South Molton, Devon EX36 3BU
e-mail: visitsouthmolton@btconnect.com
Tel: 01769 574122

TAVISTOCK

Town Hall, Bedford Square, Tavistock,
Devon PL19 0AE
e-mail: tavistocktic@westdevon.gov.uk
Tel: 01822 612938

TEIGNMOUTH

The Den Sea Front, Teignmouth,
Devon TQ14 8BE
e-mail: teigntic@teignbridge.gov.uk
Tel: 01626 215666

TIVERTON

Phoenix Lane, Tiverton, Devon EX16 6LU
e-mail: tivertontic@btconnect.com
Tel: 01884 255827

TORQUAY

The Tourist Centre, Vaughan Parade, Torquay
Devon TQ2 5JG
e-mail: holiday@torbay.gov.uk
Tel: 01803 211211

TORRINGTON

Castle Hill, South Street, Great Torrington,
Devon EX38 8AA
e-mail: info@great-torrington.com
Tel: 01805 626140

TOTNES

The Town Mill, Coronation Road, Totnes,
South Devon TQ9 5DF
e-mail: enquire@totnesinformation.co.uk
Tel: 01803 863168

WOOLACOMBE

The Esplanade, Woolacombe, Devon EX34 7DL
e-mail: info@woolacombetourism.co.uk
Tel: 01271 870553

Towns, Villages and Places of Interest

TOWNS, VILLAGES AND PLACES OF INTEREST

226

TRAVEL PUBLISHING ORDER FORM

To order any of our publications just fill in the payment details below and complete the order form. For orders of less than 4 copies please add £1.00 per book for postage and packing. Orders over 4 copies are P & P free.

Name:

Address:

Tel no:

Please Complete Either:

I enclose a cheque for £ _____ made payable to Travel Publishing Ltd

Or:

Card No: Expiry Date:

Signature:

Please either send, telephone, fax or e-mail your order to:

Travel Publishing Ltd, Airport Business Centre, 10 Thornbury Road, Estover, Plymouth PL6 7PP

Tel: 01752 697280   Fax: 01752 697299   e-mail: info@travelpublishing.co.uk

	Price	Quantity
HIDDEN PLACES REGIONAL TITLES		
Cornwall	£8.99	....
Devon	£8.99	....
Dorset, Hants & Isle of Wight	£8.99	....
East Anglia	£8.99	....
Lake District & Cumbria	£8.99	....
Lancashire & Cheshire	£8.99	....
Northumberland & Durham	£8.99	....
Peak District and Derbyshire	£8.99	....
Yorkshire	£8.99	....
HIDDEN PLACES NATIONAL TITLES		
England	£11.99	....
Ireland	£11.99	....
Scotland	£11.99	....
Wales	£11.99	....
OTHER TITLES		
Off the Motorway	£11.99	....
Garden Centres & Nurseries	£11.99	....

	Price	Quantity
COUNTRY LIVING RURAL GUIDES		
East Anglia	£10.99	....
Heart of England	£10.99	....
Ireland	£11.99	....
North East	£10.99	....
North West	£10.99	....
Scotland	£11.99	....
South of England	£10.99	....
South East of England	£10.99	....
Wales	£11.99	....
West Country	£10.99	....

TOTAL QUANTITY:

POST & PACKING:

TOTAL VALUE:

READER REACTION FORM

The *Travel Publishing* research team would like to receive reader's comments on any visitor attractions or places reviewed in the book and also recommendations for suitable entries to be included in the next edition. This will help ensure that the *Hidden Places series of Guides* continues to provide its readers with useful information on the more interesting, unusual or unique features of each attraction or place ensuring that their visit to the local area is an enjoyable and stimulating experience. To provide your comments or recommendations would you please complete the forms below and overleaf as indicated and send to:

The Research Department, Travel Publishing Ltd,
Airport Business Centre, 10 Thornbury Road, Estover, Plymouth PL6 7PP

Your Name:

Your Address:

Your Telephone Number:

Please tick as appropriate:

Comments ☐   Recommendation ☐

Name of Establishment:

Address:

Telephone Number:

Name of Contact:

READER REACTION FORM

COMMENT OR REASON FOR RECOMMENDATION:

....

....

....

....

....

....

....

....

....

....

....

....

....

....

....

....

....

....

....

READER REACTION FORM

The *Travel Publishing* research team would like to receive reader's comments on any visitor attractions or places reviewed in the book and also recommendations for suitable entries to be included in the next edition. This will help ensure that the *Hidden Places series of Guides* continues to provide its readers with useful information on the more interesting, unusual or unique features of each attraction or place ensuring that their visit to the local area is an enjoyable and stimulating experience. To provide your comments or recommendations would you please complete the forms below and overleaf as indicated and send to:

**The Research Department, Travel Publishing Ltd,
Airport Business Centre, 10 Thornbury Road, Estover, Plymouth PL6 7PP**

Your Name:

Your Address:

Your Telephone Number:

Please tick as appropriate:

Comments ☐   Recommendation ☐

Name of Establishment:

Address:

Telephone Number:

Name of Contact:

READER REACTION FORM

COMMENT OR REASON FOR RECOMMENDATION:

....

....

....

....

....

....

....

....

....

....

....

....

....

....

....

....

....

....

....

....

INDEX OF ADVERTISERS

Index of Advertisers

PLACES OF INTEREST